Seattle Children's Theatre
Volume Two

A Smith and Kraus Book
Published by Smith and Kraus, Inc.
177 Lyme Road, Hanover, NH 03755
www.SmithKraus.com

Copyright ©2000 by Smith and Kraus
All rights reserved
Manufactured in the United States of America
Cover and text design by Julia Hill Gignoux, Freedom Hill Design

First Edition: September 2000
10 9 8 7 6 5 4 3 2 1

The Library of Congress Cataloging-In-Publication Data
Seattle Children's Theatre volume two: six plays for young audiences /
Deborah Lynn Frockt, editor. —1st ed.
p. cm. —(Young actors series)
includes bibliographical references
Summary: A collection of plays dealing with family, friendship, freedom, and courage.
ISBN 1-57525-158-2
1. Children's plays, American—Washington (State)—Seattle.
2. American drama—20th century. [1. Plays—Collections.]
I. Frockt, Deborah Lynn. II. Series.
PS625.5.S43   1996
812'.540809282—dc20   96-18740
CIP
AC

Seattle Children's Theatre
Volume Two

SIX PLAYS
FOR YOUNG AUDIENCES

DEBORAH LYNN FROCKT, EDITOR

Young Actors Series

SK
A Smith and Kraus Book

CONTENTS

INTRODUCTION

In twenty-five years of producing professional theatre, Seattle Children's Theatre has been committed to creating a new breed of play that is truly ageless. While the young audience member is always foremost in our minds, we believe that in the theater, an intergenerational habitat can emerge.

I say we, because the six scripts in this book represent a shared vision of many minds. First and foremost, these scripts bear witness to the talent, commitment, and passion this group of playwrights has offered our audiences. But in another sense, they represent the work of many who share the singular vision that audiences of any and all ages deserve theater of the highest quality. While these plays can be read, rehearsed, and even produced again, they are unique historical documents—the single most important, tangible aspect of our ever-ephemeral art form.

These plays are first imagined and wrought in solitude—given birth to in quiet rooms of exquisite joy and horrific torture. They grow and change and transform under the playwrights' care and guidance, as many hands reach to sometimes caress and sometimes prod them along in the arduous process of maturing.

I believe playwrights commit themselves and their work to a process of development and production for the same reason I do. We are all striving to create work that speaks to an existing audience while creating an open invitation to a new one. I believe that people are hungry for a place where age is neither a barrier nor a restriction nor a requirement. I believe that an eleven-year-old and sixty-three-year-old might respond to a piece of theater together. I believe that people still yearn for some shared experience with their children, parents, and grandparents—some experience that is not tailor-made for and suited only to a single demographic group defined by an adman in Manhattan, Silicon Valley, or the mall.

I am not suggesting that the intergenerational audiences that see and read these plays will have the same experience. On the contrary, each individual has his own point of entry for each work. Our belief at SCT has been that variety of experience adds to the depth, flavor, and ultimately the quality of the theatrical event.

In *The King of Ireland's Son* a young person may be captivated by Sean's desire for adventure and empathize with his impatient struggle to escape his father's protective restraints. An older person may feel the resonance of Shaking Head's longing to have lived his life better. As the elder focuses on a mother's relief as she regains her lost child in *Still Life with Iris*, the child may delight in Iris' delight as she reunites her family, literally and figuratively bringing the dawn of new day to her home.

In *Great Expectations* and *Cyrano*, the ageless audience can discover that it has something in common with timeless classics—agelessness. In maturity we may despair for Pip and his desire for all the wrong things; but in youth we may identify most strongly with the boy's hope and ambition. With experience, we may come to see that Cyrano has proscribed his own tragic fate. Earlier in life, we may feel Cyrano's self-conscious anxiety most poignantly.

As Tuc and his father struggle to find true communication in *The Taste of Sunrise: Tuc's Story*, we as children identify with the child's desire that our parents might understand us; we as parents identify with the parent's desire that our children might understand us. And in *The Book of Ruth*, we empathize with Ruth's youthful and human desire to keep a loved one near her, always alive. And we witness Hannah's desperate need to leave something behind to help her heartbroken loved one keep living.

This group of plays spans time and space and defies categorization by genre. Four are original stories for the stage, one is adapted from a great piece of literature, and the other is a re-envisioning of a classic play. Reading them as a piece, you will travel across continents and through centuries. You will find thematic confluences alongside a multiplicity of theatrical languages. And in each, I hope that you will find characters and stories that remain indelibly with you, as they have with me.

Linda Hartzell
Artistic Director
Seattle Children's Theatre

STILL LIFE WITH IRIS

by Steven Dietz

For Linda Hartzell

THE AUTHOR

Steven Dietz's plays and adaptations have been seen at over one hundred regional theaters in the United States, as well as Off-Broadway. International productions have been seen in England, Japan, Germany, France, Australia, Sweden, Argentina, Slovenia, Peru, and South Africa. Mr. Dietz received the 1994 PEN USA West Award in Drama for his play, *Lonely Planet,* which has now been translated into several languages; the Kennedy Center's Fund for New American Plays Award for *Still Life with Iris,* the first play for young audiences to receive such an award; and the Yomuiri Shimbun Award as one of the top five plays produced in Japan for his adaptation of Shusaku Endo's novel, *Silence.* Other widely produced plays include *God's Country, Private Eyes, Rocket Man, Trust, The Nina Variations, Handing Down the Names, Halcyon Days, Ten November, Foolin' Around with Infinity,* and *More Fun than Bowling.* His stage adaptations include Joyce Simmons Cheeka's *The Rememberer,* which was awarded the 1994 Lila Wallace/Reader's Digest Award; Bram Stoker's *Dracula; Force of Nature,* from a novella by Goethe; and *Paragon Springs,* a new play based on Ibsen's *An Enemy of the People.*

ORIGINAL PRODUCTION

Still Life with Iris was originally produced by Seattle Children's Theatre on September 19, 1997. This play was originally produced with the assistance of the Fund for New American Plays, a project of the John F. Kennedy Center for the Performing Arts with support from American Express Company in cooperation with the President's Committee on the Arts and Humanities. It was directed by Linda Hartzell. Deborah Lynn Frockt was the dramaturg. This production featured the Image Influenced Illusions of Steffan Soule and Cooper Edens. Kara L. Mullen* was the stage manager. The cast was:

Thunder Bottler/Mister Matternot . . . . John Abramson
Thunder Bottler/Mozart . . . . Jeff Cummings*
Leaf Monitor/Annabel Lee . . . . Allison Gregory*
Mom/Miss Overlook . . . . Sue Guthrie*
Hazel/Gretta Good/Captain Also . . . . Leslie Law*
Elmer/Grotto Good/Third String . . . . William Salyers*
Memory Mender/Rain Maker/
Mister Otherguy/Ray . . . . David Scully*
Iris . . . . Julyana Soelistyo*
Butterfly Trainer/Flower Painter/
Bolt Bender/Mister Himtoo . . . . Steffan Soule
Understudies—Teresa Castracane*, John Holyoke
*Members of Actors' Equity Association, the union for stage professionals

Still Life with Iris (in this published version) was subsequently produced by Childsplay, Inc. (Tempe, Arizona: David Saar, Artistic Director; Gary Bacal, Managing Director), in Tucson/Phoenix, Arizona, on March 14, 1998. The production was directed by David Saar; scenic design by Scott Weldin; costume design by Karen Ledger; lighting design by Rick Paulsen; sound design by Brian Jerome Peterson; magic design by Steffan Soule; and the stage manager was Marie Krueger-Jones. The cast was as follows:

Iris . . . . Katie McFadzen
Mom/Miss Overlook . . . . Kristen Drathman
Mister Matternot/others. . . . . Jere Luisi
Leaf Monitor/Annabel Lee . . . . Debra K. Stevens
Mozart/others. . . . . Jeff Goodman
Memory Mender/others . . . . Dwayne Hartford
Elmer/Grotto Good . . . . D. Scott Withers
Hazel/Gretta Good . . . . Cathy Dresbach
Flower Painter/others. . . . . David Jones

The production was mounted in association with the Arizona Theatre Company (David Ira Goldstein, Artistic Director; Jessica L. Andrews, Managing Director) and with the support of the Flinn Foundation.

CHARACTERS
(Four women, five men. Pairings indicate actor doubling.)

IRIS

MOM
MISS OVERLOOK

MAN/MISTER MATTERNOT
THUNDER BOTTLER TWO
DAD

LEAF MONITOR
ANNABEL LEE

THUNDER BOTTLER ONE
MOZART

MEMORY MENDER
RAIN MAKER

MISTER OTHERGUY
RAY

ELMER
HIS MOST EXCELLENT, GROTTO GOOD
THIRD STRING

HAZEL
HER MOST EXCELLENT, GRETTA GOOD
CAPTAIN ALSO

FLOWER PAINTER
BOLT BENDER
MISTER HIMTOO

SETTING
The Land of Nocturno—a fantastical world, whose inhabitants spend each night readying the "known" world for the next day. This is not, however, a land of night and darkness. Quite the opposite. It is a land of color and pragmatic magic. It exists in a place parallel to our days.

Great Island—a magnificent and remote inland isle. This is the home of the Great Goods, the rulers of the people of Nocturno.

PASTCOATS
All of the inhabitants of Nocturno wear long, brightly colored coats, decorated—perhaps—with a variety of small beads or other momentos. Each coat contains the *past* of the person wearing it—and are known, therefore, as their "PastCoats."

MUSIC
The music of Mozart—in all its richness, variance, and breadth—underscores the play.

TRANSITIONS
The first line of every scene is intended to immediately follow the last line of the previous scene. This obviously requires a playing space that can quickly and *simply* represent a variety of locales. This also means that the first line of any scene can be played as an "entrance" by the speaking character, and that the required scenery not already in position can move into place after the scene has begun.

And she forgot the stars, the moon, and sun,
And she forgot the blue above the trees,
And she forgot the dells where waters run,
And she forgot the chilly autumn breeze

John Keats

ACT I

The music of Mozart fills the theater as the audience arrives. Music builds as the theater darkens, and then plays under as a shaft of light rises on a tall sign. The sign reads: "WELCOME TO NOCTURNO." Attached to the sign are arrows pointing in various directions. Written on the arrows are the following destinations: "Cloud Factory," "Bird Assembly," "Plant Plant," "Rain Storage," "Fruit Coloring," "Fish School—swimming classes nightly." Standing beneath the sign—his back to us—is a Man in dark, somber attire. He wears dark gloves on his hands at all times. Unlike the residents of Nocturno, he is not wearing a PastCoat. He stands, reading the sign, as—Iris enters. She looks at the Man's back for a moment, then speaks to him.

IRIS: Are you curious or lost?

MAN: Pardon me?

(When he turns, we see that he wears a weathered sort of tool belt around his waist, containing numerous objects of practical need. The Man himself has an oddly sinister bearing.)

IRIS: It's better to be curious than lost, don't you think? Which are you?

MAN: I'm new.

IRIS: Yes, I know. I can tell by your coat. Why have you come?

MAN: I'm looking for someone.

IRIS: Well, at this time of night, everyone's at work.

MAN: Doing what?

IRIS: You name it. Whatever you see in the world by day, it's made here by night. Like that fly on your nose—

(The Man swats the unseen bug away.)

IRIS: That fly was assembled right here in Nocturno. We crank those out by the millions and teach every one of them to fly. Plus: No two are the same. Our Bug Sculptors are very proud of that.

MAN: *(Catching on.)* Just like snowflakes, then—no two alike?

IRIS: Actually—and this is privileged information—the snowflakes are made in *pairs*. But we separate them and load them into clouds bound for different locations. Don't spread that around.

MAN: I won't.

IRIS: So, you've never been here before?

MAN: Not that I remember.

IRIS: Oh, you'd remember. Unless you've got a tear in your coat. Who are you looking for?

(Lights expand to reveal the Land of Nocturno, as Hazel and Elmer—siblings, similar in age to Iris—rush on. Hazel carries a large burlap sack which is marked: "Spots." Elmer carries a wooden box.)

HAZEL: I know you took them.

ELMER: I didn't take them.

HAZEL: Where did you put them?

ELMER: I didn't take them.

HAZEL: I bet you're hiding them.

ELMER: I DIDN'T TAKE THEM. Tell her, Iris—

IRIS: What is it, Elmer?

HAZEL: *(Before Elmer can answer.)* We're almost done with our chores—all that's left is to put the spots on the Ladybugs—
(Elmer removes two large Ladybugs from the box. They're each bright orange and about the size of a cantaloupe. They are without spots.)

ELMER: But why do Ladybugs need spots, anyway? I think they look fine without them.

HAZEL: And I reach into the Spot Sack and it's filled with these— *(Hazel reaches into the sack and pulls out several long, black stripes—like those found on a zebra.)*

IRIS: Stripes.

ELMER: There must have been a mix-up.

HAZEL: We can't put stripes on the Ladybugs.

ELMER: Why not? And then we'll put the spots on the zebras.

HAZEL: *(To Iris.)* You're lucky you don't have a brother. It's like this all the time.

ELMER: Can you help us, Iris? No one can find things like you can.

IRIS: I'll help you as soon as I— *(She turns to the Man.)*

MAN: *(Interrupts her.)* Your name is Iris.

IRIS: Yes. Why?

(The Flower Painter enters. He wears a beret and has a palette and brushes on a strap over his shoulder. He goes directly to Elmer, Hazel, and Iris as, at the same instant, the Memory Mender enters, opposite, pushing a cart inscribed "Memory Mender" in large letters. The cart holds large spools of thread, extra-large buttons, scissors, etc. His hat looks like a thimble. He is a cranky but caring man, adamant about his work. Upon their entrance, the Man turns and leaves.)

MEMORY MENDER: *(Calls out across the distance.)* You there, sir—let me take a look at that coat! Sir, did you hear me?
(But the Man is gone. The Memory Mender remains at a distance, busying himself with the objects on his cart.)

FLOWER PAINTER: Elmer, Hazel—are you finished with your chores?

HAZEL: We have a problem.

IRIS: The spots are missing.

ELMER: I didn't take them.

FLOWER PAINTER: Did you talk to the Spot Maker?

HAZEL: He sent them out, just like he always does.

FLOWER PAINTER: But, the world requires Ladybugs, and Ladybugs must have their spots—

IRIS: Maybe you could paint them on.

(Elmer holds the Ladybugs out to the Flower Painter.)

FLOWER PAINTER: Out of the question. I'm a Flower Painter—nothing more. I wouldn't know the first thing about painting spots on bugs.

ELMER: *(Happily.)* I guess our chores are done—

FLOWER PAINTER: It's not that simple, Elmer. Without us, the world would come to a standstill. If I abandoned my work, the flowers of the world would look like this— *(He produces a large, dull grey flower with a long stem.)* Instead of like this—

(A flourish of music as he makes several strokes with his paint brush and produces, seemingly, the same flower—now bright yellow and red.)

FLOWER PAINTER: Now, you are Spotters and you must do your work.

HAZEL: But we've looked everywhere—

FLOWER PAINTER: I'm sure Iris can find them. She's like her Dad in that way. That man could find the moon on the blackest of nights.

ELMER: Then why has he never found his way back home?

HAZEL: *(A reprimand.)* Elmer—

ELMER: He's been gone forever.

FLOWER PAINTER: No one knows why, Elmer, and I think it's better left—

IRIS: Would you tell me if you knew?

(The Flower Painter stares at her.)

IRIS: I was only a baby, then. Even my Mom won't tell me why he left.

FLOWER PAINTER: *(Calmly, definitively.)* Because she *doesn't know,* Iris. No one does. It was the night of the Great Eclipse, and the moon was particularly hard to find. He went out to bring it in…and he's never returned.

IRIS: There's an eclipse tomorrow.

FLOWER PAINTER: The first one since that night. I doubt we'll get to enjoy it, though—

IRIS: Why not?

FLOWER PAINTER: The order just came and it's a big one.

HAZEL: An order for what?

FLOWER PAINTER: A *storm.*

ELMER: And it's a big one?

FLOWER PAINTER: Huge. *(He starts off, saying his farewell.)* Now and again.

ELMER, HAZEL, IRIS: Now and again.

HAZEL: *(Gently, to Iris.)* Sorry about my brother. He says stupid things.

ELMER: I didn't mean—

IRIS: It's not stupid. I think about it all the time, too.

ELMER: I know what would make you feel better, Iris.

HAZEL: Helping us find those spots.

ELMER: Better than that. An order has come and a storm must be assembled. Now, what does this mean to people like you and me?

IRIS: It means that somewhere in this town…right now…just *waiting for us…*is a big…fresh…wet…batch of…

IRIS, HAZEL, ELMER: *(A delicious whisper.)* …rain. *(They sigh with delight.)*

HAZEL: I bet the Rain Makers have been working nonstop—

ELMER: And it's just *sitting there,* and no one's—

HAZEL: Played in it, or—

ELMER: Tasted it, or—

IRIS: Race you there—

(As they begin to rush off they are stopped by the Memory Mender, who pushes his cart in their path.)

MEMORY MENDER: Careful, now—or you'll trip and rip your coats. And if you rip your coats I'll have to sew 'em back up for you. And you know why, don't you?

IRIS, ELMER, HAZEL: *(Having heard this a million times.)* Yes, we know why—

MEMORY MENDER: *(Quickly, quizzing them.)* Hazel, who are the rulers of Nocturno, our home?

HAZEL: The Great Goods.

MEMORY MENDER: Iris, where do the Great Goods live?

IRIS: Across the water, on Great Island.

MEMORY MENDER: And, Elmer, how deep is the water that surrounds Great Island?

ELMER: Umm—

IRIS: I know!

HAZEL: I know, too!

ELMER: *(Sharp, to the girls.)* So do I.

MEMORY MENDER: Well?

ELMER: It's—umm—

MEMORY MENDER: You knew it when I asked you last week.

ELMER: It's—oh, I don't know. Why do I always get the hard questions?!

MEMORY MENDER: Let me see your coat.

(Elmer walks over to the Mender, who discovers a tiny rip in the sleeve of Elmer's PastCoat. He sews it back up as he speaks.)

MEMORY MENDER: See there. A little rip in your coat and your memory is harmed. It makes me crazy. You've got to take care of your coat because your coat holds your *past*. Every stitch, every pocket, every button and sleeve—it's your whole life in there! Think you can just go out and get a past like you can get a glass of milk?! Think again. *(He is finished sewing Elmer's coat.)* There we are. Now, Elmer, how deep is the water that surrounds Great Island?

ELMER: *(Touching the new stitches in his coat.)* Ninety-nine thousand and twenty-three feet.

MEMORY MENDER: Exactly. Now, don't trip and get a rip. *(To Iris, referring to her coat.)* Iris, have your Mom keep an eye on that button. It's getting loose.

IRIS: I will.

MEMORY MENDER: *(Taking Iris aside.)* And one thing more: The Fog Lifter is retiring today. After all these years, she can still set the fog down in the morning—but she just can't lift it up anymore. She'd like you to take her place, Iris.

IRIS: *(Honored.)* Thank you.

MEMORY MENDER: Now and again.

IRIS, ELMER, HAZEL: Now and again.

(Music, as the Memory Mender exits, pushing his cart, and lights shift to reveal the Leaf Monitor—Hazel and Elmer's mom—standing near a tree. She holds several large leaves and a clipboard. Near her are two large sacks with leaves protruding out of the tops of each. One is marked "OLD" and one is marked "NEW." Iris, Elmer and Hazel rush past her.)

LEAF MONITOR: Hazel.

(Hazel stops. Elmer and Iris also stop, and stand behind her.)

LEAF MONITOR: Where are you going?

HAZEL: *(Innocently.)* What, Mom?

LEAF MONITOR: You heard me. Where are you rushing off to? Did you finish your chores?

HAZEL: Why don't you ever ask Elmer that question?

LEAF MONITOR: Because you're the oldest.

ELMER: And you always will be.

(Hazel glares at Elmer.)

LEAF MONITOR: I need you to help me balance these books. I keep checking and double-checking, but I'm still *one leaf off.*

ELMER: *(Quickly.)* I didn't take it.

LEAF MONITOR: In all my years as the Leaf Monitor, I've never encountered this. We must be certain that for every new leaf we put on a tree, an old one falls. *(To Hazel.)* But, where could the missing one be?

(The Thunder Bottlers enter, pushing a tall crate on wheels which is marked: "THUNDER." Stacked inside the crate are bottles, sealed with bright red lids. Other bottles in the crate are empty and unsealed. The men are busy bottling the thunder, as follows: Holding a bottle to their mouths, they use a funnel of some kind and make a loud, vocal sound of thunder into the bottle. Then they quickly seal up the bottle with a red lid and place it inside the crate. They repeat this, throughout the following.)

THUNDER BOTTLER ONE: How many is that?

THUNDER BOTTLER TWO: That's thirty-four thunders.

THUNDER BOTTLER ONE: And that's not enough?!

THUNDER BOTTLER TWO: The order was for a forty-thunder storm.

ELMER: I've never seen so much thunder.

THUNDER BOTTLER TWO: We've been bottling it up all night.

THUNDER BOTTLER ONE: Gonna be a monster. *(He thunders into a bottle.)*

THUNDER BOTTLER TWO: We gotta be ready. *(He thunders into a bottle.)*

THUNDER BOTTLER ONE: Word is the Color Mixer has outdone himself. For this storm, he's come up with a brand new shade of *stormy sky blue-black.*

IRIS: Really?

THUNDER BOTTLER TWO: Gonna be something. *(He thunders into a bottle.)*

THUNDER BOTTLER ONE: We gotta be ready. *(He thunders into a bottle.)*

LEAF MONITOR: *(To Bottler One.)* Keep an eye out for a missing leaf.

THUNDER BOTTLER ONE: Did you take it, Elmer?

ELMER: Why does everyone always—

LEAF MONITOR: Once the storm comes and they start *swirling*—I'm afraid I'll never find it.

THUNDER BOTTLER TWO: It's not the BEST leaf that's missing, I hope.

HAZEL: Why not?

LEAF MONITOR: The BEST leaf must be sent to the Great Goods. You know that.

THUNDER BOTTLER ONE: Have Iris help you—if it's lost, she'll find it.

(The Bolt Bender enters, carrying a piece of lightning, about four feet long. He's bending it in various ways, trying to get the right shape. Other lightning bolts poke out of a quiver he wears over his shoulder.)

THUNDER BOTTLER ONE: *(Greeting the Bolt Bender.)* Almost day.

BOLT BENDER: *(Nods, greets them all.)* Almost day, indeed—and I can't get the lightning right. Even the best Bolt Bender gets tired of making the same old lightning bolt, over and over again.

IRIS: But, when there's thunder, people expect lightning to go with it.

BOLT BENDER: But, why couldn't it be something else?

ELMER: Like what?

BOLT BENDER: Open up one of those thunders and let's experiment. Instead of *lightning bolt* lighting up the sky, maybe it's—

(The Bolt Bender reaches into his quiver, as Bottler One opens up one of the sealed bottles of thunder. A huge, quick crack of thunder fills the theater, as the Bolt Bender produces a bolt in the shape of a cactus—or some other incongruous object—and holds it high above his head. If possible, it lights up.)

BOLT BENDER: —THIS!

THUNDER BOTTLER ONE: That's a possibility.

THUNDER BOTTLER TWO: *(Holding up the original lightning bolt.)* The Great Goods would never approve. As long as they've been our rulers, the lightning has always looked like *this*. *(With seriousness.)* And, believe me, you don't want to get on the bad side of the Great Goods.

HAZEL: What can happen to you?

THUNDER BOTTLER ONE: *(Directly to Hazel.)* If you disobey the Goods, your punishment is great.

HAZEL: Mom. *(Hazel reaches into her PastCoat and brings out a large, beautiful autumn leaf.)* I'm sorry. I didn't mean to offend the Goods. But it was so pretty.

ELMER: It's the best leaf of them all.

(The Leaf Monitor holds out her hand, and—reluctantly—Hazel hands her the leaf. The Leaf Monitor gently brushes a strand of hair from Hazel's face.)

LEAF MONITOR: Someday, Hazel, when *you're* the Leaf Monitor—you'll understand. Now, finish up your chores. It's almost day.

(The Leaf Monitor exits, as the Bolt Bender lifts the lightning bolt, saying—)

BOLT BENDER: *(As he leaves.)* It's gonna be huge.

THUNDER BOTTLER ONE AND TWO: *(As they leave.)* We gotta be ready.

(The Thunder Bottler's thunder into their bottles and leave, along with the Bolt Bender.)

ELMER: *(Whispers to Iris and Hazel.)* Come on, it's our last chance before the storm.

(The kids rush away and arrive at a very large rain barrel. It is wooden, with notches on its side [or a ladder] that enables it to be climbed. A large label

on the barrel reads: "RAIN. Batch #7893392." The kids see the barrel. They stop, stunned. All take a deep breath and are about to cheer loudly with delight—but realize they might be heard and get caught—so they exhale by quieting each other.)

IRIS, HAZEL, ELMER: *(To each other.)* SSSSSSSSShhhhhhhhhhhh! *(They approach the barrel, looking around to make sure they're not being seen. They each roll their pant legs up a little ways. They begin to climb up the side/back of the barrel. Their voices remain soft, urgent.)*

HAZEL AND ELMER: *(To themselves, overlapping each other.)* Please don't let my mom call my name—please don't let my mom call my name—please don't let my mom call my name—please don't let—

IRIS: Hey, Hazel.

HAZEL: Yeah?

IRIS: Why is that?

HAZEL: Why is what?

IRIS: Why is it that no matter how far away from our mom we get, if she says our name—we can still hear her?

HAZEL: I don't know. But I wish we could *change it.*

ELMER: Let me ask you both a question: Are we going to *gab*…or are we going to *splash?!*
(Iris and Hazel nod. All climb up and then stop—looking down into the barrel below them. They look at each other. They each pull back one of their sleeves, exposing the whole of their arm. They take a deep breath—then they each shove their arms down into the freezing cold water.)

IRIS, HAZEL, ELMER: *(A joyous scream.)* AAAAAAAAAAAAAUUUUUU-UWGGGGGGGGGGGHHHHHHHHHH!
(They laugh. They shiver. They cup their hands and drink water [which we see] from the barrels. They laugh and play some more, splashing a bit of water on each other, all the while repeating, under their breath, overlapping.)

IRIS, HAZEL, ELMER: Please don't let my mom call my name—please don't let my mom call my name—please don't let my—
(Shafts of light discover Iris' Mom, and the Leaf Monitor, or their amplified voices are heard.)

IRIS' MOM: *(Simultaneously.)* Iris!

LEAF MONITOR: *(Simultaneously.)* Hazel and Elmer!

IRIS' MOM AND LEAF MONITOR: Time to come home!
(The kids freeze, poised over the water, exasperated.)

IRIS, ELMER, HAZEL: HOW DO THEY *DO* THAT?!
(Music, as the Rain Maker backs onto the stage, not seeing the kids. He wears

a long apron covered with bright raindrops. He holds bright orange batons in his hands—and is using them to direct an unseen approaching cloud into place.)

RAIN MAKER: *(Backing in.)* Okay, let's back her on in. Good. Little to your left. Good. Man, they keep building these clouds bigger and bigger. I don't know how they even get off the ground. Okay. Good. Keep her coming— *(The kids have climbed down from the barrels, unseen.)*

IRIS: *(Whispering.)* Now and again.

HAZEL AND ELMER: Now and again.

(They run off in separate directions and are gone.)

RAIN MAKER: Okay, fellas. Let's load 'er up. We got some rain to drop.

(Music changes to what will become recognized as the "Still Life" music, as lights reveal Iris' home. It consists, in total, of a white wooden table with three white chairs. On the table is a simple glass vase. Nothing else. Iris arrives home. Just before entering the scene, she stops and rolls her pant legs back down. As she does so, she watches, unseen, as her Mom puts an iris in the vase and sets a steaming cup of cocoa on the table. She pulls Iris' chair away from the table. She goes to the middle chair and touches it, looks down at it. Then, she moves to her own chair, pulls it away from the table, and sits. She looks at the iris in the vase, admiring it. Note: This is the "Still Life"—the image that Iris will remember throughout the play. Iris stares at this picture for a long moment, as the music plays, then she enters.)

IRIS: Hi, Mom.

MOM: How was the rain?

IRIS: What rain?

(Mom looks at her.)

IRIS: Good. Cold.

(Mom smiles. Iris sits, the cocoa in front of her.)

IRIS: Mom, they asked me to be the Fog Lifter.

MOM: *(Knowing this in advance.)* I'm very proud of you, Iris.

IRIS: And we saw all the thunder they're bottling up.

MOM: This storm means a lot of extra work for me. A lot of wind to be taught.

IRIS: Why doesn't the wind remember how to whistle?

MOM: The wind has no memory. Just like us if we lost our PastCoats. So every storm, I've got to start from scratch. And, this being a big storm, I've got to teach not only whistling—but *howling.*

IRIS: Did Dad used to help you?

(Silence. Mom stares at her.)

MOM: Yes, in fact, he did.

IRIS: And did you ever help him?

MOM: Iris, I've told you, it's better forgotten, it's better not to think about—

IRIS: Did he leave because of me?

(Pause, Mom stares at her.)

IRIS: Because he didn't want to be my dad?

MOM: *(Gently.)* No.

IRIS: Why, then?

MOM: I wish I knew. The night of the Great Eclipse he went in search of the moon—but it was so dark, Iris. I'm afraid he lost his way and was captured by that black night. I stood at the door, waiting for him—but all that arrived was the wind…moving through the house, not making a sound. Your dad was gone.

IRIS: *(Moving into the center chair.)* I know you haven't forgotten him. I know he's still part of your coat. *(Iris touches Mom's coat near her heart.)* Please, Mom. Tell me about him.

(Silence. Mom looks at her, then speaks, a revery.)

MOM: Every night he roped the moon. And he pulled it down out of the sky. Then he'd give the signal— *(Palm open, fingers spread, arm extended—she raises her hand slowly in front of her.)* —to raise the sun into place. That was his job. He was the Day Breaker.

(Silence, as Iris smiles at the memory—then grows more serious.)

IRIS: There's another eclipse tomorrow.

MOM: Yes, there is.

IRIS: And who will find the moon?

(Mom stares at Iris for a long moment.)

MOM: He left something for you, Iris. A leather pouch. He wore it every night while he worked.

IRIS: Why haven't you ever given it to me?

MOM: I was afraid it would make you sad. All these years, I've tried to protect you from that.

IRIS: *(Simply.)* Please don't. Not any more.

(Mom stares at her, then gently touches Iris' face.)

MOM: You're right. It's time it was yours.

(Mom starts to exit, as Iris lifts her cocoa from the table.)

MOM: Careful. That's hot.

(Iris nods and sips her cocoa. Then she speaks to Mom offstage.)

IRIS: Sometimes I get mad at him, Mom. Sometimes I wish I could find him and make him tell me why he left. I've waited so long for him to come home.

(Music under, as from the direction Mom exited, the Man we saw earlier enters. His name is Mister Matternot.)

MISTER MATTERNOT: Your waiting is over, Iris.

(Iris turns and sees Matternot.)

MISTER MATTERNOT: You've been selected.

IRIS: Mom——?

MISTER MATTERNOT: You needn't call for your mother, you needn't think of your father, anymore——

IRIS: *(Growing more frightened.)* What are you doing here? You were lost——you were looking for someone——

(Matternot approaches Iris.)

MISTER MATTERNOT: And I've found her.

IRIS: But, I don't know who you are——

(Iris tries to run off to find her Mom. Matternot stands in her way.)

IRIS: MOM!

MISTER MATTERNOT: You're a special girl, Iris. I'm told you can find missing things.

(Iris is confused, scared, staring up at Matternot.)

IRIS: Yes, but I don't——

MISTER MATTERNOT: And because you are special, you've been chosen.

IRIS: Chosen by whom?

MISTER MATTERNOT: Why, by the rulers of Nocturno——the Great Goods. No one can travel to Great Island without their permission. But you, Iris, have been chosen to make the voyage.

IRIS: I don't want to visit Great Island. I want to know what's happened to my mom, where did she——?

MISTER MATTERNOT: Listen to me, Iris, you have not been chosen to *visit* Great Island. You have been chosen to *live there.*

IRIS: Live there? What are——?

MISTER MATTERNOT: They have, you see, only the BEST of everything on Great Island——but, until this moment, they have never had a little girl. Now, they will have you. You will be their daughter.

IRIS: I don't want to be their daughter! *(Iris runs again in the direction her mom left.)* I belong here with my mom——!

(As Iris says this, Mom appears and faces her. She looks the same as before, however, she is not wearing her PastCoat. Iris throws her arms around Mom, desperately. Mom does not respond at first, but then puts her arms gently around Iris, sympathetically. Iris is crying, holding tightly onto Mom as she speaks.)

IRIS: Make him go away! He's scaring me—I don't want to go to Great Island—please, Mom, make him go away!
(Music fades out, as Mom continues to hold Iris.)
MOM: *(To Matternot, concerned.)* Why is this girl calling for her mother? Isn't there something we can do? Where is her family? Where is her home?
IRIS: *(Pulling away.)* What are you saying? What is— *(For the first time, Iris notices that her Mom's PastCoat is gone. She speaks, quietly.)* Mom. Where's your coat?
MOM: What's that?
IRIS: *(To Matternot.)* Her coat—where is it?
MOM: What coat is she talking about?
IRIS: She went in there to bring me a pouch—a leather pouch—and now she—
MOM: *(Holds out the old and weathered leather pouch.)* You must mean *this*. I found it in the next room. Is it yours?
(Matternot takes the pouch from Mom.)
IRIS: *(Desperately.)* Yes. It belonged to my dad—
MISTER MATTERNOT: Iris, listen to me, the Great Goods do not wish to cause you any pain. And so, to remove the heartache, we must remove the coats.
(Iris wraps her PastCoat tightly around herself. She backs away, crying.)
IRIS: No. You can't. The Memory Mender said "Never let anything happen to your coat, or you'll be lost, you won't know who you are or—"
MOM: *(Overlapping, to Matternot.)* If the little girl wants to keep her coat, I think she should be allowed to—
MISTER MATTERNOT: Iris, I want to tell you something—
IRIS: Stay away from me—
MISTER MATTERNOT: Iris—
IRIS: *(Looking at Mom.)* YOU'VE TAKEN AWAY HER COAT—
MOM: *(To Matternot.)* We should find her Mother. We should take her home.
IRIS: *(Crying.)* LOOK AT HER! SHE DOESN'T KNOW WHO I AM!
MISTER MATTERNOT: *(Grabbing her, holding her.)* IRIS. *(Quieter now.)* Listen to me. *This is what's done.* I don't like it, but it's what the Great Goods desire and therefore it must be done. Believe me, its better to let me have your coat. If you keep it, you will be haunted by your past. You will think of your mother all the time. You will think of your home and your friends and your life here—and *you will never stop missing it.* It will be an ache that will never vanish from your heart.
(She looks up at him, holding her PastCoat tightly around her. Matternot now reaches out his hands to her, asking for the coat.)
MISTER MATTERNOT: Now…please.

IRIS: But if you take my past, who will I be?

MISTER MATTERNOT: You will be Iris. You'll be the girl you are now, but you'll remember nothing that happened before this moment.

IRIS: I'll never think of my mother again?

MISTER MATTERNOT: And therefore, you'll never be saddened by your loss. *(Looking at Mom.)* Nor will she. *(To Iris.)* It's the only way, Iris. It's the only way to make it not hurt.

IRIS: *(Stares at him.)* Let me keep the pouch.

MISTER MATTERNOT: Iris—

IRIS: Please?

MISTER MATTERNOT: It will mean nothing to you once your coat is gone.

IRIS: *Please?*

(Matternot hands her the pouch. She attaches it around her waist, or over her shoulder. Then, she looks over at Mom, with some final hope of recognition.)

IRIS: Mom…?

MOM: *(Kindly.)* I do hope you find her, Iris. Whoever she is. Wherever she's gone.

(Iris looks back at Matternot. He holds out his hand, awaiting the coat. She stares at him. She looks down at her coat. She looks over at her Mom, one final time. She wraps her PastCoat around herself very tightly for a moment…closing her eyes…and then, eyes still closed, she slowly removes her coat and holds it out away from her. A long mournful gust of wind is heard, as Matternot takes the coat in his arms. He then goes to the table and removes the iris from the vase. The table and chairs are taken away. The sound of wind fades. Iris' eyes remain closed. The three of them stand there in silence for a moment. Then, finally, Matternot speaks.)

MISTER MATTERNOT: *(Gently.)* Iris. Open your eyes.

(Iris opens her eyes. He stands before her, speaks kindly.)

MISTER MATTERNOT: My name is Mister Matternot.

IRIS: *(Pleasantly.)* Hello.

MISTER MATTERNOT: And this is Miss Overlook.

MISS OVERLOOK [formerly Mom]: Hello, Iris. It's a pleasure to meet you.

IRIS: It's nice to meet you, too. Where are we?

MISTER MATTERNOT: A little girl and her mother once lived here. We came to visit them. But, now we're on our way to Great Island.

IRIS: Why's it called that?

MISTER MATTERNOT: Because everything on the island—every single thing— is the BEST of its kind. And you, Iris, will continue that tradition.

IRIS: *(Looking at the pouch.)* And what's this?

MISS OVERLOOK: That's your pouch, Iris. It belongs to you.

MISTER MATTERNOT: One thing more. *(He holds up Iris' PastCoat.)*

IRIS: What a wonderful coat. Is that mine, too?

MISTER MATTERNOT: It belonged to the little girl who lived here. *(Testing her.)* Would you like it?

IRIS: Really?

MISTER MATTERNOT: She won't be needing it anymore. Would you like to wear it?

IRIS: Is it cold where we're going?

MISTER MATTERNOT: Not at all. The temperature on Great Island is always perfect.

IRIS: *(Simply.)* Then I won't need it. Thank you, anyway.

MISTER MATTERNOT: *(Smiles.)* As you wish. *(To Overlook.)* Miss Overlook, I'll see you on Great Island.

(Matternot exits, taking the PastCoat with him. Iris begins to follow him, as Overlook sees something on the ground. She reaches down and picks it up: It is a button from Iris' PastCoat.)

MISS OVERLOOK: Iris?

(Iris stops, turns back to her.)

MISS OVERLOOK: Did you drop this? *(She holds up the button.)*

IRIS: What is it?

MISS OVERLOOK: It's a button.

IRIS: It must have fallen off that girl's coat.

MISS OVERLOOK: *(Hands Iris the button.)* Why don't you hold on to it. Maybe you'll find her in your travels.

IRIS: I'll put it in my pouch.

MISS OVERLOOK: I hope I see you again, Iris.

(Iris nods and watches Miss Overlook exit. Iris starts to put the button in her pouch. She stops, looks at the button, holding it in front of her. She closes her eyes. She rubs the button between her thumb and forefinger. As she does so music plays—the same music we heard under the "Still Life" earlier—and—lights shift, isolating only Iris and a—perhaps—miniature "Still Life," the table, cocoa, and the iris in its vase suspended in mid-air above the stage. The rest of the stage is in darkness. Iris does not look over at the "Still Life"—instead, she closes her eyes, tightly, once again. As she continues to rub the button, the light on the "Still Life" grows brighter and brighter. Then, as she opens her eyes and puts the button back in her pouch, the "Still Life" goes suddenly black. It is gone. Music out, as Mister Matternot reappears, quickly, saying—)

MISTER MATTERNOT: We're due at one o'clock, Iris, and we mustn't be late. Are you ready?

IRIS: Ready!

(Iris runs off. Mister Matternot follows her, as music plays, and lights reveal the Great Room of the Great Goods. His Most Excellent, Grotto Good stands in the room. His dashingly elegant clothes have one button, one pocket, one tassel of fringe. He wears one shoe, only. He holds a monocle in his hand, which he uses from time to time. He speaks to his servant, Mister Otherguy—dressed in the same somber manner as Matternot, and wearing a similar sort of tool belt—who is hurriedly dusting everything in the room with a single-feather duster. Music under and out.)

GROTTO GOOD: But, my fear is this, that I will handle it badly. I fear I don't know how to *maintain* a little girl. What do they *do?* What do they eat? And what will I do if she *says something to me?*

MISTER OTHERGUY: I'm sure you'll handle it well, Master Good.

GROTTO GOOD: Shouldn't they be here? It's nearly one o'clock.

(Her Most Excellent, Gretta Good enters. She is dressed in a similarly elegant style to her husband. She, too, wears, only one shoe. She has one ring on her finger. She is affixing her one earring as she arrives.)

GRETTA GOOD: I must tell you, a terrifying thing just happened to me.

GROTTO GOOD: What was it, my dear?

GRETTA GOOD: I found a *second earring.* It was just lying there, next to this one.

GROTTO GOOD: My good, what did you do?

GRETTA GOOD: I threw it away, instantly.

GROTTO GOOD: Oh, thank good.

GRETTA GOOD: It set me back, I must tell you. A shock like that.

GROTTO GOOD: Don't think of it again. Now, Gretta dear, I've been assured by Mister Otherguy that I needn't be nervous about meeting a little girl.

GRETTA GOOD: We'll be fine, Grotto dear. We've chosen the best of the best.

GROTTO GOOD: But what do they *do*—these *children?* That's all I'd like to know. And what if she *says something to me?*

(Gretta shrugs: "I don't know.")

GROTTO GOOD: Mister Otherguy?

(Otherguy shrugs—imitating Gretta.)

GROTTO GOOD: Oh, my good.

(The door flies open quickly, revealing Iris. She now wears an overlayer of clothing that is similar to the Great Goods—elegantly eccentric, very different than her Nocturno attire. She wears one very shiny shoe. The Goods gesture for her to take a step into the room. She does so. She stands stiffly, with a pleasant, forced smile on her face. The clock chimes, once. For a moment,

they all just stand and nod at each other. Finally, Iris turns to Grotto Good and speaks in as friendly a way as possible.)

IRIS: Hello. I'm Iris. What an odd place this is.

(Grotto nods at her for a moment, then turns quickly to Otherguy.)

GROTTO GOOD: My good, *she said something to me.*

(Otherguy gestures for Grotto to respond. Grotto looks at Iris, looks at Gretta, looks back to Iris…then finally speaks, smilingly, definitively.)

GROTTO GOOD: You are a girl.

IRIS: Yes.

GROTTO GOOD: *(Smiling throughout.)* And now you are here.

IRIS: Yes, I am.

GROTTO GOOD: And I am speaking to you.

IRIS: Yes, you are.

GROTTO GOOD: *(Still smiling.)* And now I am finished. *(Turns to his wife.)* Gretta?

GRETTA GOOD: *(Walks toward Iris, calmly.)* You must forgive my husband. He's never spoken to a little girl before. You are the first one to ever arrive on Great Island.

IRIS: I see.

GRETTA GOOD: But, you are welcome here, Iris. More than welcome, you are *treasured.*

GROTTO GOOD: You will now be the greatest of our goods.

GRETTA GOOD: Have you nothing to say?

IRIS: Umm…thank you…

GRETTA GOOD: And?

IRIS: And where's my other shoe?

GROTTO GOOD: Oh, my.

GRETTA GOOD: You are wearing the finest shoe under the sky. Have you *looked* at it?

IRIS: Yes, I have, and its beautiful—maybe the most beautiful shoe I've ever seen. But, still, one of them is missing and the one I'm wearing really hurts my foot. Is there another pair I could wear?

GROTTO GOOD: Oh, my.

IRIS: They don't have to be as nice as these—

GROTTO GOOD: Oh, my.

IRIS: Just a little more comfortable, so I can—

GRETTA GOOD: Iris.

IRIS: Yes, Mother Good?

GRETTA GOOD: There are no other shoes for you. We have only what's BEST on this island and to ensure the value and importance of each item, *we have only one of everything. (To Otherguy.)* Bring her something to drink. *(Otherguy nods and brings a goblet, as well as a small, sealed glass container, on a tray to Iris.)*

IRIS: One of everything—what do you mean?

GROTTO GOOD: Look around, Iris! Everything here is unrivaled in its goodness. Like, for example, our BOOK. Or this—our DRAPE. Or our CHAIR.

IRIS: You only have one chair?

GROTTO GOOD: Isn't it a beauty? *(He brings it to her and insists she sit in it during the following.)*

GRETTA GOOD: So, you see, Iris, that is why you have only one shoe.

IRIS: What happened to its mate?

GROTTO GOOD: It is now in the Tunnel of the UnWanted.

GRETTA GOOD: *(Sees that Iris' drink is ready.)* Oh, here we are. Thirsty?

IRIS: Very.

(Otherguy offers Iris the goblet. She takes it and looks in it—it is empty. Otherguy opens the sealed glass container. He tips it over and pours its contents into the goblet: one long, slow, perfect drop of water. The Goods nod approvingly, as Iris looks into the goblet.)

IRIS: What is this?

GROTTO GOOD: It's a perfect raindrop.

IRIS: This is all the water you have?

GRETTA GOOD: It's all we need. For, at daybreak, another perfect drop will arrive. There's a land near here, where they work all night to see to our pleasure each day.

GROTTO GOOD: So, drink up!

(Iris looks at them, looks at the goblet, then drinks. She, of course, barely tastes it. As she swallows, the Goods sigh, audibly, blissfully.)

GRETTA GOOD: Perfect, isn't it?

IRIS: I guess.

GRETTA GOOD: Now, Iris, we've heard you have a gift for finding things. Is that true?

IRIS: I don't know. Maybe. I don't remember finding *anything*.

GROTTO GOOD: You'll help us find PERFECT THINGS for the Island, I'm sure. Now, we've prepared the best of the best for you—

IRIS: What exactly do you *do* here?

GRETTA GOOD: We enjoy our goods in the greatest of ways.

IRIS: Don't you work?

GROTTO GOOD: Certainly not.

GRETTA GOOD: But we are ever on the lookout for flaws. We musn't let anything that is not the BEST invade Great Island. *(Gretta sees the pouch that Iris wears.)* Like *this* for example. What is the meaning of this old pouch?

GROTTO GOOD: And what's inside?

IRIS: A button. It belongs to a little girl I'm looking for.

GROTTO GOOD: There are no other girls, Iris. You're the only one here.

GRETTA GOOD: Mister Otherguy, show Iris her toy box.

(Otherguy raises the lid of the toy box, as Iris continues to stare at Grotto.)

IRIS: There's no one else to play with?

GRETTA GOOD: We're still searching for a little boy.

GROTTO GOOD: One who's perfect—like you.

IRIS: You brought me here because you think I'm perfect?

GROTTO GOOD: Of course we did.

IRIS: I'm not perfect.

GRETTA GOOD: *(After a quick look at Grotto.)* Really?

IRIS: Not perfect at all.

GROTTO GOOD: Very well. Tell us something you've done that *wasn't perfect.* Some day when you did a bad thing. Something from your *past,* Iris.

(The Goods look at her.)

GROTTO GOOD: Well?

(Silence. Iris thinks.)

IRIS: I can't think of anything.

GROTTO GOOD: You see!

IRIS: But, I know I'm not—

(The Goods leave happily, in a flourish, saying—)

GROTTO GOOD: Enjoy your toys, Iris!

GRETTA GOOD: And if you find anything that is not the BEST of its kind—

GROTTO GOOD: We'll discard and replace it immediately!

GRETTA GOOD: A great good pleasure to meet you!

GROTTO GOOD: A great good pleasure, indeed!

(Music, as lights pull down to isolate Iris near the toy box. The face of the clock remains lit, as well. Mister Otherguy lifts something out of the toy box: a doll encased in glass. On the side of the glass is a small lock. The doll is dressed identically to Iris. Otherguy holds the doll out to Iris. Iris looks at him…then takes it from him. She looks at the doll, then tries to open the lock to take the doll from the case—but it won't open.)

IRIS: It's locked. How can I play with her if she's locked inside?

(Mister Otherguy simply shrugs and exits. Music builds as Iris sits on the closed

toy box, her hands pressed against the glass that houses the doll, as the face of the clock grows brighter and brighter. The clock chimes, once. Lights rise fully on the room, once again, as Mister Matternot enters.)

MISTER MATTERNOT: Hello, Iris.

IRIS: What day is it today?

MISTER MATTERNOT: It's the BEST day of the week—just like it always is.

IRIS: And how long have I been here?

MISTER MATTERNOT: You've been on Great Island for one month—the BEST month of the year.

(Iris is silent. She takes off her lone shoe and tosses it aside.)

MISTER MATTERNOT: Is something wrong? Are you unhappy?

IRIS: I don't remember being happier and I don't remember being sadder. But there must have been a time when I had someone to play with.

MISTER MATTERNOT: Iris, the Goods have filled your toy box with the finest toys under the—

(Iris finishes his sentence with him. She goes to the toy box and pulls out the following items as she describes them.)

IRIS: *(Simultaneous with Matternot.)* "—finest toys under the sky." Yes, I know— and maybe *you'd* like to play with them. Would you like to play cards, well…here's the CARD. Or maybe you'd like to do a jigsaw puzzle, well… here's the PIECE.

MISTER MATTERNOT: What is it you want to do, Iris?

(She now begins to play "Jacks"—with the ball and the one—very beautiful—jack.)

IRIS: I want to—I don't know—I want to go fishing.

MISTER MATTERNOT: But the Goods have already *caught* a fish—a remarkable fish—

IRIS: I don't care! I wouldn't mind TWO of something. Like maybe two jacks instead of one. Or maybe two kids that I could play with.

MISTER MATTERNOT: Perhaps you'd like to go *find* something—the perfect leaf, the perfect stone?

IRIS: There's no need— *(She holds up a picture frame. Framed within it is the leaf we saw Hazel give to the Leaf Monitor.)* The perfect leaf arrived today. Where do these things come from?

MISTER MATTERNOT: A land near here.

IRIS: Is that where the little girl lived? The girl whose coat you offered me?

MISTER MATTERNOT: I don't recall.

IRIS: Of course you do. She lived there with her mother. May we go see her?

MISTER MATTERNOT: She's gone, Iris.

IRIS: Where did she go?

MISTER MATTERNOT: She can't be found.

IRIS: But, I need to return something to her.

MISTER MATTERNOT: Put it out of your mind.

IRIS: Show me the way—I'll find her myself.

MISTER MATTERNOT: I've told you: No one leaves the island without the permission of the Goods.

IRIS: Then I'll—

MISTER MATTERNOT: And the Goods intend to keep you here.

IRIS: Here in this room? Forever?

(Mister Matternot stares at her, saying nothing, as Mister Otherguy and Mister Himtoo enter.)

MISTER OTHERGUY: Iris, the Goods have denied your request.

(Iris lifts the doll still in the glass case and holds it.)

MISTER MATTERNOT: What request?

IRIS: I asked for the key to unlock this case.

MISTER HIMTOO: She is to remain under glass.

MISTER OTHERGUY: It is the word of the Goods.

MISTER MATTERNOT: *(Attempting to cheer her.)* I'm sure you'll find a way to play with her, Iris. She's the BEST doll under the—

IRIS: *(Simply.)* My toy box does not suit me.

MISTER MATTERNOT: *(Thrown by this new tone in her voice.)* I beg your pardon?

IRIS: I am a Good now and I deserve the best of the best, isn't that correct?

MISTER MATTERNOT: Well, yes, of course, but—

IRIS: This box is flawed and I can no longer abide it. I want it replaced.

MISTER MATTERNOT: If I may ask…what is wrong with it?

IRIS: It…has TWO handles! One on either side! It's intolerable! The Goods asked me to tell them if something was not satisfactory—and this, clearly, is not. I want it replaced immediately.

(Matternot stares at her, then turns to Otherguy and Himtoo.)

MISTER MATTERNOT: Inform the Goods.

(Otherguy and Himtoo exit.)

IRIS: Mister Matternot?

MISTER MATTERNOT: Yes?

IRIS: Why are there three of you?

MISTER MATTERNOT: What do you mean?

IRIS: You all work for the Goods. And they have only one of everything. How come they have three of you?

MISTER MATTERNOT: *(A fact, without pity.)* Because we're ordinary. We're not special in the least. *(Pause, going to her.)* It's only been one month, Iris. In time, you'll come to love it here.

(She looks up at him.)

MISTER OTHERGUY: What better place could there be?

IRIS: I don't know. But there must be something. Somewhere.

(She removes the button from her pouch. As she rubs it, music plays and lights rise on the miniature "Still Life" once again.)

IRIS: Because when I hold this button in my hand and close my eyes…I see a picture in my mind. Why would that happen?

MISTER MATTERNOT: May I see that button?

(Iris holds the button out to him. He removes his gloves and takes hold of the button, inspecting it. The "Still Life" is now gone. The music fades out.)

IRIS: And why don't I know what that picture means?

MISTER MATTERNOT: *(Gently, close to her.)* Iris. Some things are the way they are because the way they are is the least likely to bring sadness or bad memories.

IRIS: I don't have any bad memories. Do *you?*

(She sees the open palms of his hands—still holding the button. She touches one of his hands, saying.)

IRIS: You have scars on your hand. Long, red scars. Where did they come from?

(Mister Matternot looks at her, then quickly hands the button back to her— and pulls his gloves back over his hands. He exits, as the Goods' voices are heard, opposite.)

VOICE OF GROTTO GOOD: OH, IRIS!

VOICE OF GRETTA GOOD: WE HAVE YOUR NEW TOY BOX!

(Iris looks off in the direction of their voices, then looks at the toy box next to her. An idea! She opens the toy box and climbs into it, closing the lid and disappearing just as the Goods enter, followed by Mister Otherguy and Mister Himtoo who carry a new, larger, more ornate toy box—with only one handle.)

GROTTO GOOD: Here we are!

GRETTA GOOD: *(Looking around.)* Iris?

GROTTO GOOD: She must be with Matternot. We'll leave it here and surprise her.

(As Gretta speaks, Grotto gestures to Otherguy and Himtoo—showing them where the new toy box should be placed. They follow his instructions.)

GRETTA GOOD: I'm so proud of her, Grotto. She found fault with something! She's become a Good through and through.

GROTTO GOOD: *(Points to the "old" toy box.)* Look at that—it's an abomination! Away with it this instant!

(Mister Otherguy and Mister Himtoo lift, or roll, the "old" toy box—exchanging a quick, curious look regarding its weight—and then exit, taking it away, as Mister Matternot enters, passing them.)

GRETTA GOOD: Ah, there you are.

MISTER MATTERNOT: Where are they going?

(Grotto is putting Iris' toys—the puzzle piece, the card, etc., into the new toy box.)

GROTTO GOOD: In with the best, out with the rest.

GRETTA GOOD: Is Iris with you?

MISTER MATTERNOT: No. I left her right here.

GRETTA GOOD: That's impossible.

(Grotto spots Iris' shoe on the ground.)

GROTTO GOOD: Gretta.

GRETTA GOOD: What?

(Grotto lifts the shoe.)

GRETTA GOOD: Oh my good.

GROTTO GOOD: I fear she's escaped.

GRETTA GOOD: Escaped? But where would she go?

GROTTO GOOD: Every inch of the island must be searched.

GRETTA GOOD: *(To Matternot.)* Well, don't just stand there—

GRETTA AND GROTTO GOOD: START SEARCHING!

(Music, as lights shift to night. A beach on Great Island. One very large seashell, or stone, is prominent, upstage. Music fades into the sound of waves. Iris enters, exhausted, worried. She is barefoot. She looks around in all directions, calling out.)

IRIS: Hello!

(No answer.)

IRIS: Is anybody out there, across the water?!

(No answer.)

IRIS: Can you tell me where I am?! *(Iris climbs atop the shell and calls out.)* HEL-LLOOOOO!

(An echo comes back to her from the water.)

ECHO: HELLLOOOOO!

(Iris looks into the distance, trying to locate the echo. Note: If possible, both live and recorded voice are used to make the "echo" come from a variety of directions in the theater.)

IRIS: WHERE AM IIIIII?

ECHO: WHERE AM IIIIII?

(Iris gradually climbs down and approaches the water, downstage. Liking the sound of the "IIIIIII"—she continues.)

IRIS: IIIIIII!

ECHO: IIIIIII!

IRIS: I!

ECHO: I!

IRIS: IIIIIII'M—

ECHO: IIIIIII'M—

IRIS: IIIIIIIRIS!

ECHO: IIIIIIIRIS!

IRIS: IIIIIII'M IIIIIIIRIS!

ECHO/VOICE OF ANNABEL LEE: IIIIIII'M ANNABEL LEE!

IRIS: *(Jumps back away from the water's edge.)* Who's there?

VOICE OF ANNABEL LEE: An echo waiting to be free.

(Iris stares into the distance, still unable to locate the voice.)

IRIS: Can you help me get away from here? I'm lost.

VOICE OF ANNABEL LEE: Yes, we both seem to be.

IRIS: Really? Where do you live?

(Annabel Lee, a young woman of the sea, appears. She wears a tattered gown of dark blues and greens and the boots and belt of a pirate. Her belt holds a small telescope. Her hair is entwined with seaweed. And, most prominently, she has a long chain (or rope) attached to her wrist, or ankle with a large padlock, which leads far out into the sea, offstage. Iris stares at her, amazed.)

ANNABEL LEE: *(As she enters.)* In a kingdom by the sea. Have you never seen an Annabel Lee?

IRIS: Never. How did you—

ANNABEL LEE: For years I've been locked away—held against my will—but now you, Iris, you've set me free.

IRIS: How?

ANNABEL LEE: By loosing these chains that bind me to the sea.

IRIS: But how did you get here?

ANNABEL LEE: Through your wishing, I assume. What else could it be?

IRIS: I did wish for someone to play with. And I wished for someone to help me get across this water.

ANNABEL LEE: And I wished I would find my ship.

IRIS: You have a ship?

ANNABEL LEE: *(Looking through her telescope.)* It's what I'm searching for, and my ship is searching for me.

IRIS: How do you know?

ANNABEL LEE: I listen at night, locked away, in my kingdom by the sea.
And as the waves crash and fall—
I can hear in the squall—
My ship's voice calling to me—

IRIS: What does it say?

ANNABEL LEE: For the moon never beams without bringing me dreams
Of the beautiful Annabel Lee;
And the stars never rise, but I see the bright eyes
Of my captain, Annabel Lee.

IRIS: *(Smiles.)* Your ship really calls out to you?

ANNABEL LEE: I'm so close to finding it, Iris. It's just out of reach.

IRIS: I see a picture like that, sometimes. A picture of a room. But I don't know where it is.

ANNABEL LEE: What have you been using to navigate with? Have you been using the stars?

IRIS: There's more than *one?*

ANNABEL LEE: Of course there are. Look.

(She hands Iris the telescope, and Iris looks through it at a sky full of stars.)

IRIS: Oh, my. From the palace of the Great Goods, you can only see *one* star.

ANNABEL LEE: Why is that?

IRIS: It's the best one. They chose it.

ANNABEL LEE: There's no best in stars. They're like waves upon the sea. A multitude of many; far as the eye can see. *(Shakes the chain with her arm.)* Now, if you'll free me from this, I'll find my ship and together we'll sail away.

(Iris goes to her and tries to pry the lock from Annabel Lee's arm.)

IRIS: It's locked shut. Maybe we could cut the chain.

ANNABEL LEE: It's too strong—I've tried.

IRIS: *(Looks closely at the lock.)* Then we have to pick the lock. We need something long and narrow and flat. *(Iris looks around, but sees nothing that will work.)*

ANNABEL LEE: Maybe something in your pouch?

IRIS: No. *(Showing her.)* All I have is this button. *(Still looking.)* There must be *something* we can use.

ANNABEL LEE: *(Looking up to the sky.)* I think I know what it is.

IRIS: You do?

(Annabel Lee nods.)

IRIS: What is it?

(Annabel Lee sits, leaning against the shell, looking up at the stars.)

ANNABEL LEE: The same thing that brought me here to you.

IRIS: But that was must me—wishing.

ANNABEL LEE: Exactly. *(Gestures for Iris to join her.)* C'mon, Iris. Your wishes will be our vessel. And the stars will be our map. And with courage and faith as our captain and mate, the ship I've lost and room you seek may fall into our lap.

(Annabel Lee begins to hum "Twinkle Twinkle Little Star," softly and beautifully. After a moment, Iris sits next to her and joins her. They whistle/hum the song together, happily. As they are about to repeat the song, they hear a piano playing the same melody, nearby. They stop whistling/humming. They look around—not knowing where it's coming from. As they stand up and look around, the piano stops. Iris and Annabel Lee whistle/hum a phrase of the song, and the piano echoes the phrase. Note: If possible, the piano phrases should come from a variety of directions in the theater, similar to the "echo" earlier in this scene. Iris and Annabel Lee look around. Then they rush downstage and whistle/hum a phrase of the song, and the piano echoes the phrase. Still looking for the source, Iris and Annabel Lee rush upstage and whistle/hum the next phrase of the song and the piano again echos the phrase, and then, unseen—at first—by Iris and Annabel Lee, Mozart, age eleven, appears downstage, at the edge of the water. He is playing a small piano that is attached to his waist like a drum. The song is the "Twelve Piano Variations in C" [which we know as "Twinkle Twinkle Little Star"]. He is dressed in the clothes of his day. A white handkerchief cascades from his breast pocket. In between phrases, he repeatedly jumps back away from the unseen waves and shakes water from his shoes—all the while continuing to play, avidly. Iris and Annabel Lee turn and stare at him, curiously. They've never seen a person like this before. Mozart finishes the song with a flourish, as Annabel Lee and Iris—behind him—applaud. Mozart turns, surprised.)

MOZART: *Guten tag! Bon jour!* Good day! *(A quick look up at the stars, speaks urgently.)* Or *night.* Why is it night? How long has it been night? And how close are we to morning? It's crucial that I find out. Can you tell me?!

IRIS: Who *are* you?

MOZART: Oh. Yes. Where are my manners? I must have left them in Vienna where manners seem to be all that matters. *(Steps toward them, bows.)* I am Mozart. Wolfgang Amadeus Mozart.

(Iris and Annabel Lee mimic his bow, as they speak, simultaneously.)

IRIS: Hi.

ANNABEL LEE: Hello.

MOZART: But you can call me Motes. I prefer that. Where are we?

IRIS: On the shores of Great Island.

ANNABEL LEE: Isn't it a beautiful beach?

MOZART: *(Sincerely, wiping away some water.)* Yes—but why must it be so close to the water?

IRIS: *(Smiles.)* I'm Iris. And this is Annabel Lee.

MOZART: Are you a pirate?

ANNABEL LEE: My mother was.

MOZART: Your *mother* was?

ANNABEL LEE: And my father was the sea.

MOZART: And I thought *my* family was strange.

ANNABEL LEE: Why must you know when the night ends?

MOZART: I've been searching for something. Something that's *just out of reach.*
    (Iris and Annabel Lee look at each other.)

MOZART: It's a song I work on at night. Only at night. *(With one finger, he plays the first few phrases of the Serenade in G—the Allegro movement from "Eine kleine Nachtmusik." He stops—abruptly—one note prior to completing the second phrase. He looks back at them.)* But, that's it. I can't seem to finish it, because when the sun rises…the melody vanishes. If only I could stop time—if only I could find a way to make the sun wait *just a few seconds more before rising*—I think the song would come to me.

ANNABEL LEE: I know that feeling. Something just out of reach, like my ship—
    (Iris removes the button from her pouch and shows it to them.)

IRIS: Like when I hold this button in my hand.
    (She closes her eyes, as the "Still Life" is illuminated once again. The music that accompanied it plays softly, under, as Iris describes it.)

IRIS: There is a table. And on the table, a vase. And in the vase, an iris.

MOZART: Is it a memory?

IRIS: I'm not sure. This button belonged to a little girl. If I can find her, maybe she'll tell me.
    (The "Still Life" vanishes. The music fades.)

ANNABEL LEE: Is she on this island?

IRIS: I've looked everywhere—and I've found a lot of things for the Great Goods and I found the two of you—but I can't find that little girl.

MOZART: *(As he searches once again for the final note of his melody.)* If she's that elusive, she must be worth the search. Like a melody which hovers in the ether—anonymous and unknown—until it is captured and rendered unforgettable.

IRIS: *(Looking at Mozart's tiny piano.)* That's it.

ANNABEL LEE: What?

(Iris approaches Mozart and points to something on his piano.)

IRIS: May I see that note?

MOZART: That is not, technically, a *note*. It is rather a *key*.

IRIS: Then, it's perfect. May I have it?

MOZART: *Have it?*

IRIS: Just for a moment—yes.

ANNABEL LEE: Iris, what are you—

MOZART: But I may need it. It may be part of the melody I'm searching for—

IRIS: *(Pointing to another one.)* Then give me that one—or that one—or that one. Surely you can do without one of your notes.

(Mozart looks at her, then chooses a key from the piano and hands her the thin, ivory top of it.)

MOZART: *(Reluctantly.)* Here. *(A reprimand.)* And, as I said, it is not, technically, called a *note*. It is—rather—

(Iris inserts the piano key into Annabel Lee's lock, and frees her from the chain, saying—)

IRIS: —a *key*.

ANNABEL LEE: *(Happily tossing the chain aside.)* Thank you, Iris! And thank you, Motes! Now, if we find my ship, we can go in search of that little girl.

MOZART: Did you say "ship"?

ANNABEL LEE: Yes.

MOZART: As in wood which floats precariously over deep, freezing water?

ANNABEL LEE: Yes.

MOZART: *(Moving away.)* Could you point me to Vienna?

ANNABEL LEE: Are you afraid of the water?

MOZART: *(Taking his "key" back from Iris.)* I prefer to be anchored to a piano bench.

ANNABEL LEE: But water is like a rush of music—it is the common language of the world. *(To Iris.)* Isn't that right, Iris?

IRIS: Well, I don't remember if—

ANNABEL LEE: When you're on the water, your heart pounds with delight. And your past is a tide which crashes inside and you speak aloud the story of your life. *(To Iris.)* Isn't that so, Iris?

(Silence. Iris stares at Annabel Lee.)

IRIS: I can't say.

ANNABEL LEE: But, Iris—

IRIS: I have no story to tell.

MOZART: But what about your past? What's the first thing you remember?

IRIS: The face of Mister Matternot. A woman standing with him. And this button.

ANNABEL LEE: And that's all?

IRIS: That's all.

(A huge crash of thunder/crack of lightning, followed by the sound of rain. Iris, Annabel Lee, and Mozart stare at the sky in wonder.)

MOZART: Look at that.

ANNABEL LEE: I've never seen the sky that color. What would you call that?

IRIS: Stormy sky blue-black.

ANNABEL LEE: It's so lovely.

MOZART: And so…*wet.*

(Iris and Annabel Lee are about to playfully grab Mozart and push him toward the water, as a voice is heard, nearby.)

VOICE OF MISTER MATTERNOT: IRIS? IRIS, IS THAT YOU?

(They freeze. Annabel Lee and Mozart turn to Iris.)

MOZART: *(Whispers.)* Who's that?

IRIS: *(Whispers.)* They'll take me back to the Great Goods.

ANNABEL LEE: Hide, Iris. We'll take care of it.

MOZART: We will?

(Annabel Lee gestures for Mozart—still wearing his piano—to run offstage. She then exits, opposite. Iris hides behind the large shell or stone, as Mister Matternot and Mister Otherguy rush on, looking around.)

MISTER OTHERGUY: I heard her voice. I know I did.

MISTER MATTERNOT: *(Calling out.)* THE GOODS ARE VERY DIS-PLEASED WITH YOU, IRIS.

(No response.)

MISTER MATTERNOT: If you don't let me bring you home, I'm afraid they'll punish you. They'll throw you into the Tunnel of the UnWanted and you'll never be found again.

(No response.)

MISTER MATTERNOT: IRIS?

(Otherguy realizes Iris must be behind the shell. He signals to Matternot and they begin to approach slowly, from either side. As they are about to look behind it and find Iris, a voice comes from a distant place, offstage.)

VOICE OF ANNABEL LEE: Here I am!

(Matternot and Otherguy turn in the direction of the voice. Iris too, peeks up—briefly—from behind the shell.)

MISTER OTHERGUY: Over there!

(Matternot and Otherguy start to rush off in the direction of the voice, as a

piano plays a quick phrase of music from a distant place, offstage, opposite. Matternot and Otherguy stop, turn in the direction of the piano.)

MISTER MATTERNOT: What was that?

(As Matternot and Otherguy start to rush off in the direction of the piano, the voice of Annabel Lee calling "Here I am!" and the phrase of Mozart music begin to repeat and overlap each other—coming from seemingly every possible direction all at once. Matternot and Otherguy freeze—trying to decide which way to go. They look at each other. They decide to split up and head off in opposite directions. They rush off, calling out.)

MISTER MATTERNOT AND MISTER OTHERGUY: IRIS!

(As they disappear...the voice and piano fade away and are gone. Silence, as Iris slowly emerges from behind the shell. She walks downstage, calling off to either side of the stage in a whispered voice.)

IRIS: It's safe. They're gone.

(Silence. Iris looks around for them.)

IRIS: You can come out now.

(Silence. She continues to look.)

IRIS: Motes? Annabel Lee?

(Silence. She stares in disbelief, heartbroken.)

IRIS: Oh, no. I made you up. *(Iris sits on the ground, sadly.)* I made you up, and now you're gone—

(Music up, as suddenly Annabel Lee and Mozart are revealed, standing in the back of the theater [or pop up from behind the shell]. They call out to Iris, gesturing for her to follow them.)

ANNABEL LEE: Come on, Iris!

MOZART: Off we go!

(Iris stands and breaks into a big smile as music crescendos, and lights snap out, quickly.)

END OF ACT ONE

ACT II

Music, as lights reveal a small, downstage area. Mister Matternot leads Iris, Mozart, and Annabel Lee onstage. They stand in a line, facing the audience, as Matternot addresses them.

MISTER MATTERNOT: The Goods will be with you in a moment. Please—for your own safety—wait here until they're ready for you. Great Island can be a dangerous place to get lost.

IRIS: We weren't lost, we were curious. And how can that be dangerous? If everything here is the BEST under the sky, what harm can befall us?

MISTER MATTERNOT: The Goods only allow the best of things to be *seen*. But, elsewhere on the island, hidden away in the Tunnel of the UnWanted, are all the OTHERS—all the angry, forgotten, discarded things which are common and unremarkable. You must take care to avoid them.

ANNABEL LEE: You don't understand. All she wants to do is—

MISTER MATTERNOT: Are you her friend?

ANNABEL LEE: Yes, I am.

MISTER MATTERNOT: Then convince her of this: *(Approaches Iris and speaks to her.)* The Great Goods are willing—as you might expect—to forgive you...once. But after that, they may lock you up behind glass.

IRIS: Like a decoration.

MISTER MATTERNOT: Wait here. *(Mister Matternot exits.)*

MOZART: I know the feeling, Iris. Everyone just stares at you all the time like you're perfect and you'll never change and you'll never make a mistake—

IRIS: And everyone makes mistakes—

MOZART: *(Simply.)* I don't. But, I'm *afraid* I might. I'm afraid I'll disappoint my father and never amount to anything and just be another guy in Vienna named Wolfgang Amadeus Mozart.

ANNABEL LEE: If you hadn't been so afraid of the water, we'd have gotten away. There was only that ONE wave.

MOZART: But it was HUGE! Crashing and returning—over and over again.

IRIS: And the wind was so strong—but you couldn't hear it blow. It was completely silent.

ANNABEL LEE: And the fog—thick as cotton—blanketing the horizon in every direction. I think that fog has captured my ship.

IRIS: I wonder when it will finally lift?

MOZART: I miss Vienna. I miss the little streets. I miss the way my sister makes me hot cocoa. I *adore* hot cocoa, don't you?

(Lights expand to reveal the Great Room of the Great Goods. The Goods enter, followed by Mister Matternot and Mister Himtoo. Gretta Good is carrying a candelabra—with one candle, of course—which she sets on a beautiful piano that has been added to the room. Grotto Good walks down the line past Iris, Mozart, and Annabel Lee—as though inspecting them.)

GROTTO GOOD: *(With typical definitiveness.)* Well, here we are—gathered and assembled and brought together here in the very midst of each other— right now, presently, at this time. Gretta?

GRETTA GOOD: *(To Mister Matternot.)* The shoe.

(Matternot produces Iris' tight, shiny shoe and places it on her foot during the following.)

GRETTA GOOD: We're glad to see it restored to your foot, Iris. And as for your clothes which became quite disheveled during your maladventure on the beach—a tailor is on his way to the island to sew you a new, best outfit.

(Matternot gives Iris a look which prompts her to say.)

IRIS: *(Quietly.)* Thank you.

GROTTO GOOD: *(To Mozart.)* You, young man, will be staying with us.

GRETTA GOOD: We've been looking for a little boy.

GROTTO GOOD: We think you'll do nicely.

(Gretta removes the tiny piano that Mozart wears—and hands it to Himtoo.)

GRETTA GOOD: And you won't be needing this—

MOZART: But that's my piano—

GROTTO GOOD: *(Standing by the new piano in the room.)* From now on—THIS is your piano.

MOZART: *(Excitedly, seeing the other piano.)* May I play it?

GROTTO GOOD: Not now, son.

GRETTA GOOD: *(To Annabel Lee.)* And as for you, Miss Lee, the numbers are not in your favor. *(Indicating Iris.)* For you see, we already have a girl on Great Island.

GROTTO GOOD: You're superfluous and we're sorry.

ANNABEL LEE: But, I'm helping Iris find her home—

GROTTO GOOD: And you've succeeded. Now—

(He claps his hands. Mister Himtoo takes hold of Annabel Lee.)

GRETTA GOOD: You'll be shown to the Tunnel.

GROTTO GOOD: The Tunnel of the UnWanted.

(Mister Himtoo begins to pull Annabel Lee away.)

ANNABEL LEE: Don't worry, Iris—I'll find my ship and I'll—

(Matternot steps in and stops them.)

MISTER MATTERNOT: Is this truly necessary, Master Good?

GROTTO GOOD: Did you just *speak to me without consent?!*

MISTER MATTERNOT: My apologies, Master Good. But, perhaps we can make room for another—

GROTTO GOOD: Perhaps we can make room for *you* in the *Tunnel.*

GRETTA GOOD: Off with you, now.

(Matternot and Himtoo lead Annabel Lee offstage. The following three speeches are spoken simultaneously.)

ANNABEL LEE: Have courage and faith, Iris—

IRIS: Please—don't do this!

MOZART: Let her stay!

(Annabel Lee is gone. Smiling widely, the Goods put their arms around Iris and Mozart, as if posing for a quick photograph.)

GROTTO GOOD: And now here we are, a FAMILY at last!

(The clock chimes, once. The Goods step away, admiring their children.)

GRETTA GOOD: Do you like spaghetti?

GROTTO GOOD: We've procured the BEST noodle in all the world!

MOZART: *(Whispers quickly to Iris.) One* noodle?

IRIS: *(Whispers quickly to Mozart.)* I told you.

GRETTA GOOD: What a special treat it is to welcome our new son!

GROTTO GOOD: The newest of our Goods!

GRETTA GOOD: *(To Mozart.)* Your father and I want you to know that you mean the world to us, and we shall provide for your every happiness here on Great Island. The tailor will measure you for your new, best clothing.

GROTTO GOOD: A perfect room shall be prepared for you.

GRETTA GOOD: And, we shall employ the best piano teacher in the world to come and give you lessons.

IRIS: Motes doesn't need a piano teacher. He's pretty good at it, already.

GRETTA GOOD: He is not a "Pretty Good." Nor are you, Iris, a "Pretty Good." We are—all of us—*Great Goods.* And that must never be forgotten!

MOZART: May I play the piano?

GROTTO GOOD: Not now, son.

MOZART: But, it's *night*—and I need to play as much as I can. The song that I'm searching for can only be captured at night. So, please, Father Good— may I play? Would that be all right?

(Grotto looks to Gretta. She does not have an answer. She stares right back at him. He's on his own.)

GROTTO GOOD: Well—I'm not sure if it *is* all right—I've never had a little boy—

or a piano—so, I don't—YES—absolutely—that would be fine—I mean—actually—in fact—NO—certainly not. Is that clear?

(Mozart just stares at him.)

IRIS: I want to see the Tunnel.

GROTTO GOOD: That's out of the question.

IRIS: Mister Matternot told us about it. He said—

GRETTA GOOD: *(Looking to Grotto.)* Mister Matternot will be reprimanded.

GROTTO GOOD: You don't want to see the Tunnel, Iris. I assure you.

IRIS: Why not?

GROTTO GOOD: Because— *(Looking at Gretta.)*

GRETTA GOOD: Because— *(Looking at Grotto.)*

IRIS: Yes?

GROTTO GOOD: Because...

GRETTA GOOD: ...you're *afraid of the Tunnel.*

IRIS: I am?

GRETTA AND GROTTO GOOD: Yes.

(Silence. Iris looks at them, curious and hopeful.)

IRIS: So, I've been there before?

GRETTA GOOD: Yes. *Many times*—when you were younger.

GROTTO GOOD: And you asked us to never show it to you again.

IRIS: I did?

GROTTO GOOD: Yes.

IRIS: Why don't I remember that?

(Silence. The Goods stare at her, then look away.)

MOZART: Iris, ask them about the room.

IRIS: Did we have a white table with three chairs? And on the table was there a—

GROTTO GOOD: I think you know that *three chairs* would be out of the question.

GRETTA GOOD: Yes, now let's—

IRIS: *Tell me things.* Please. Tell me things that happened when I was little.

GRETTA GOOD: But, why, Iris?

IRIS: Because I don't remember. I want you to tell me about when I was a baby.

(Gretta Good look at one another.)

IRIS: Please? Tell me anything—even if its little. Tell me what my first word was. Or what my favorite toy was. Or what games we used to play.

(Silence. The Goods stare at her. Her tone becomes more serious.)

IRIS: Did we used to be happy? If we were, please tell me about that. What did that feel like?

(The Goods stare at her for a long moment—saying nothing. Then, Grotto turns quickly to Mozart, saying.)

GROTTO GOOD: It's time to play the piano, son.

GRETTA GOOD: A great good idea.

(Mozart is still looking at Iris, as Grotto seats him at the piano bench.)

GROTTO GOOD: You mustn't dawdle. You mustn't hesitate. You must do what you're asked when you are asked to do it.

(The Goods prepare to listen.)

GRETTA GOOD: Ah, the delights of a castle above us and our family around us, and now, the sweet caress of music, like water from a distant well, filling our—

(Mozart begins to play: It is, once again, the beginning of the serenade from "Eine kleine Nachtmusik." He plays it with a huge, pounding rhythm—loud and showy—but, stops briefly at the end of his incomplete phrase each time…and then immediately starts into the opening notes again, louder still, avidly searching for the song. The Goods' reaction is horrified and immediate.)

GROTTO GOOD: Oh, my.

GRETTA GOOD: Oh, my good.

GROTTO GOOD: Oh, good help us.

IRIS: I told you he was pretty good!

(Mozart does not hear them, does not stop playing. They step toward the piano and exclaim.)

GRETTA GOOD: Great good son—

GROTTO AND GRETTA GOOD: STOP THIS INSTANT!

(Mozart looks up at them, stops playing.)

MOZART: *(Innocently.)* What is it, Mother Good?

GRETTA GOOD: Grotto?

GROTTO GOOD: My son, you are now a Good. And a Good must be…*selective.* A Good must not fritter away his time in a variety of directions. A Good must always gravitate to that which is great.

MOZART: I'll show more respect, Father Good.

GROTTO GOOD: I knew you would.

(Mozart begins to play again. He plays the identical, still incomplete passage, but this time with a languorous, melancholy feeling. Again, after a few notes, the Goods step forward. They each take hold of one of his hands, stopping him.)

GROTTO AND GRETTA GOOD: *(Firmly, not with anger.)* No, son.

(Mozart looks up at them, as they hold his hands.)

IRIS: Why did you stop him? He's playing for you, he's—

GROTTO GOOD: Quiet, Iris.

GRETTA GOOD: You are very talented, my son. This talent gives you many choices.

GROTTO GOOD: And so, you must *make one.*

MOZART: Make one *what?*

GRETTA GOOD: Make one choice.

GROTTO GOOD: You must pick the Greatest Note and play *only it.*

(*Mozart looks up at them. They release his hands. He looks back down at the keyboard—then back up at them.*)

MOZART: One note?

GROTTO AND GRETTA GOOD: Yes.

MOZART: And *only* one?

(*They nod. Mozart smiles.*)

MOZART: Surely you're joking!

GROTTO AND GRETTA GOOD: No.

(*Mozart stops smiling. The Goods move away and prepare to listen once again. Mozart removes one of the keys—as he did earlier with his tiny piano—and holds it up, offering it.*)

MOZART: What if I gave you one and kept the rest?

(*The Goods shake their heads. Mozart returns the key to the keyboard, as the Goods wait, expectantly.*)

GRETTA GOOD: Now, our great good son, we are ready.

MOZART: But may I say, that is not music. Music is the sound of many things coming together.

GRETTA GOOD: We await your note.

MOZART: (*Standing.*) But there are eighty-eight keys, there are—

GROTTO GOOD: And ONE of them must be the best of all!

IRIS: (*At Mozart's side.*) Why? Why must everything have a "best"? With so many things in the world, it makes no sense to—

GROTTO GOOD: I warn you to say no more—

IRIS: This island is not Great—it is *small.*

GRETTA GOOD: Iris—

IRIS: A "great" island would have *hundreds* of things and not just ONE!

GROTTO GOOD: (*Forcefully, to Iris.*) You must be silent.

GRETTA GOOD: (*Forcefully, to Mozart.*) And you must *choose.*

(*Silence. Mozart looks at them…then sits back down at the bench, solemnly. He looks at the Goods. They nod. Then, they close their eyes, expectantly, awaiting the playing of the "note." Mozart looks back at the keyboard. His hands move—tentatively—up and down the keys…looking for the "perfect" place to land.*)

GROTTO GOOD: (*Whispers.*) Oh, the expectation!

GRETTA GOOD: *(Whispers.)* Quiet!

> *(After another moment of searching, Mozart slowly lowers his finger to the keyboard and plays a note, a beautiful, low A-flat. The Goods both sigh, rapturously, and speak simultaneously.)*

GROTTO GOOD: Oh, my good…

GRETTA GOOD: Yes, that's it…

MOZART: *(Lifts his finger from the keyboard, looks back at the Goods and tries to smile.)* Are you pleased?

GROTTO AND GRETTA GOOD: Oh, yes.

GRETTA GOOD: *(To Grotto.)* Shall we hear it again?

GROTTO GOOD: *(Deliciously.)* Do you think we *dare*?

GRETTA GOOD: Yes, let's do!

> *(The Goods close their eyes again and wait, expectant, as Mozart turns back to the keyboard and looks down at the "note." He pauses…then plays the same note again. Then he plays the incomplete phrase of "Eine kleine Nachtmusik" using only the ONE note. The Goods sigh again, audibly.)*

IRIS: Motes…

MOZART: *(Broken, looking down at the keys.)* It's over. I've failed. I'm never going to find that song.

> *(Mister Himtoo enters and announces.)*

MISTER HIMTOO: Master Good, the tailor has arrived.

> *(The Memory Mender enters. He does not have his cart. He has, instead, a leather case that has "Memory Mender" printed on the outside. He looks around with part dread/part curiosity—never having been to Great Island before.)*

GRETTA GOOD: *(Approaching the Memory Mender.)* We require measurements of our new son—

GROTTO GOOD: *(Also approaching.)* And a garment made for him that will be the finest under the—

MEMORY MENDER: *(Having just seen Iris.)* Iris?

IRIS: How do you know my name?

GRETTA GOOD: Yes, that is—in fact—our daughter, Iris.

GROTTO GOOD: *(A firm threat.)* And beyond saying her name—you will say *nothing more*. Do you understand?

> *(The Memory Mender looks at them, looks at Iris.)*

GRETTA GOOD: *(Coldly.)* There is a place for people who *speak more than they should*. Do you know of it?

> *(The Memory Mender nods.)*

GRETTA GOOD: Splendid. We have an understanding.

(Grotto Good snaps his fingers, and Himtoo brings the piano bench to center. The Memory Mender gestures for Mozart to stand on the stool. During the following, the Memory Mender measures Mozart with a brightly colored measuring tape.)

IRIS: Father Good, I wonder if I could ask the tailor a question.

GROTTO GOOD: *(After a look at Gretta.)* Very well.

IRIS: *(Pointing to his leather case.)* What do these words mean? What is a "Memory Mender"?

MEMORY MENDER: Well, Iris, where we— *(Quickly corrects himself, looking at the Goods.)* where *I* come from, our memories are—

GRETTA GOOD: Your memory is perfect, Iris. It holds nothing but the best of thoughts.

IRIS: Yes, but I—

GROTTO GOOD: We've arranged for you to have an unblemished past—free from sadness, free from—

IRIS: But it's not free. It's *incomplete.*

MOZART: There's a picture in her mind, and she doesn't know what it—

GROTTO GOOD: The mind plays tricks!

GRETTA GOOD: That's it!

GROTTO GOOD: Tricks and nothing more!

GRETTA GOOD: *(Firmly, to the Memory Mender.)* Tell her.

MEMORY MENDER: *(Choosing his words carefully.)* Well—as they say—the mind can be mistaken. If one's memory is harmed—or lost—or *taken*—

GROTTO GOOD: *(Stepping in very close to him.)* You've said *enough.*

IRIS: *(To the Memory Mender.)* May I look at your buttons?

(Iris looks at the buttons on the Memory Mender's PastCoat.)

IRIS: I'm looking for a girl who had a coat like yours. *(Iris reaches into her pouch and removes the button. She hands it to the Memory Mender.)* And she lost this button. Do you know where I might find her?

GROTTO GOOD: Of course he doesn't know! He's not from this Island! He's a common tailor, for good's sake!

IRIS: I want him to answer me!

GRETTA GOOD: Iris—

IRIS: Why are you so afraid of him?!

GROTTO GOOD: Afraid of him?!

GRETTA GOOD: Don't be silly—

IRIS: He's a common tailor—or so you said—why won't you let him answer me?!

(The Goods look at Iris. Then, they turn and look at the Memory Mender, threateningly.)

GRETTA GOOD: *(Quietly, firmly.)* He will *answer you—*

GROTTO GOOD: *(Quietly, firmly.)* *—carefully.* Won't you?

(The Memory Mender nods. He turns to Iris.)

MEMORY MENDER: I know the girl of whom you speak. I made her this button myself.

IRIS: You did?

(The Goods step in, looking at the Memory Mender.)

MEMORY MENDER: *(Looking into Iris' eyes.)* But…I don't know where she is now. She should be very nearby…but I'm afraid that that girl—as I knew her— is gone.

(The Goods smile, relieved. The Memory Mender leans in more closely to Iris and hands her the button, saying.)

MEMORY MENDER: I will tell you this, though: If you find her coat…you will find *her.*

(Iris looks at him. Mozart has heard this, as well. The Goods now begin to rush the Memory Mender out of the room—with Himtoo's help.)

GROTTO GOOD: Is your measuring complete?

MEMORY MENDER: Well, yes, but I—

GRETTA GOOD: We expect the garment to be the best of the best.

MEMORY MENDER: Good luck, Iris—

GROTTO GOOD: Off we go, now—

IRIS: Good-bye.

(The Memory Mender and Himtoo are gone.)

GRETTA GOOD: *(Happily, to Mozart.)* And now, son, before supper, why don't you play us another *note?*

(Mozart stares at her, as lights shift to a dark, forgotten room on Great Island. All that is required is a dirty old brown table with one chair. Nearby are two other dirty chairs, lying about, broken. Miss Overlook sits at the table. She wears dark clothing, similar to Mister Matternot, Mister Otherguy, etc. She is busy polishing several dark, dirty pots and pans with a wire brush. It is filthy, tedious work. Matternot enters, carrying a large box. He speaks, officiously.)

MISTER MATTERNOT: Miss Overlook, the supplies for the island have arrived from Nocturno.

MISS OVERLOOK: And the paint I requested? Did it arrive?

MISTER MATTERNOT: Your request was denied by the Goods.

MISS OVERLOOK: I only wanted to give this dark room some light.

MISTER MATTERNOT: There is, however, paint which was ordered by the Goods that—due to a flaw in its creation—will be of no use to them. It was to be thrown into the Tunnel. You're welcome to it.

MISS OVERLOOK: What flaw?

MISTER MATTERNOT: It is white. All of it. Each and every can.

MISS OVERLOOK: Why is that?

MISTER MATTERNOT: An accident in Nocturno. The Color Mixer has died. He fell from his Color Wheel during last night's storm—thrown to the ground by a great rush of wind.

MISS OVERLOOK: That's terrible.

MISTER MATTERNOT: He was given no warning. The wind, it is said, remained perfectly silent as it blew through the town. *(He sets the paint in front of her.)* You're an excellent worker, Miss Overlook. The Goods are pleased with you.

MISS OVERLOOK: I've never even met them.

MISTER MATTERNOT: That is a sign of their satisfaction. *(He starts to leave.)* Have a great good evening.

MISS OVERLOOK: Mister Matternot.

MISTER MATTERNOT: I've work of my own to do, excuse me—

MISS OVERLOOK: You once told me that I'd always lived here and always done this work. Is that true?

MISTER MATTERNOT: That is the word of the Goods.

MISS OVERLOOK: I'm not asking the Goods. I'm asking *you.* Is it true? Have I truly spent my life in this dark, musty room. Have I never seen the sky, never felt the wind?

MISTER MATTERNOT: *(Challenging her.)* What sky are you speaking of? What wind do you remember?

MISS OVERLOOK: *(A pause as she thinks, then quietly.)* None. None at all.

MISTER MATTERNOT: Then you have your answer.

MISS OVERLOOK: But I've dreamt of such things. And my dreams hold a picture—a picture of a family, a house, a table set for three.

MISTER MATTERNOT: I am a worker, Miss Overlook. I do not dote on wishes and dreams. Nor should you. Be thankful for the *generosity* of the Goods—that they have provided you with a room and a function. Better that than to be thrown into the Tunnel—the home of the angry, forgotten, unremarkable things. At least you and I are *needed* here.
(She stares at him…and then nods.)

MISTER MATTERNOT: You have the paint you requested. But as for seeing the sky, don't think of it again.

(Mister Matternot turns to leave, just as Iris and Mozart appear at the entrance to the room.)

MISTER MATTERNOT: What are you doing here?

IRIS: We were just…

MOZART: …*looking.*

MISTER MATTERNOT: For what?

IRIS: For the way to the Tunn— *(Stops.)*

MISTER MATTERNOT: The way to the what?

MOZART: *Cocoa.* The way to the cocoa.

IRIS: Yes.

MOZART: Is it through here?

MISTER MATTERNOT: I'll have Miss Overlook find you some cocoa.

MISS OVERLOOK: I'd be happy to.

MISTER MATTERNOT: This room is not for the children of the Goods, it is for workers.

MISS OVERLOOK: *(To Iris.)* Did you ever find your Mother? Your name is Iris, isn't it?

IRIS: Yes.

MISS OVERLOOK: I met you once. You were looking for your mother.

MISTER MATTERNOT: And she found her. The Goods are her parents. Now, it's time to—

IRIS: *(Opens her pouch and removes the button.)* I just remembered, you gave me this button. It had fallen off a little girl's coat. It's my oldest memory.

MISS OVERLOOK: I remember that as well. And you put the button in your pouch.

IRIS: Yes—

(Matternot removes one of his gloves and reaches out his hand toward the button.)

MISTER MATTERNOT: It's time you gave me that, Iris. It doesn't belong to you.

IRIS: But, it's my—

MISTER MATTERNOT: I'll return it for you.

IRIS: Do you know where that little girl is?

MISTER MATTERNOT: Yes, I do.

IRIS: Then, why won't you tell me?

MOZART: We needn't ask his help, Iris. If we find that coat, we'll find her.

(Iris puts the button back in her pouch.)

MISTER MATTERNOT: Who told you that?

MOZART: My tailor, if you must know.

MISTER MATTERNOT: Enough, now. There is to be no more discussion of coats and button and—

MISS OVERLOOK: But you were there, Mister Matternot. I remember that as well. You were there the day it happened.

MISTER MATTERNOT: *(Forcefully.) Do you not know what can happen to you?*
(He points in a specific direction—which Iris and Mozart observe.)

MISTER MATTERNOT: Do you not know what awaits you in the Tunnel if you displease the Goods?!

IRIS: But she didn't—

MISTER MATTERNOT: Iris, you are *never to come to this room, again.* You don't belong here. *(Indicating Miss Overlook.)* This woman is ordinary—just as I am—and you're not to trouble yourself with that which is ordinary. Now, return to your parents—both of you!
(Iris and Mozart exit—but Matternot does not see that they exit in the direction of the Tunnel.)

MISTER MATTERNOT: Miss Overlook, have I made myself clear?

MISS OVERLOOK: You were there. I saw you.
(As Matternot puts his glove back on—Overlook takes hold of his ungloved hand, saying.)

MISS OVERLOOK: Your hands. There are long red scars on the palms of your hands. Why is that?

MISTER MATTERNOT: Excuse me, I need to—
(She holds tightly to his hand, not letting him leave.)

MISS OVERLOOK: Have you always been here, as well?

MISTER MATTERNOT: Yes.

MISS OVERLOOK: And these scars on your hands. Where are they from?

MISTER MATTERNOT: *(Pause, simply.)* I don't remember.

MISS OVERLOOK: *(Quietly.)* It's terrible, isn't it? To forget so much. What would cause that, I wonder?
(Music plays, as lights shift quickly to the Tunnel. The music under the scene is joined by the sound of the angry, forgotten things that live in the Tunnel— the random cries of people and animals and discarded objects. The sound of water dripping is heard, as well. Note: A live hidden microphone causes all the following dialogue to reverberate as a slight echo. Iris and Mozart are crawling on their hands and knees. Iris has abandoned her shoe once again and is barefoot.)

IRIS: *(Whispering.)* How much further?

MOZART: *(Also whispering.)* I wish I knew.

IRIS: *(Calling out.)* ANNABEL LEE!

(A frightening echo comes back at them—filled with the sound of the angry, forgotten things.)

MOZART: What are those noises?

IRIS: The angry, forgotten things, I guess.

MOZART: I had no idea there'd be so many of them. Is that what will happen to us, someday? Discarded and forgotten—known only for the noise we once made? *(Sees something.)* Iris?

IRIS: Yes.

MOZART: *(Lifting it.)* Here's your other shoe.

(It is, indeed, the mate to the fancy shoe she wore earlier.)

IRIS: I don't want it.

MOZART: No one does.

(Mozart tosses the shoe aside. As it lands, a noise is heard: the rolling of wheels, the clanging of metal.)

MOZART: What was that?

IRIS: I think *someone's coming*—

(Another, louder noise.)

MOZART: Or *some THING*—

(Another, still louder noise is heard.)

IRIS: Motes, c'mon—we've got to get—

(As they start to stand and run, they immediately encounter a rusty, beat-up metal shopping cart. The cart is filled with discarded items. On the side of the shopping cart is a hand-lettered sign that reads: "Your Name Here." Sitting in the shopping cart is Captain Also—she wears dark, raggedy clothing with a huge number "2" on her chest. She wears a colander as a hat and mismatched gloves on her hands. Pushing the cart is Third String—a man in similarly raggedy clothing with hundreds of "Third Place" ribbons pinned to his clothing. He wears an old football helmet with no face mask, and holds a single ski pole in his hand. With them is Ray—who wears a long, dark raggedy coat, with a small, battered black umbrella attached to his head as a hat. He also wears dark sunglasses. Note: The effect of these individuals is that of a strange, eccentric menace.)

CAPTAIN ALSO: OUT OF HERE? Is that what you started to say? You've got to get OUT OF HERE?! Well, fat chance there is of THAT. You're DOWN UNDER, now. You're in the middle of the mediocre middle.

(Iris and Mozart try to turn and run the other way—but Ray intercepts them and blocks their way.)

CAPTAIN ALSO: And now that you're here, you've got to answer to ME.

IRIS: Who are you?

CAPTAIN ALSO: I'm Captain Also, the Dean of the Discards, the Chairman of the Abhorred. I'm second best to all the rest. And this is Third String—

THIRD STRING: *(Menacingly.)* Have a nice *grey.*

CAPTAIN ALSO: Third String is not a winner and he's not a loser. He is undeniably *average.* So, I made him my CEO.

THIRD STRING: Chief *Extra* Officer.

CAPTAIN ALSO: We are the Top of what's on the Bottom, the most Famous of the Forgotten!

(Captain Also reaches into the shopping cart and pulls out some items, tossing them at Iris and Mozart.)

CAPTAIN ALSO: You want a TOASTER?—we got millions of 'em. HANGERS— PLASTIC TUBS—BRIDESMAID DRESSES—we got *millions of 'em.* Everybody wanted 'em ONCE—

THIRD STRING: —and nobody wants 'em NOW.

CAPTAIN ALSO: We are the Orphans of the Ordinary!

THIRD STRING: Unexceptional—

CAPTAIN ALSO: —and Unnecessary!

MOZART: And who's that?

THIRD STRING: That's Ray.

IRIS: Is he ordinary, too?

CAPTAIN ALSO: No, he's displaced. Ray used to work for the Sun. He did outreach. Show 'em, Ray—

(Ray opens his coat to reveal its brilliantly yellow lining.)

CAPTAIN ALSO: You ever wonder what happens to the sun when you shade your eyes, or step under a tree to cool off? Ever wonder where those Rays of Sun end up once they're not needed, anymore?

(Ray closes his coat.)

CAPTAIN ALSO: You got it. They end up right here. Just like the two of you.

THIRD STRING: What's your business here? Who threw *you* out?

IRIS: Nobody threw us out.

CAPTAIN ALSO: What?!

THIRD STRING: Then what are you doing in the Tunnel?!

MOZART: We're searching for our friend.

RAY: "Friend"—what's that? Won't find any of those down here.

IRIS: Why not?

RAY: If you're a friend—somebody wants you. There's no one like that down here.

MOZART: You see, we were living with the Goods, but we—

CAPTAIN ALSO: The GOODS?! We've got a couple of GOODS here?! Get 'em!

(Third String surprises Iris and Mozart from behind, putting his ski pole under their chins—trapping them in place. Ray moves in on them, as well.)

CAPTAIN ALSO: Oh, we've been waiting for this moment. Haven't we, Ray?

RAY: Since the day they turned me into shade.

CAPTAIN ALSO: And we're not alone. Do you hear them?

(The sound of the angry forgotten things begins to grow louder and louder.)

CAPTAIN ALSO: Do you hear all the angry, forgotten things? They've been waiting for you and now they'll have their revenge!

(Captain Also gestures, quickly and dramatically, and the sound of the angry forgotten things stops, instantly.)

THIRD STRING: Tell us your story, so we can devise your punishment.

CAPTAIN ALSO: Yeah—tell us what makes you SPECIAL. *(To Mozart.)* You first.

MOZART: Me? Oh, nothing, really. Nothing in the least.

THIRD STRING: C'mon. You're a Good. Spill the beans.

MOZART: I've just written a few songs.

THIRD STRING: A few?

MOZART: Well, ten sonatas and three symphonies by the age of nine—

CAPTAIN ALSO: I see.

MOZART: But there's a song—or part of a song—that I'm still looking for.

RAY: You won't find it here. People *want* music—so, there's no music down here.

THIRD STRING: *(To Iris.)* And what about you?

CAPTAIN ALSO: Yeah—what's your *story?*

IRIS: I don't have one.

THIRD STRING: Sure you do. Everybody's got a story. Even Ray.

RAY: It all started on a sunny day in a—

CAPTAIN ALSO AND THIRD STRING: Shut up, Ray.

IRIS: I wish I had one. But, I don't.

THIRD STRING: She's lying.

IRIS: All I have is a picture in my mind.

CAPTAIN ALSO: A picture of when you were *wanted?* A picture of your *home?*

IRIS: Yes, I think so—

CAPTAIN ALSO: Well, FORGET ABOUT IT. Because you'll never get back to it.

THIRD STRING: Nobody ever leaves the Tunnel.

MOZART: But, why?

CAPTAIN ALSO: Because *the only way out of here is to be WANTED*—

THIRD STRING: To be USEFUL—

RAY: So, we're TRAPPED—

CAPTAIN ALSO: Just like *you.*

(They tighten their grips on Iris and Mozart, as Annabel Lee enters, holding a wooden ship's wheel in her hand. Strapped over her shoulder is what appears to be a large, fabric satchel of some kind. She goes directly to Captain Also, Third String, and Ray.)

ANNABEL LEE: Unhand them this instant and prepare to set sail!

MOZART: *(Simultaneously.)* Annabel Lee!

IRIS: *(Simultaneously.)* There she is!

CAPTAIN ALSO: You know her?

ANNABEL LEE: There's a speedy escape should you do what I say—
Or a watery grave should you me disobey.

RAY: Who are you?

ANNABEL LEE: When the fog is lifted and the tide is high—
We will sail our ship and bid the Goods good-bye!

THIRD STRING: Ship? What ship?

ANNABEL LEE: Now, unhand them and see to your duties!

CAPTAIN ALSO: We don't answer to you, Miss WhoeverYouAre. These Goods are our prisoners here, and—

ANNABEL LEE: And I am your *captain.*
(She tosses the ship's wheel to Captain Also—who catches it and holds it, proudly. Silence, then.)

THIRD STRING: You mean…

CAPTAIN ALSO: …you *need us?*

ANNABEL LEE: I can't sail without you.

THIRD STRING: You mean…

RAY: …you'll *free us from the Tunnel?*

ANNABEL LEE: If you'll unhand my friends and serve as my crew—
Your discarded days will vanish from view.
(Captain Also, Third String and Ray release their grip on Iris and Mozart.)

ANNABEL LEE: Now, fall in.
(Third String and Ray line up next to Captain Also's shopping cart—forming a line. Annabel Lee walk past them, taking stock of her new crew.)

ANNABEL LEE: The ship waits—trapped in fog—at the far end of this Tunnel.
There are sails to mend! rigging to ready, and provisions to load.
Are you able, willing and sufficiently brave—
To conquer the sea and make fear your slave?

CAPTAIN ALSO, THIRD STRING, RAY: *(Saluting.)* We are!

ANNABEL LEE: Now, to the ship!
(Annabel Lee gestures off, and the three of them rush off, pushing Captain Also who steers with the ship's wheel. Iris and Mozart approach Annabel Lee.)

IRIS: How did you find the ship in all that fog?

ANNABEL LEE: I was looking for parts of your picture—the table, the flower, the vase. So, I kept following the Tunnel, on and on. And I saw something shining in the distance—a shimmering patch of light—and when I reached it—

(She removes the satchel from over her shoulder—and we see that it is actually a faded and weathered PastCoat that she has used to carry an object. She unwraps the object. It is a vase—identical to that in the "Still Life.")

ANNABEL LEE: —I found vases. Hundreds of them. Discarded in a huge pile.

(Annabel Lee hands the vase to Iris.)

IRIS: Just like the picture in my mind.

ANNABEL LEE: And there the Tunnel empties into a cove, shrouded in fog. And when I lifted this vase, the light cut through the fog and there it was…my ship, awaiting me.

(Iris has discovered the weathered PastCoat.)

IRIS: Motes, look.

MOZART: Is that the coat you're looking for? Is it missing a button?

IRIS: (Looking closely at the coat.) No. And it's too big to be a little girl's.

ANNABEL LEE: There are hundreds of those coats, piled up at the far end of the Tunnel.

IRIS: We'll need to get all of them. (To Annabel Lee.) Can you make it back there?

ANNABEL LEE: (Nods.) I found a shortcut through the water.

IRIS: Good. And take Motes with you.

(Iris takes the vase and rewraps it in the PastCoat.)

MOZART: (To Annabel Lee.) Wait…did you say water?

ANNABEL LEE: (Tossing him a discarded life preserver.) It's an easy swim. There's only that ONE wave—

MOZART: I would like to rethink our entire plan—

(Annabel Lee ushers Mozart off, and Iris exits, opposite, as lights shift to Miss Overlook's room. The table is now white. One of the chairs is painted white. Another is half-painted. The third remains a dirty brown. An open can of paint sits nearby. Miss Overlook enters and sets a steaming cup of cocoa on the table in front of the one painted chair. She looks down at the table for a moment, touching the back of the white chair, as Iris enters, carrying the wrapped vase.)

IRIS: Miss Overlook—

MISS OVERLOOK: Is Mozart with you? I have his cocoa for him.

IRIS: He'll be here. I wanted to ask you something.

MISS OVERLOOK: What do you have there?

(Iris unwraps the vase and sets it on the table—however, her focus is clearly on the PastCoat.)

IRIS: It's something we found in the Tunnel. Would you hold onto it for me?

MISS OVERLOOK: By all means.

IRIS: What I wanted to ask you about was *this*.

(Iris holds up the PastCoat, showing it to Overlook.)

IRIS: Have you ever seen this before?

(Silence, as Overlook looks at the coat.)

MISS OVERLOOK: Not that coat, Iris. But one like it. On the day I met you.

IRIS: Yes, I remember that as well. It belonged to a little girl.

MISS OVERLOOK: It belonged to you. *(Pause.)* You had a coat like this.

IRIS: What happened to it?

MISS OVERLOOK: It's better that you don't know, Iris. That's what Mister Matternot said and I see now that he was right.

IRIS: But why would he say that?

MISS OVERLOOK: He took your coat from you. I watched him as he did it. *(Pause.)* At the time, I thought he was very kind. For before he took your coat, you were very upset—you were calling for your mother.

IRIS: My mother?

MISS OVERLOOK: Yes. But then, a moment later, he took your coat from you…and you were fine. *(Pause.)* He did it to protect you.

IRIS: I don't want that. Not any more. *(Iris stares at her—then rushes out of the room, taking the coat with her.)*

MISS OVERLOOK: Iris—!

(As lights shift quickly to the Great Room. Mister Otherguy and Mister Himtoo are putting a large, ornate glass case in place. It is an exact replica of the small case that held Iris' doll—including the lock on one side of it. Mister Matternot enters, watching, as Gretta and Grotto Good enter, opposite.)

MISTER MATTERNOT: Master Good, if I may ask, what is the meaning of this?

GROTTO GOOD: You may not ask. You may not ask it at all.

GRETTA GOOD: You were given a task, Matternot. You were told to bring us a little girl and make certain that she felt at home.

GROTTO GOOD: You were to remove any vestige of her past.

MISTER MATTERNOT: And that's what I did!

GROTTO GOOD: To the contrary—this girl, Iris, has grown curious about her Before-Good life.

GRETTA GOOD: You have displeased us—

GROTTO GOOD: —And we have your Fate under consideration.

MISTER MATTERNOT: And Iris—what of her? You can't hope to keep her here. Now that she is curious, she will—

GROTTO GOOD: It's no longer your concern.

GRETTA GOOD: We've found a fine place for her.

GROTTO GOOD: A fitting home for the greatest of our Goods!

(The Goods start off, as Iris enters—carrying the old, tattered PastCoat—and goes directly to Mister Matternot. Seeing Iris, the Goods stop at a distance, listening. Mister Otherguy and Mister Himtoo stand on either side of the glass case.)

IRIS: Mister Matternot—

MISTER MATTERNOT: (Seeing the coat in her hand.) Iris, what do you have in your—

IRIS: The coat you showed me. It was *mine*, wasn't it? Tell me the truth. It was mine and you took it from me.

MISTER MATTERNOT: You had been *chosen*, Iris. The Great Goods had—

IRIS: You lied to me—

MISTER MATTERNOT: I was trying to save you—

IRIS: Save me?

MISTER MATTERNOT: From your sadness. From the loss of your home. Believe me, it was the only way I could—

IRIS: But why would you take my coat?

MISTER MATTERNOT: It holds your *past*, Iris—it holds the story of your life.

GROTTO GOOD: (Stepping in.) Matternot—!

IRIS: Take me back there.

MISTER MATTERNOT: I can't—

IRIS: Take me back to that room—

MISTER MATTERNOT: That room is gone. (Forcefully.) Just like your mother. It is gone and you must forget about it.

IRIS: Who was she? Tell *me*.

(The Goods approach.)

GRETTA GOOD: Your life is here with us, Iris.

GROTTO GOOD: We've given you the BEST things in all the world—

IRIS: You've given me everything but the thing I want most: *the story of who I am*. Even the common, forgotten things know where they came from—but I don't. I wish I was one of them.

GRETTA GOOD: (Simultaneously.) Don't say that—

GROTTO GOOD: (Simultaneously.) Iris, that's enough—

IRIS: (To Mister Matternot, desperately.) I want you to take me to that room!

MISTER MATTERNOT: (Simultaneously.) But, Iris, I—

GRETTA GOOD: *(Simultaneously.)* Put it out of your mind.

GROTTO GOOD: We have a greater place for you, Iris!

(Grotto and Gretta clap their hands, and Otherguy and Himtoo step forward and grab Iris. The old, tattered PastCoat falls to the ground.)

MISTER MATTERNOT: What are you doing?

IRIS: Let go of me—

GRETTA GOOD: You will be the glory of Great Island!

(Music, as Matternot runs toward Iris, but is restrained by Otherguy, as Himtoo takes Iris to the glass case. The Goods remove the lock and open the door to the case.)

MISTER MATTERNOT: You can't do this. You must tell her—you must tell her the truth!

GRETTA GOOD: Had you done your job well, this could have been avoided—

IRIS: *(Cries out.)* No—please don't do this—

GRETTA GOOD: But, now she must pay for your mistakes—

MISTER MATTERNOT: No, listen to me—

GROTTO GOOD: Her pain is your doing, Matternot. Her sadness is your curse.

(Iris is placed inside the glass case. The lock is attached by Grotto—who holds the large key ring with the one key aloft, proudly. Iris stands, trying to plead with the Goods through the glass, "Why are you doing this?" "Please, don't leave me in here!" etc., but she cannot be heard. The Goods exit, followed by Otherguy and Himtoo. Iris stares out, helplessly, as Matternot tries to talk to her through the glass.)

MISTER MATTERNOT: *(Painfully, from his heart.)* I was afraid, Iris—afraid of the wrath of the Goods—that they'd send me to the Tunnel and I would die alone and forgotten. But worse than the Tunnel is what I've done to you— given you glimpses of your home and nothing more. *(Pause.)* What our memory leaves unfinished, our heart completes with ache.

(Matternot puts his ungloved hand up and presses it against the glass. Iris looks at him—then matches his gesture with her hand.)

MISTER MATTERNOT: *Forgive me,* Iris.

(Annabel Lee and Mozart rush on, Mozart carries a huge bundle of PastCoats in his arms.)

ANNABEL LEE: What have you done with her?!

MISTER MATTERNOT: I was trying to—

MOZART: *(Dropping the coats to the ground.)* You've locked her up behind glass.

MISTER MATTERNOT: No, it was the Goods who—

(The Goods rush on, followed by Mister Otherguy and Mister Himtoo.)

GRETTA GOOD: What is all the motion and commotion?!

GROTTO GOOD: *(Seeing Annabel Lee.)* And what are you doing here?! You were discarded!

ANNABEL LEE: Well, I'm *back.*

(Matternot is now standing near the pile of PastCoats.)

MISTER MATTERNOT: *(Forcefully, to the Goods.)* Now I see what you've done! *(He kneels amid the coats, lifting armfuls of them as he speaks.)* All these years—I had no idea!

GRETTA GOOD: *(Simultaneously.)* What is that?

GROTTO GOOD: *(Simultaneously.)* What's there?

MISTER MATTERNOT: *Coats.* Look at all of them!

GRETTA GOOD: We've given each of them a Great Good life.

MISTER MATTERNOT: You told me there were only *two.* Only Iris and her mother. But, there have been HUNDREDS!

GROTTO GOOD: Not another word, Matternot—

MISTER MATTERNOT: *(Referring to Himtoo and Otherguy.)* You've done this to *all of us,* haven't you?!

GROTTO GOOD: *(Throwing the key ring to Otherguy.)* Lock him away as well! *(As Otherguy catches the key ring and starts toward Matternot, Matternot throws one of the PastCoats from the pile to Otherguy, saying.)*

MISTER MATTERNOT: You've ripped the past from each and every one of us! *(Upon catching the coat, Otherguy stops. He looks down at the coat, holding it tightly in one hand, the key ring in the other, then he looks at the Goods— puzzled, wanting an answer.)*

GRETTA GOOD: You've been given an order, Mister Otherguy—

MISTER MATTERNOT: *(To Otherguy.)* That's not your name. Your name was stolen from you by the Goods—

GROTTO GOOD: Mister Himtoo—take that coat from him! *(As Himtoo rushes at Otherguy, Matternot throws a coat from the pile to Himtoo—who, upon catching it, immediately stops. He, too, looks at the coat, then up at the Goods—puzzled, wanting an answer.)*

MISTER MATTERNOT: It's too late—now they know the truth. *(Otherguy and Himtoo look at their coats, at each other. Then they put their coats on and approach the Goods with menace.)*

GROTTO GOOD: This, Gretta, is a great good problem. *(Matternot lifts the pile of PastCoats from the ground—inadvertently leaving behind the single, tattered PastCoat that is laying elsewhere—and rushes off, saying.)*

MISTER MATTERNOT: Soon everyone will know!

GROTTO GOOD: *(Simultaneously.)* No—

GRETTA GOOD: *(Simultaneously.)* MATTERNOT—

(The Goods start to rush off after Matternot—but are stopped by Otherguy and Himtoo. Annabel Lee takes the key from Otherguy and opens the glass case, freeing Iris, saying.)

ANNABEL LEE: Don't worry, Iris. My ship is rigged and ready—

MOZART: And her crew is second to none—

ANNABEL LEE: And the moment the fog is lifted, we shall sail away and be gone.

IRIS: Thank you, both—

(Otherguy and Himtoo begin to place the Goods inside the glass case.)

GROTTO GOOD: *(To Otherguy and Himtoo.)* You wouldn't dare!

GRETTA GOOD: Grotto, dear, what will become of us?!

(Annabel Lee tosses the key back to Otherguy—and the Goods are locked inside, silently pleading for help.)

MOZART: Now, let's get off this island before being a Good gets any worse.

(Annabel Lee sees the tattered PastCoat that was left behind. She lifts it.)

ANNABEL LEE: Mister Matternot left this behind—the old and tattered one.

IRIS: *(Taking it from her.)* I'll bring it with me. C'mon—

(Iris rushes off, followed by Annabel Lee and Mozart, as music changes to that of the "Still Life," and lights shift to Miss Overlook's room. Miss Overlook holds a paintbrush in her hand, making a few final brush strokes on the third and final white chair. The table and chairs in the room are now all painted white. She positions the vase in the center of the table. She moves the cocoa slightly—so that it is now in the exact position seen in the "Still Life." The "Still Life" is now lacking only the iris. Overlook takes a long look at the table, then exits—exactly as she did in Act One, as Mister Matternot enters, opposite. He now carries only one PastCoat in his arms. He stops when he sees the white table and vase.)

MISTER MATTERNOT: Miss Overlook?

(No response. Matternot takes a long look at the table, then he lowers the coat, revealing something he is holding in his hands…it is an iris. He places the iris in the vase. The "Still Life" is now complete. Music continues as Matternot steps away from the table, and Iris enters, carrying the old, tattered PastCoat. Iris stops when she sees the "Still Life." She steps toward the table. Walks around it, slowly. Iris takes the button from her pouch. She closes her eyes and rubs it in her hand, as the light on the table grows brighter and brighter. She opens her eyes and compares the picture in her mind with the picture in front of her. They are identical. The music fades away.)

IRIS: *(Quietly.)* That's it. *(Iris moves to the table. She pulls "her" chair back from the table—exactly as she did in Act I. She sits. She looks at the vase, the flower,*

*the cocoa in front of her. Then—just as she did in Act I—she begins to reach
for the cocoa, as Miss Overlook enters.)*

MISS OVERLOOK: *(Simply.)* Careful. That's hot.

IRIS: *(Looks at her. Then, simply, quietly.)* Mom.

MISS OVERLOOK: Yes, I know, Iris. I know you miss her. Whoever she is, wherever she's gone.

*(Matternot takes the PastCoat and walks toward Overlook. She looks at him,
puzzled.)*

MISS OVERLOOK: Mister Matternot?

MISTER MATTERNOT: I'd like you to meet someone.

*(Matternot helps Overlook put on the coat—her PastCoat. When it is on, she
looks first at the table...and then at Iris.)*

MOM [formerly Miss Overlook]: *(Quietly.)* Iris.

(Iris and Mom embrace.)

MOM: Oh, Iris. I'm right here. And now wherever you are, no matter how far
away—

IRIS: —when you call my name, I'll hear you.

MOM: Thank you, Mister Matternot. *(Mom turns and looks at Matternot. Then,
she approaches him.)* I'd like to see your hands, if I could.

*(Mom helps Matternot remove his gloves. He stares at her, puzzled. Mom hands
the gloves to Iris. Iris takes them, confused.)*

MOM: Here, Iris. These gloves belong in your pouch. *(Mom touches the palms
of Matternot's hands as she looks into his eyes, speaking softly.)* These scars
on your hands. They belong to the man who roped the moon every night,
and hauled it down out of the sky. And then he'd give the signal for the
sun to rise...

IRIS: *(Looking at Matternot.)* ...and the day to break.

*(Mom holds out her hand, and Iris hands her the tattered PastCoat. Mom
helps Matternot put his PastCoat on.)*

MOM: Do you remember us?

DAD [formerly Mister Matternot]: *(Quietly.)* Yes.

MOM: Even with your coat tattered and torn?

DAD: Your name is Rose.

MOM: Yes. *(Pause.)* And, this is your daughter...Iris.

(Iris and Dad stare at each other.)

IRIS: I thought you left us.

DAD: The Great Goods took me away, Iris. Just like you.

IRIS: Do you remember me?

DAD: You were just a baby. And my coat is old and worn—

IRIS: Don't worry, Dad—we'll be your coat. We'll tell you everything you missed.
> (*Dad and Iris embrace, as Annabel Lee and Mozart enter. Annabel Lee is carrying a smaller PastCoat in her arms.*)

MOZART: The coats have all been returned, Iris.

ANNABEL LEE: We've given everyone back their Pasts.

MOM: And what of the Goods?

DAD: The Goods reign is over. They work for *us* now.

ANNABEL LEE: They're loading Motes' piano onto my ship.

MOZART: (*Deliciously.*) One note at a time.

ANNABEL LEE: (*Holding up the coat.*) There's one coat left, Iris.
> (*Dad takes the coat from Annabel Lee. Mom and Dad put the PastCoat on Iris, and then stand, holding each other, arm in arm.*)

IRIS: Thank you. (*Turning to Annabel Lee and Mozart.*) I hope you find your song, Motes.

MOZART: I'll try again tonight. Perhaps I'll find it just before the sun rises.

IRIS: (*Giving Annabel Lee the button.*) Annabel Lee, this is for you.

ANNABEL LEE: But this button—it's part of your coat—

IRIS: And now I'm part of yours.
> (*Annabel Lee smiles.*)

IRIS: I'll lift the fog for you as soon as I get home.
> (*Annabel Lee and Iris embrace.*)

MOZART: Hey, Iris—

IRIS: What?

MOZART: Are you going to drink that cocoa?

IRIS: (*Smiles and hands the cup of Cocoa to Mozart.*) Take it with you, Motes.
> (*Annabel Lee and Mozart leave.*)

ANNABEL LEE: (*Simultaneously.*) Good sailing, Iris!

MOZART: (*Simultaneously.*) Adieu!
> (*Iris looks at her Mom and Dad—who have taken their places at the table. Iris joins them.*)

IRIS: But how will *we* get home?

DAD: (*Simply.*) By *remembering.*

MOM: (*Quietly.*) What do you see, Iris?

IRIS: (*Slowly, quietly.*) I see an iris in a vase. And the vase is on a table. And the table is in a house. And the house is—
> (*A flourish of music, as lights reveal the Land of Nocturno, once again—identical to the beginning of the play. The WELCOME TO NOCTURNO sign is there. The rain barrel is there—marked with the number of a new batch.*)

And, approaching the table are Hazel and Elmer—each holding a still-spotless Ladybug; and the Flower Painter—painting a rose.)

IRIS: *(Opens her eyes, saying.)* —in Nocturno, our home!

ELMER:: *(Simultaneously.)* Hazel, look—!

HAZEL: *(Simultaneously.)* Iris!

FLOWER PAINTER: *(Simultaneously.)* Here they are!

(Iris, Mom, and Dad step away from the table.)

IRIS: Does it look the same to you, Dad?

DAD: *(Looking around.)* Some of it does...

(The Flower Painter gives the rose to Mom, as Hazel and Elmer approach Iris.)

FLOWER PAINTER: Welcome home, Rose. The wind's been silent without you.

MOM: *(Smiles.)* You'll hear it again in no time.

HAZEL: *(To Iris, like she never left.)* Did you find the spots, Iris?

IRIS: The what?

ELMER: *(Holding up his Ladybug.)* For the Ladybugs?

(Iris reaches into her PastCoat and removes one large, black spot. She hands it to Elmer.)

IRIS: Where I was, Elmer, they only had *one.*

(Hazel smiles and embraces Iris, as Elmer looks puzzled, and the Memory Mender pushes his cart into the midst of the celebration, cranky as ever.)

MEMORY MENDER: Well, look at this, a bunch a people huggin' and pattin' each other on their coats—when they oughtta be takin' care of each sleeve and button and—

DAD: *(Approaches the Memory Mender, with a smile of recognition.)* Well, one thing in Nocturno hasn't changed. You're still as cranky as ever!

(A pause, while the Memory Mender stares at Dad, trying hard to place him in his memory. The others looks on. The Memory Mender looks hard at Dad—while at the same time touching various parts of his own coat, saying.)

MEMORY MENDER: Wait—wait—wait—don't tell me—

(After a few tries the Memory Mender touches a small button at the end of his sleeve, saying.)

MEMORY MENDER: The Day Breaker! Husband of Rose, father of Iris.

DAD: *(Shaking his hand.)* That's me.

MEMORY MENDER: I gotta tighten that button down before I *lose you completely.*

(To Iris.) I see you found your coat, Iris. Welcome home.

IRIS: Thank you.

MEMORY MENDER: *(To Dad.)* And you know, I had to rope the moon for you every night, while you've been gone. It's awful hard on the hands—

DAD: Yes, it is.

MEMORY MENDER: In fact, I just now put her away for the day.

DAD: Have you given the sun her signal to rise?

MEMORY MENDER: Have at it. I got coats to sew. *(He moves away, still talking.)* People 'round here think the past's just some kind of toy that their mind plays with, but you gotta take care of it or you'll trip and get a rip— *(The Memory Mender moves upstage and looks on as he sews. The others turn and look at Dad.)*

DAD: *(Turning to Iris and her Mom.)* Ready? *(From a great distance…music plays…the first few phrases of the Serenade in G from "Eine kleine Nachtmusik," as before. Dad reaches out his arm in front of him—preparing to raise it, as Iris steps in, interrupting him.)*

IRIS: Wait, Dad. Wait one…more…moment. *(As soon as Iris has said this, the full Mozart serenade continues and plays on—uninterrupted—for the first time. Iris nods to her Dad, smiling. Everyone looks out at the horizon. Iris stands next to her Dad, as he reaches his arm out in front of him, preparing to give the sun its "signal," preparing to break the new day.)*

IRIS: Almost day.

DAD: Almost day, indeed. *(Dad lifts his arm, dramatically, in front of him, as upstage, a huge sun lifts into place and a brilliant orange glow illuminates all of them. The music builds and fills the theater as the people of Nocturno gradually return to their work, except for Iris, who stands front, home at last, looking up into the glorious morning light.)*

END OF PLAY

GREAT EXPECTATIONS

Adapted by Barbara Field
from the novel by Charles Dickens

ORIGINAL PRODUCTION

Great Expectations was originally produced by Seattle Children's Theatre on September 30, 1983. It was directed by Richard Edwards. Lisa Ruble was the stage manager. The cast was:

Young Pip . . . . Jonathan Bridgman/Isaac Benjamin Sterling
Magwitch . . . . Robert I. Lee
Joe Gargery/Aged Parent/Porter/Prison Doctor . . . . . . John Pribyl
Mrs. Joe/Molly . . . . Mary Thielen
Pumblechook/Wemmick/Drummle . . . . Todd Jefferson Moore
Lieutenant/Tailor/Herbert Pocket . . . . Geoffrey Alm
Jaggers/Compeyson . . . . Rex Allen
Estella . . . . Katharine Kramer
Miss Havisham/Miss Skiffins . . . . Barbara McKean
Biddy/Clara . . . . Michelle Blackmon
Young Herbert Pocket . . . . Joshua Ramsell/Jason Tanner
Pip . . . . Brett Keogh
Joe's Boy . . . . Mark Branom
Understudy for Joe's Boy—Michaelangelo Von Dassow

CHARACTERS

Six men, four women to double as follows:
Pip
Herbert Pocket, Lieutenant , Tailor
Wemmick, Pumblechook, Bentley Drummle
Jaggers, Compeyson**, Clergyman
Joe Gargery, Aged Parent, Porter, Prison Doctor
Magwitch, A Pocket
Miss Havisham, Miss Skiffins
Estella
Biddy, Clara Barley, A Pocket
Mrs. Joe Gargery, Molly, A Pocket

Although in the first production children were used to play Young Pip, Herbert, and Estella, adult actors have subsequently played the characters throughout the play.

** The actor playing Jaggers can double as Compeyson, except for a few non-speaking crossovers in Act II. Since the character is heavily muffled, other actors may take turns at Compeyson during these scenes.

ABOUT THE NARRATION

The premise of this adaptation is that *all* of the actors tell the story; it is a shared effort in storytelling. Narration is assigned at the director's discretion. Narrating actors may be solitary and removed, may be part of the scene, or may be narrating while assisting in a scene change.

One interesting choice is to let narration *about* a particular character be spoken by the actor playing that role. For example, another member of the company can speak the line "The next morning early, after fortifying themselves with…" etc. But Pip might take the line, "Pip was puzzled."

SET

There are over fifty scenes in this adaptation, in more than a dozen locales. It is imperative that scene changes take no more time than the narrative dialogue that accompanies them takes to deliver.

The set is a neutral platform, with upstage scaffolding. This scaffolding performs several functions:

1. A (movable) part of it must become Miss Havisham's iron garden gate, allowing entrances from behind the scaffolding onto the stage.

2. It must contain a couple of functioning prop shelves for the actors to use.

3. If possible, the scaffolding should contain an upper level, with visible stairs.

There should also be one or two smallish wagons, which can be preset offstage with the few big set pieces (Miss Havisham's table with the bride cake, for instance), then wheeled onstage either by actors or mechanically. Chairs can be hung on pegs at the sides of the stage or on the scaffolding. In any case, the furniture used should be as spare as possible, and should be manipulated rapidly.

The Thames River scenes have been written with a large map of the Thames estuary in mind—to be used on the floor if the stage is raked. Model boats manipulated by actors can travel on the map. The actors provide, in effect, a kind of voice-over for the action.

With one or two obvious exceptions, costume changes should be minimal.

Responsibility for most sound effects should also belong to the acting company, who can ring all the bells, make the rural sounds, etc., in view of the audience.

The premise on which this adaptation stands is that simple, honest storytelling and open use of the stage *as a stage* will be more effective than any literal-minded or realistic set.

ACT I

The entire company is assembled onstage, except for the actor playing Magwitch, who is already hiding behind the tombstone.

NARRATION: His family name being Pirrip and his own name being Philip, in the beginning the boy could make of both names nothing longer than…Pip. So he called himself Pip, and came to be called Pip. The family name, Pirrip, he had on the authority of a certain tombstone, his father's, and on the authority of his older sister, Mrs. Joe Gargery, who was married to the town blacksmith. They lived in the marsh country of Kent, where the Thames ran down to the sea. In that dark, flat wilderness was a village churchyard where, one day, Pip found his parents.

(Churchyard. A few tombstones. Pip kneels in front of one of them, reads haltingly.)

PIP: "Philip Pirrip, late of this parish." *(Pause.)* "Also Georgiana, wife of the above…"

NARRATION: The boy, a small bundle of shivers, began to cry, when—
(Magwitch pops up from behind a tombstone.)

MAGWITCH: Keep still, you little devil, or I'll cut your throat!

PIP: Oh don't, sir!

MAGWITCH: Tell us your name quick, then!

PIP: Pip, sir.

(Magwitch lifts him abruptly, sets him atop the stone, searches him. He finds a crust of bread, which he gnaws.)

MAGWITCH: Lookee here, then—where's your mother?

PIP: There, sir.

(Magwitch starts.)

PIP: There— "Also Georgiana." That's my mother.

MAGWITCH: Hah. And that's your father, alonger your mother?

PIP: Yes, sir. "Late of this parish."

MAGWITCH: Hah. And who d'ye live with now, supposin' I kindly let you live, which I haven't made up my mind about?

PIP: My sister, Mrs. Joe Gargery. She's wife to the blacksmith.

MAGWITCH: Blacksmith, eh? *(He looks down at his leg irons.)* Lookee here: The question being whether or not you're to be let live—you know what a file is?

PIP: Yes, sir.

MAGWITCH: And you know what wittles is?

PIP: Wittles is food, sir.

MAGWITCH: You bring me a file and you bring me some wittles, or I'll have your heart and liver out. Bring 'em tomorrow at dawn—and don't say a word about having seen me—and I'll let you live.
(Pip nods.)

MAGWITCH: But mind, I'm not alone, if you're thinking that. No indeed, there's a young man hid with me, in comparison with which young man *I* am an angel. So you must do as I tell you.

PIP: Yes, sir.

MAGWITCH: *(Magwitch pulls out a little Bible.)* Swear—say "Lord strike me dead if I don't."

PIP: "Lord strike me dead if I don't."
(Magwitch gives him a dismissing nod. The boy backs away, then bolts. Magwitch huddles by the tombstone.)

(The forge kitchen.)

NARRATION: Pip's sister, Mrs. Joe Gargery, was more than twenty years older than the boy. She had established a great reputation as a foster parent, because she had brought the boy up *by hand.*
(As Pip races in, she slaps him.)

NARRATION: She was neither a good-looking woman, nor a cheerful one.
(Joe steps in to protect Pip.)

NARRATION: Pip had the impression that she must have made Joe Gargery marry her *by hand,* too.
(She slaps Joe, as well.)

MRS. JOE: Where've you been, young monkey? I'm worn away with fret and fright over you.

PIP: I've only been to the churchyard.

MRS. JOE: Churchyard! If it weren't for me, you'd have been in the churchyard long ago. Bad enough being a blacksmith's wife, and him a Gargery, without being your mother as well. You'll drive *me* to the churchyard one of these days, between the two of you.
(As she talks, she butters a slice of bread, hands it to Pip with another slap. He takes a bite, then when she isn't looking, he secretes the rest in his pocket. Joe notices, however. Mrs. Joe turns to Pip.)

MRS. JOE: Where's your bread? Did you swallow it whole? This boy has the manners of a swine!

JOE: Oh no, my dear, I don't think he—

MRS. JOE: Don't my dear me! I'm not your dear. *(She hands Pip a slate, some chalk.)*

NARRATION: Pip felt little tenderness of conscience toward his sister. But Joe he loved.

(Joe watches Pip writing laboriously on the slate.)

JOE: I say, Pip, old chap, what a scholar you are!

PIP: I'd like to be. *(He writes.)* How do you spell Gargery?

JOE: I don't spell it at all.

PIP: But supposing you did?

JOE: It cannot be supposed—though I am oncommon fond of reading.

PIP: Are you, Joe? I didn't know that.

JOE: Oncommon—give me a good book and I ask nothin' better.

PIP: *(Pause.)* Did you ever go to school?

JOE: My father, he were given to drink, Pip; and whenever he were overtook with drink, he'd beat my mother and me, most onmerciful. We ran away a time or two, and my mother would find a job. "Joe," she'd say, "now you shall have some schooling, please God." And so I'd start school. But my father was such a good-hearted man, he couldn't bear to live without us, so he'd hunt us down and drag us home. Then he'd beat us up again to show how he'd missed us. Which you see, Pip, were a serious drawback to my learning.

(Mrs. Joe takes Pip's slate away.)

MRS. JOE: Time for bed, boy. *(She gives him a slap for good measure.)*

JOE: Time for bed, Pip, old chap. *(Whispers.)* Your sister is much given to government, which I meantersay the government of you and myself. *(He hugs Pip.)*

(There is a distant boom of a cannon.)

MRS. JOE: Hark, the guns.

JOE: Ay. It must be another conwict off, eh?

PIP: Off?

MRS. JOE: Escaped, escaped.

PIP: Please, Joe, where's the shooting come from?

MRS. JOE: Ask no questions, you'll be told no lies.

JOE: It comes from the Hulks, Pip, old chap.

PIP: Please, Joe, what's the Hulks?

MRS. JOE: This boy! Answer one question and he'll ask a dozen more!

JOE: Hulks is prison ships.

PIP: And please, Joe—

MRS. JOE: No more! Time for bed! Bed! Bed! Bed!

NARRATION: Conscience is a dreadful thing when it accuses a boy. Pip labored with the thought that he was to become a thief the next morning...Which was Christmas Day.

(The cannon booms.)

NARRATION: Pip scarcely slept that night. When pale dawn came he crept into the forge where he stole a file, and thence into the pantry where he stole a loaf of bread, some brandy, and a beautiful, round firm pork pie. As he ran toward the marshes, the mist, the wind, the very cattle in the field seemed to accuse him. Stop thief! Stop that boy!

(The churchyard. Pip runs toward the convict, whose back is to Pip. The man turns at Pip's whistle—but it is not the same man! Both gasp, then the man runs off. Pip empties his pockets, then Magwitch appears. He grabs the brandy.)

MAGWITCH: What's in the bottle, boy?

PIP: Brandy.

(Magwitch stuffs the food into his mouth. He shivers as he eats.)

PIP: I think you've caught a chill, sir.

MAGWITCH: I'm much of your opinion, boy. *(He pauses, listens.)* You brought no one with you?

(Pip shakes his head.)

MAGWITCH: I believe you. You'd be a mean young hound if you could help hunt down a wretched warmint like me, eh?

(Pip watches him eat.)

PIP: I'm glad you enjoy your food, sir.

MAGWITCH: Thankee, boy, I do.

PIP: But I'm afraid you haven't left much for him.

MAGWITCH: Who's him?

PIP: That young man you spoke of, who's with you.

MAGWITCH: Oh, *him.* *(He grins.)* He don't want no wittles.

PIP: He looked as if he did—

MAGWITCH: —Looked? When? *(He rises.)*

PIP: Just now.

MAGWITCH: —Where?!

PIP: Right here, a few minutes ago. I thought it was you—he wore gray, like you, and he wore…he had the same reason for wanting a file. He ran away.

MAGWITCH: Did he have a scar on his face?

PIP: *(Nods.)* Here.

MAGWITCH: Give us that file, boy. *(Magwitch starts to file his leg irons.)* And then ye'd best go—they'll be missing you!

(Pip nods, then runs off.)

NARRATION: As Pip ran home, he could still hear the file sawing away at the convict's fetters. He fully expected to find a constable waiting to arrest him when he got home. But there was only Mrs. Joe, readying the house for Christmas dinner.

(The Forge kitchen.)

MRS. JOE: —And where the deuce ha' you been now? Company's expected!

PIP: I was…down to hear the carolers.

(She gives him a crack on the head.)

JOE: Merry Christmas, Pip, old chap.

NARRATION: Dinner was set for half-past one. There was one guest…Mr. Pumblechook, wealthy seed-and-corn merchant in the nearby town. He was Joe's uncle, but he was Mrs. Joe's ally.

PUMBLECHOOK: Mrs. Joe, I have brought you a bottle of sherry wine, and I have brought you a bottle of port wine, in honor of the Day.

MRS. JOE: You was ever the soul of generosity, Uncle.

(They sit at table. She cuffs Pip.)

MRS. JOE: Stop fidgeting, boy—he wriggles as if he had a guilty conscience.

PUMBLECHOOK: Then he must indeed have one. Boys, Joseph—a bad lot!

MRS. JOE: Will you say the blessing, Uncle Pumblechook?

PUMBLECHOOK: For that which we are about to receive, may the Lord make us truly thankful.

ALL: Amen.

PUMBLECHOOK: D'you hear that, boy? Be ever thankful to them what has brought you up by hand.

PIP: Yes, sir.

PUMBLECHOOK: Joseph, why is it the young are never thankful? I declare, boys are naturally wicious!

MRS. JOE: Too true, Uncle Pumblechook.

JOE: Have some gravy, Pip? *(He ladles it onto Pip's plate.)*

PUMBLECHOOK: Not too much—the Lord invented the pig as an example of gluttony to the young. *(To Mrs. Joe.)* He's no end of trouble to you, is he, ma'am?

MRS. JOE: Trouble? You cannot know what trouble he's been.

JOE: More gravy, Pip old fellow, old chap, old friend?

PUMBLECHOOK: I suppose this boy will be apprenticed to you, soon, Joseph?

MRS. JOE: Not for another year. Till then he'll eat me out of house and home— but I'm forgetting! I've a delicious pork pie, yet!

(Pip drops his fork.)

PUMBLECHOOK: Ah, pork pie! A morsel of pie would lay atop any dinner you might mention, and do no harm, eh?

MRS. JOE: I'll just go fetch it. *(She goes.)*

(Pip rises in terror, rushes to the front door to escape. Simultaneously, a sharp knock at the door, and a scream from Mrs. Joe. At the door, Pip is confronted by a pair of handcuffs, held by a soldier.)

LIEUTENANT:	MRS. JOE: *(Off.)*
Hello, young fellow—	Stop! Stop, thief, my
Does the blacksmith live here?	pie—it's been stolen.
Well?	

PUMBLECHOOK: This is the blacksmith's, yes.

LIEUTENANT: Sorry to disturb your Christmas dinner—

PUMBLECHOOK: Think nothing of it, my good man.

LIEUTENANT: —But we've caught two convicts, and need these irons repaired. Can you do it?

PUMBLECHOOK: Not me, him. He's the smith. Certainly he can do it.

(Mrs. Joe enters, distraught.)

MRS. JOE: My pork pie—it's gone—

LIEUTENANT: *(To Joe.)* By the way, is this your file?

JOE: *(Examines it.)* Which it are!

LIEUTENANT: It was found in the churchyard—

MRS. JOE: Thieves, thieves…

(Pumblechook is already pouring port wine down her throat.)

NARRATION: Christmas dinner was over. When Pip arrived at the boat landing with Joe, he recognized *his* convict—and the other, with the scarred face.

(The convicts glare at each other. The lieutenant takes the handcuffs from Joe, snaps them on Magwitch. The other man, Compeyson, lunges at Magwitch, is pulled off by soldiers.)

MAGWITCH: I took 'im! I caught the villain! I turned 'im in, don't forget.

COMPEYSON: This man—this man has tried to murder me!

MAGWITCH: See what a villain he is—look at his eyes! Don't forget, I caught 'im for ye!

(Magwitch turns, notices Pip. Pip gives him a tiny shake of the head.)

MAGWITCH: I wish ter say something respectin' this escape. It may prevent some persons from lying under suspicion alonger me.

LIEUTENANT: You'll have plenty of chance later—

MAGWITCH: —But this is a separate matter. I stole some wittles up in the willage yonder. Likewise a file—

JOE: Halloa, Pip?

MAGWITCH: And some liquor. And a pie. *(To Joe.)* Sorry to say, I've eat your pie.

JOE: God knows you're welcome to it, as far as it was ever mine. We don't know what you have done, but we wouldn't have you starved to death for it, poor miserable fellow. Would us, Pip?

(Pip shakes his head. The lieutenant calls out, "Ready! Move!" The prisoners are marched off, Magwitch stops, turns back. He and Pip stare at each other for a moment, then he goes off. Darkness.)

(The forge kitchen.)

NARRATION: It was not long after the incident on the marsh that Mrs. Joe returned home in the company of Mr. Pumblechook, in a state of rare excitement.

(Joe smoking his pipe in a chair, Pip on the floor beside him. Mrs. Joe and Pumblechook burst in.)

MRS. JOE: If this boy ain't grateful this night, he never will be!

(Pip tries to look grateful.)

MRS. JOE: It's only to be hoped she won't fill his head with silly ideas.

PUMBLECHOOK: I doubt it. She knows better.

JOE: Which someone mentioned a *she?*

MRS. JOE: Unless you call Miss Havisham a he—

JOE: Miss Havisham? That odd, solitary lady in the town?

MRS. JOE: She wants this boy to go play there. Of course he's going—and he'd better play, or I'll work him! *(She cracks Pip on the head.)*

JOE: Well, to be sure. I wonder how she come to know Pip?

MRS. JOE: Noodle—who says she knows him? *(She cracks Joe on the head.)* Couldn't she ask Uncle Pumblechook if he knew of a boy to go play there?

Isn't it barely possible that Uncle Pumblechook may be a tenant of hers; and might he go there to pay his rent? And couldn't Uncle, out of the goodness of his heart, mention this boy here—to whom I have ever been a willing slave?

PUMBLECHOOK: Now, Joseph, you know the case.

MRS. JOE: No, Uncle, Joseph does not know the case. *(To Joe.)* For you do not know that Uncle, aware that this boy's fortune might be made by Miss Havisham, has offered to deliver Pip to her tomorrow, with his own hands! What do you say to that?

JOE: *(Mystified.)* Thankee kindly, Uncle Pumblechook.

PUMBLECHOOK: My duty, Joseph. *(To Pip.)* Boy, be ever grateful to those what brought you up by hand. *(He gives Pip a box on the ear.)*

NARRATION: Miss Havisham's house was of dismal bricks. Most of its windows were boarded up. There was a tall iron gate before which Mr. Pumblechook and Pip appeared at ten the next morning.

(Miss Havisham's. The garden; then a room. Mr. Pumblechook rings the bell.)

PUMBLECHOOK: Right on the dot of ten, boy.

PIP: No sir, I believe we're early. See, her big tower clock says twenty to nine.

PUMBLECHOOK: It must have stopped. My timepiece is always correct.

(Estella appears.)

ESTELLA: What name?

PUMBLECHOOK: Pumblechook.

ESTELLA: Quite right.

(She unlocks the gate. Pumblechook pushes Pip through.)

PUMBLECHOOK: This is Pip.

ESTELLA: This is Pip, is it? Come in, Pip.

(Pumblechook tries to follow.)

ESTELLA: Do you wish to see Miss Havisham?

PUMBLECHOOK: I'm sure Miss Havisham wishes to see me.

ESTELLA: Ah, but you see, she don't. *(She shuts the gate in his face, leads Pip on.)* Don't loiter, boy.

NARRATION: Although she was about Pip's age, to him she seemed years older— Being beautiful and self-possessed— And being a girl.

(She leads Pip upward, with a candle in her hand. She knocks. A voice says "come in." Estella gestures Pip into the room, then leaves. It is dark. There is a banquet table with a huge cake. Miss Havisham is seated before it.)

HAVISHAM: Who is it?

PIP: Pip, ma'am.

HAVISHAM: Pip?

PIP: Mr. Pumblechook's boy, ma'am. Come to play.

HAVISHAM: Come nearer, let me look at you. Come closer.

NARRATION: Once Pip had been taken to see a waxwork at a fair. Once he had been taken to an old church to see a skeleton in the ashes of a rich robe, which had been dug out of a vault. Now waxwork and skeleton seemed to have dark eyes that moved, and looked at him.

HAVISHAM: Come closer. Ah, you are not afraid of a woman who has never seen the sun since you were born?

PIP: …No.

HAVISHAM: You know what I touch here?

PIP: Your heart.

HAVISHAM: Broken. *(Pause.)* I am tired. I want diversion. Play.

(Pip does not move.)

HAVISHAM: I sometimes have sick fancies; and I have a sick fancy that I'd like to see someone play. Play. Play, play!

(Pip does not move.)

HAVISHAM: Are you so sullen and obstinate?

PIP: I'm very sorry, but I can't play just now. I would if I could, but it's all so new here…so strange and fine and…melancholy.

HAVISHAM: So new to him, so old to me; so strange to him, so familiar to me; so melancholy to us both.

(Estella enters.)

HAVISHAM: Let me see you play cards with this boy.

ESTELLA: With this boy!? Why, he's nothing but a common laboring boy!

HAVISHAM: *(Aside to Estella.)* Well? You can break his heart.

ESTELLA: What do you play, boy?

PIP: Only "Beggar My Neighbor," miss.

(Estella brings out a deck of cards, deals. They play. Pip drops some cards.)

ESTELLA: He's stupid and clumsy—look at his hands, so coarse!

(They play.)

HAVISHAM: *(To Pip.)* You say nothing of her. What do you think of her, tell me in my ear.

PIP: *(Whispers.)* I think she is very proud.

HAVISHAM: Anything else?

PIP: I think she is very pretty.

HAVISHAM: Anything else?

PIP: I think she is very insulting and I'd like to go home.

HAVISHAM: You may go soon. Finish the game.

(*They play.*)

NARRATION: The girl won. Her name was Estella. Pip was asked to return the next week. Estella took the candle and led him out.

ESTELLA: (*Going.*) You're crude. You're clumsy. Your boots are ugly!

NARRATION: The girl saw tears spring to Pip's eyes. Pip saw her quick delight at having been the cause of them. And for the first time, he was bitterly aware that life had been unjust to him. He quickly dried his eyes so she would not catch him weeping.

ESTELLA: Why don't you cry again, boy?

PIP: Because I don't want to.

ESTELLA: Yes you do. You cried before, and you'll cry again—

NARRATION: Pip headed for home with the shameful knowledge that his hands were coarse and his boots were ugly, and that he was much more ignorant than he had thought himself the night before.

(*The forge kitchen. Pumblechook, Mrs. Joe, and Joe wait eagerly. Pip enters.*)

PUMBLECHOOK: Well, boy? How did you get on?

PIP: Pretty well, sir.

PUMBLECHOOK: "Pretty well?" Tell us what you mean by pretty well, boy.

PIP: I mean pretty well.

PUMBLECHOOK: And what is she like?

PIP: Very tall and fat.

MRS. JOE: Is she, Uncle?

(*Pause. Pumblechook nods vaguely.*)

PUMBLECHOOK: Now, tell us what she was doing when you went in?

PIP: She was sitting in a big black velvet coach.

(*His listeners are amazed. Pip smiles.*)

PIP: Miss Estella handed her wine and cake, into the coach. We all had wine and cake—on golden plates!

(*Astonished pause.*)

PUMBLECHOOK: Was anyone else there?

PIP: Four black dogs.

PUMBLECHOOK: Large or small?

PIP: Immense!

PUMBLECHOOK: That's the truth of it, ma'am, I've seen it myself the times I've called on her.

(*He bows, exits with Mrs. Joe. Pip whistles a tune to himself.*)

NARRATION: After Mr. Pumblechook departed, Pip—or his conscience—sought out Joe.

PIP: It was all lies, Joe.

JOE: Really? The black velvet coach was a lie?

PIP: Yes.

JOE: Even the golden plates?

PIP: I wish my boots weren't so thick, Joe, I wish— *(He throws his arms around Joe, buries his face in Joe's shoulder.)*

NARRATION: He told Joe how miserable he'd been made to feel, by Uncle Pumblechook and Mrs. Joe, and by the very beautiful young lady who had called him common.

JOE: One thing, Pip, lies is lies and you mustn't tell any more of 'em. That ain't the way to stop bein' common. As for that, in some ways you're most oncommon. You're oncommon small. You're an oncommon scholar.

PIP: I'm not, I'm ignorant and clumsy.

JOE: Pip? Even the four black dogs was lies?

NARRATION: Although Pip could not improve the quality of his boots, he set about to remedy the quality of his education by taking lessons from Mr. Pumblechook's great-aunt's grand-niece—Biddy—who lived in the neighborhood.

BIDDY: *(Holds up a slate to Pip.)* Six times four.

PIP: Twenty-four.

BIDDY: Seven times four?

PIP: Twenty-eight.

BIDDY: Eight times four?

(A pause. Pip isn't sure of the answer and, to tell the truth, neither is Biddy.)

PIP: Thirty-four?

(She nods approval.)

NARRATION: And a week later he returned to Miss Havisham's at the appointed hour.

(Miss Havisham's. The garden, then a room.)

ESTELLA: Follow me, boy. Well?

PIP: Well, miss?

ESTELLA: Am I pretty?

PIP: Very.

ESTELLA: Am I insulting?

PIP: Not so much as you were last time.

ESTELLA: No? *(She slaps his face.)* Coarse little monster, why don't you cry?

PIP: I'll never cry for you again.

(As they cross, they pass Mr. Jaggers coming from the other direction.)

NARRATION: As Estella led him through the gloomy house, they encountered a singular-looking gentleman coming toward them.

JAGGERS: Well, well, what have we here?

ESTELLA: A boy.

JAGGERS: Boy of the neighborhood?

PIP: Yes, sir.

JAGGERS: How d'you come to be here?

ESTELLA: Miss Havisham sent for him, sir.

JAGGERS: Well, behave yourself. I've a pretty large experience of boys, and you're a bad set of fellows. Behave! *(He continues out.)*

(Estella and Pip enter Miss Havisham's room.)

HAVISHAM: So, the days have worn away, have they? A week. Are you ready to play?

PIP: I don't think so, ma'am.

HAVISHAM: Are you willing to work, then?

(Pip nods. She takes his arm, leans against his shoulder.)

HAVISHAM: Help me to walk, boy.

(They circle the table.)

HAVISHAM: This is where I shall be laid when I am dead. *(She points with her stick.)* What do you think that is?

PIP: I cannot guess.

HAVISHAM: It's a great cake. A bride-cake. Mine.

PIP: There are mice in it, ma'am.

HAVISHAM: Yes. This cake and I have worn away together, and sharper teeth have gnawed at me.

NARRATION: Breathing the heavy air that brooded in the room, Pip suddenly had an alarming fancy that all was decaying—that even he and Estella might presently begin to decay.

HAVISHAM: Now you must play at cards.

(Estella gets the deck.)

HAVISHAM: Is she not pretty, Pip?

(Pip sighs, nods. Estella deals.)

NARRATION: And so the visits ran, with little to distinguish one from another.

Estella always won at cards. Once, some relations called upon Miss Havisham.

A POCKET: How well you look, ma'am.

A POCKET: Happy birthday, cousin—

A POCKET: —And many happy returns of the day.

HAVISHAM: You see, Pip? The vultures have descended again, my Pocket relations. But the Pockets shall not have a penny of mine, never! You may go, Pip.

NARRATION: Pip was all too glad to take his leave. He was about to let himself out by the garden gate, when he was stopped by a pale young gentleman. *(Young Herbert appears, munching an apple.)*

YOUNG HERBERT: Halloa, young fellow. Who let you in?

PIP: Miss Estella.

YOUNG HERBERT: *(Pleasantly.)* Do you want to fight? Come on. *(He tosses the apple over his shoulder, strips off his cap, jacket, and shirt.)* I ought to give you a reason for fighting. There— *(He claps his hands together under Pip's nose, gently pulls his hair. He dances around Pip, fists doubled.)* Standard rules, is that agreeable?

(Pip nods. Herbert dances around, throwing punches that miss Pip. Pip finally gets one off, and it levels Herbert. Estella peeps out to watch.)

PIP: Oh dear, I'm sorry—

YOUNG HERBERT: Think nothing of it, young fellow!

(He jumps to his feet, squeezes a sponge of water over his head, dances around again. Pip lands another punch, Herbert falls.)

PIP: Oh, look, I'm really so sorry, I—

YOUNG HERBERT: Perfectly all right. *(He gets up, picks up the sponge, throws it.)* See, I'm throwing in the sponge. That means you've won.

(He offers his hand. They shake.)

PIP: Can I help you?

YOUNG HERBERT: No thankee, I'm fine.

(He picks up his jacket and cap. As he goes off, Estella passes him, sticks out her tongue. He shrugs, leaves. Pip stares after him. Estella comes to him.)

ESTELLA: You may kiss me, if you like.

(He kisses her on the cheek, then, overwhelmed, he flees.)

NARRATION: If Pip could have told Joe about his strange visits— If he could have unburdened himself about his love for Estella, or even about his fight with the pale young gentleman— But of course he could not, for Joe's hands were coarser and his boots thicker than Pip's own! So Pip confided in Biddy—it seemed natural to do so. He told her everything, And Biddy had a deep concern in everything he told her.

(Pip and Biddy are strolling, sharing a piece of toffee.)

PIP: Biddy, I want to be a gentleman.

BIDDY: Oh, I wouldn't if I was you, Pip.

PIP: I've my reasons for wanting it.

BIDDY: You know best, but wouldn't you be happier as you are?

PIP: I am not happy as I am! I am disgusted with my life.

BIDDY: That's a pity for you, isn't it?

PIP: I know. If I was half as fond of the forge as I was a year ago, life would be simpler. I could become Joe's partner someday. Who knows, perhaps I'd even keep company with you. I'd be good enough for *you,* wouldn't I, Biddy?

BIDDY: Oh yes, I am not over-particular. *(Pause.)* Is it Estella?

PIP: It's because of her I wish to be a gentleman.

BIDDY: Do you wish to be a gentleman to spite her or to win her?

PIP: I don't know. Biddy, I wish you could put me right.

BIDDY: I wish I could...

NARRATION: But Biddy could not put Pip right. Things went on in the same way. His dreams and discontent remained. Time passed. Finally, one day Miss Havisham look at him crossly—

HAVISHAM: You are growing too tall! What is the name of that blacksmith of yours?

PIP: Joe Gargery, ma'am.

HAVISHAM: I shan't need you to come play here anymore. So you'd better be apprenticed to Mr. Gargery at once.

PIP: But—

HAVISHAM: But what?

PIP: —I don't want to be a blacksmith! I'd rather come here!

HAVISHAM: It's all over, Pip. You're growing up. Estella is going abroad to school next week. Gargery is your master now. *(She glances at Estella, whispers to Pip.)* Does she grow prettier, Pip? Do you love her? Shall you miss her? *(Pip turns away, she crosses to Estella.)*

HAVISHAM: Break their hearts, my pride and hope, break their hearts and have no mercy.

NARRATION: Pip was indentured as apprentice blacksmith to Joe Gargery the following week. Miss Havisham's parting gift of twenty-five pounds was cause for celebration in some quarters.

(Mr. Pumblechook and Mrs. Joe toast.)

NARRATION: Pip did not celebrate. He had liked Joe's trade once, but once was not now. He was wretched.

(Sound of an anvil. Glow of a forge fire.)

NARRATION: Nonetheless, Pip labored. And Pip grew. Always he would gaze into the fire at the forge and see Estella's face. He heard her cruel laughter in the wind. He was haunted by the fear that she would come home, witness his debasement, and despise him. On the surface, however, Pip's life fell into a routine. Days he worked with Joe at the forge. Evenings he became his own teacher— For he had long outstripped Biddy in learning. Once a year, on his birthday, he visited Miss Havisham.

HAVISHAM: Pip, is it? Has your birthday come round again? Ah, you're looking around for her, I see. Still abroad, educating for a lady…far out of reach and prettier than ever. Do you feel you have lost her?

NARRATION: Time wrought other changes. Mrs. Joe Gargery fell gravely ill, and lingered in a kind of twilight, tended by Biddy, who was more sweet-tempered and wholesome than ever. Pip was now a young man, old enough to accompany Joe to the local public house of an evening. And so, in the fourth year of his apprenticeship, on a Saturday night at the Three Jolly Bargemen…

(The pub. Pumblechook, Joe, and Pip at a table. Jaggers sits at a distance, in the shadows. Others are also drinking. A barmaid serves. Pumblechook is reading from a newspaper.)

PUMBLECHOOK: "The wictim is said to have spoken the name of the accused before he died, according to a witness for the prosecution. And medical testimony brought out during the third day of the trial by the prosecution points to—"

JAGGERS: I suppose you've settled the case to your satisfaction?

(Pumblechook peers into the shadows.)

PUMBLECHOOK: Sir, without having the honor of your acquaintance, I *have.* The werdict should be "guilty."

JAGGERS: I thought as much. *(He rises.)* But the trial is not over, is it? You do admit that English law supposes each man to be innocent until he is proved—*proved*—guilty?

PUMBLECHOOK: Certainly I admit it, sir.

JAGGERS: And are you aware, or are you not aware, that none of the witnesses mentioned in that questionable journal you read has yet been cross-examined by the defense?

PUMBLECHOOK: Yes, but—

JAGGERS: I rest my case. *(He peers around the room.)* From information I have received, I've reason to believe there's a blacksmith among you by the name of Joseph Gargery. Which is the man?

PUMBLECHOOK: There is the man. What have you done, Joseph?

JAGGERS: And you have an apprentice who is commonly known as Pip—is he here?

PUMBLECHOOK: Aha! I knew that boy would come to no good!

JAGGERS: I wish a conference with you two—a private conference.
(The others drift away, grumbling.)

JAGGERS: My name is Jaggers, and I am a lawyer in London. I'm pretty well known there. I've some unusual business to transact with you.
(Pip and Joe glance at each other.)

JAGGERS: Know first that I act as the confidential agent of a client. It is his orders I follow, not my own. Having said that: Joseph Gargery, I've come with an offer to relieve you of this apprentice of yours.

JOE: Pip?

JAGGERS: Would you be willing to cancel his indentures, for his own good?
(Joe thinks, nods.)

JAGGERS: You'd ask no money for doing so?

JOE: Lord forbid I should want anything for not standing in Pip's way.

JAGGERS: Good. Don't try to change your mind later. *(With great formality.)* The communication I have come to make is…that this young man has great expectations.
(Pip rises. He and Joe gape.)

JAGGERS: I'm instructed to inform him that he will come into a handsome fortune; that he is to be immediately removed from his present sphere of life and from this place, that he is to be brought up as a gentleman—in a word, as befits a young man of great expectations.
(Joe and Pip stare wordlessly for a moment.)

PIP: Joe—

JAGGERS: —Later. First, understand that the person from whom I take my instruction requests that you always bear the name of Pip. You've no objection, I daresay? Good. Secondly, *Mr.* Pip, the name of your benefactor—

PIP: —Miss Havisham—

JAGGERS: —the name of your benefactor must remain a secret until that person chooses to reveal it. Do you accept this condition? Good. Good. I've already been given a sum of money for your education and maintenance. From now on, you will please consider me your guardian.

PIP: Thank you—

JAGGERS: —Don't bother to thank me, I am well-paid for my services, or I shouldn't render them. Now then, education: You wish a proper tutor, no doubt? Good. Have you a preference?

PIP: Well…I only know Biddy, that's Mr. Pumblechook's great-aunt's grand-niece—

JAGGERS: —Never mind, there's a man in London who might suit well enough, a Mr. Matthew Pocket.

PIP: Pocket—is he a cousin of Miss Havisham?

JAGGERS: Ah, you know the name. He is. When do you wish to come to London?

PIP: Soon—directly!

JAGGERS: Good. You'll need proper clothes—here is twenty guineas. You'll take the hackney coach up to London—it's a five-hour trip. Shall I look for you a week from tomorrow? Good. Well, Joseph Gargery, you look dumb-founded.

JOE: Which I am.

JAGGERS: It was understood you wanted nothing for yourself.

JOE: It were understood and it are understood and ever will be.

JAGGERS: But what if I was instructed to make you a present, as compensation for the loss of his services—?

JOE: —Pip is that hearty welcome to go free with his services to honor and fortune, as no words can tell him. But if you think as money can compensate me for the loss of the little child what—what come to the forge and…and…ever the best of friends. *(He weeps.)*

PIP: Oh, Joe, don't…I'm going to be a gentleman!
(Darkness.)

NARRATION: That night Pip sat alone in his little room at the forge, feeling sorrowful and strange that this first night of his bright fortune should be the loneliest he had ever known. The next morning, things looked brighter—only seven days until his departure. Seven *long* days. But there was much to do. First he visited a tailor.

PIP: *(Rings bell.)* I beg your pardon…

TAILOR: *(Unimpressed.)* I beg yours.

PIP: I am going to London.

TAILOR: What of it?

PIP: I shall need a suit of fashionable clothes.

(Pip drops coins one-by-one into the hand of the tailor, who becomes obsequious. During the following Pip goes behind a screen and changes his clothes as:)

TAILOR: I beg your pardon, my dear sir. Fashionable clothes, is it? For London! You've come to the right place, you shall be quite correct, I assure you, quite the thing! Indeed, one might call you the "glass of fashion." We'll turn you out from top to toe as fine as any London gentleman could wish!

NARRATION: And thence, to Mr. Pumblechook's, to receive that great man's blessing.

PUMBLECHOOK: *(Raising a glass.)* Beloved friend, I give you joy in your good fortune. Well-deserved, well-deserved! And to think that I have been the humble instrument leading up to all this…is reward enough for me. So here's to you—I always knew you had it in you! And let us also drink thanks to Fortune—may she ever pick her favorites with equal judgement!

NARRATION: And thence to Miss Havisham's, with barely suppressed excitement…and gratitude.

(Pip emerges from behind the screen. His London suit is almost comical in its exaggeration of high fashion. It is de trop.)

HAVISHAM: This is a grand figure, Pip.

PIP: Oh, ma'am, I have come into such good fortune!

HAVISHAM: I've learned of it from Mr. Jaggers. So, you've been adopted by a rich person, have you?

PIP: Yes, Miss Havisham.

HAVISHAM: Not named?

PIP: Not named.

HAVISHAM: You've a promising career before you. Deserve it! You're always to keep the name of Pip, you know?

(He nods.)

HAVISHAM: Good-bye then, Pip.

(She puts out her hand, he kisses it clumsily.)

NARRATION: Finally, the morning of his departure dawned.

(The forge kitchen.)

PIP: You may be sure, dear Joe, I shall never forget you.

JOE: Ay, old chap, I'm sure of that.

PIP: I always dreamed of being a gentleman.

JOE: Did you? Astonishing! Now me, I'm an awful dull fellow. I'm only master in my own trade, but…ever the best of friends— *(He flees in tears.)*

PIP: *(To Biddy.)* You will help Joe on, won't you?

BIDDY: How help him on?

PIP: Joe's a dear fellow, the dearest that ever lived, but he's backward in some things, Biddy…like learning and manners.

BIDDY: Won't his manners do, then?

PIP: They do well enough here, but if I were to bring him to London when I come into my property—

BIDDY: —And don't you think he knows that? Pip, Pip…

PIP: Well?

BIDDY: Have you never considered his pride?

PIP: His pride? Whatever do you mean? You sound almost envious—

BIDDY: If you have the heart to think so! Can't you see, Joe is too proud and too wise to let anyone remove him from a place he fills with dignity— *(Joe enters, blowing his nose.)*

JOE: It's time for the coach, Pip.

PIP: Well then. *(He picks up his valise.)*

JOE: I'll come wisit you in London, old chap, and then—wot larks, eh? Wot larks we'll have!

PIP: Good-bye, Biddy. *(He kisses her cheek.)* Dear Joe—
(Joe grabs Pip's hat, throws it up in the air, to hide his tears.)

JOE: Hoorar! Hoorar!
(With waves and cheers, the "coach" departs for London.)

NARRATION: When his coach finally left the village behind, Pip wept. Heaven knows we need never be ashamed of our tears, for they are the rain on the blinding dust of earth, overlaying our hard hearts. Pip felt better after he had cried—more aware of his own ingratitude, sorrier, gentler. But by now it was too late to turn back to Joe, so he traveled forward. The mists slowly rose and the world lay spread before him. And suddenly there was—

COACHMAN: London!

PIP: London!
(Pip climbs off the "coach," clutching his valise. He stares around him at the crowd.)

NARRATION: Not far from the great dome of St. Paul's, in the very shadow of Newgate Prison, Pip alighted and stood before an ugly stone building.

(Jaggers's office. Wemmick appears at Pip's knock. Jaggers is inside the room, washing his hands, he pours water from a pitcher into a basin, as:)

PIP: Is Mr. Jaggers in?

(Wemmick pulls him inside.)

WEMMICK: Am I addressing Mr. Pip? He's been expecting you. I'm Wemmick, Mr. Jaggers's clerk. *(He leads Pip to Jaggers.)*

JAGGERS: Well, Mr. Pip, London, eh?

PIP: Yes, sir.

JAGGERS: I've made arrangements for you to stay at Barnard's Inn. You'll share young Mr. Pocket's apartments.

PIP: My tutor?

JAGGERS: His son. I've sent over some furniture for you. And here's a list of tradesmen where you may run up bills. And you will, you will—you'll drown in debt before the year is out, I'm sure, but that's no fault of mine, is it? Good. Wemmick, take him over to Barnard's Inn, will you? I must get back to court.

(He exits. Wemmick picks up Pip's valise, they stroll.)

WEMMICK: So, you've never been to London? I was new here, once, myself. But now I know the moves of it.

PIP: Is it a very wicked place?

WEMMICK: You may get cheated, robbed, and murdered in London. But there are plenty of people anywhere who'll do that for you. Here we are, "Mr. Pocket, Jr." *(He knocks.)* As I keep the cash, we shall likely be meeting often.

(They shake hands, Wemmick goes.)

(Barnard's inn. Herbert comes to the door.)

HERBERT: Mr. Pip?

PIP: Mr. Pocket?

(They shake hands.)

HERBERT: Pray, come in. We're rather bare here, but I hope you'll make out tolerably well.

PIP: It seems very grand to me.

HERBERT: Look around. It's not splendid, because I don't earn very much at present, still I think…bless me, you're—you're the prowling boy in Miss Havisham's garden!

PIP: And you are the pale young gentleman!

HERBERT: The idea of its being you!

PIP: The idea of its being you!

(They laugh, both strike a boxing pose.)

HERBERT: I do hope you've forgiven me for having knocked you about?

(They laugh, shake hands again.)

NARRATION: Dinner was sent up from the coffeehouse in the next road and the young men sat down to get acquainted.

PIP: Mr. Pocket, I was brought up to be a blacksmith. I know little of polite manners. I'd take it as a kindness if you'd give me a hint whenever I go wrong.

HERBERT: With pleasure. And will you do me the kindness of calling me by my Christian name: Herbert?

PIP: With pleasure. My name is Philip.

HERBERT: Philip. Philip...no, I don't take to it. Sounds like a highly moral boy in a schoolbook. I know! We're so harmonious—and you have been a blacksmith...would you mind if I called you "Handel"?

PIP: Handel? Why?

HERBERT: There's a piece of music I like, "The Harmonious Blacksmith," by Handel— *(He hums the tune.)*

PIP: I'd like it very much. So...we two go way back to Miss Havisham's garden!

(They eat.)

HERBERT: Yes. She's a tartar, isn't she?

PIP: Miss Havisham?

HERBERT: I don't say no to that, but I meant Estella. You know the old lady raised her to wreak revenge on all the male sex?

PIP: No! Revenge for what?

HERBERT: Dear me, it's quite a story—which I'll begin, Handel, by mentioning that in London it's not the custom to put the knife in the mouth—scarcely worth mentioning, but... Also, the spoon is not generally used overhand, but under. This has two advantages: You get to your mouth more easily, but to your cravat less well. Now, as to Miss H. Her father was a country gentleman. There were two children, she and a half-brother named Arthur. Arthur grew up extravagant, undutiful—in a word, bad! So the father disinherited him— Have another glass of wine, and excuse my mentioning that society as a body does not expect one to be so strictly conscientious in emptying one's glass as to turn it upside down.

PIP: So sorry.

HERBERT: It's nothing. Upon her father's death, Miss H. became an heiress. She was considered a great match. There now appears on the scene—at the races, say, or at a ball—a man who courted the heiress. This is twenty-five years ago, remember. Also remember that your dinner napkin need not be stuffed into your glass. At any rate, her suitor professed love and devotion, and she fell passionately in love. She gave the man huge sums of money, against all advice—particularly against my father's; which is why she's never liked us since, and why I wasn't the boy chosen to come play with Estella— Where was I? Oh yes, the marriage-day was fixed, the wedding dress bought, the guests invited, the bride cake baked. The great day arrived—but the bridegroom failed to. Instead, he sent his regrets. That morning a letter arrived—

PIP: Which she received while she was dressing for her wedding? At exactly twenty minutes to nine?

HERBERT: Which is why she had all the clocks in the place stopped at that moment! It was later discovered that the man she loved had conspired with her brother to defraud her. They shared the profits of her sorrow.

PIP: Whatever became of them?

HERBERT: Fell into ruin and disappeared, both of 'em. Not many months after, Miss H. adopted Estella—she was a tiny child. And now, my dear Handel, you know everything I do about poor Miss H.

PIP: But I know nothing of you. If it's not rude to ask, what do you do for a living?

HERBERT: *(Dreamily.)* I'd like to go into business. I'd like to be an insurer of great ships that sail to distant ports.

PIP: I see.

HERBERT: I'm also considering the mining business…Africa.

PIP: I see.

HERBERT: Trading in the East Indies interests me.

PIP: I see. You'll need a lot of capital for all that.

HERBERT: True. Meanwhile, I'm looking about me. Temporarily employed in a counting house, but looking about me for the right opportunity…

PIP: And then…what larks.

HERBERT: Pardon?

(Pip laughs, Herbert joins him.)

NARRATION: Pip took up his studies with Herbert's father, Mr. Matthew Pocket. He was joined in his classes by another student, a haughty young man named—

DRUMMLE: —Bentley Drummle, seventh in line for a small baronetcy. And who, may I ask, are you?

NARRATION: Latin, French, history, mathematics in the mornings. In the afternoons sports, of which the favorite was rowing on the river.

DRUMMLE: No, no, no, Mr. Pip. Starboard's there. This is port!

PIP: Thank you very much.

DRUMMLE: Now you dip the *blade* of the oar into the water—that's the wide part, Mr. Pip.

PIP: You're too kind. But I did grow up near the river.

DRUMMLE: Yes, I've heard about you. Your rowing lacks form, there's no style to it, is there? Still, you're strong. One might say you've got the arm of a blacksmith!

(Pip glares at him.)

NARRATION: To his surprise, Pip enjoyed his studies with Mr. Pocket. He also enjoyed his tailor, his linen draper, his glove maker, his jeweler—

(Jaggers' office. Jaggers washes his hands. Wemmick watches.)

JAGGERS: Well, how much do you need this time?

PIP: I'm not sure, Mr. Jaggers.

JAGGERS: Fifty pounds?

PIP: Oh, not that much, sir.

JAGGERS: Five pounds?

PIP: Well, more than that, perhaps.

JAGGERS: Twice five? Three times five? Wemmick, twenty pounds for Mr. Pip.

WEMMICK: Twenty pounds in portable property, yes, sir.

JAGGERS: And now excuse me, young man, I'm late to court.

(He goes. Pip stares after him.)

PIP: I don't know what to make of that man!

WEMMICK: He don't mean you to know, either. He always acts like he's just baited a trap. He sits watching, and suddenly—snap! You're caught. By the way, if you've nothing better to do at the moment, perhaps you'd like to come home with me for supper. I live down in Walworth.

PIP: Why, that's very kind of you. Yes.

WEMMICK: You've no objection to an Aged Parent?

PIP: Certainly not.

(They stroll.)

WEMMICK: Because I have one.

PIP: I look forward to meeting her—

WEMMICK: Him. Have you been to dine at Mr. Jaggers' yet?

PIP: Not yet.

WEMMICK: He'll give you an excellent meal. While you're there, do notice his housekeeper.

PIP: Shall I see something uncommon?

WEMMICK: You will see a wild beast tamed.

(Walworth. The garden, with drawbridge.)

NARRATION: And so they arrived at Mr. Wemmick's cottage in Walworth. The place was odd, to say the least.

WEMMICK: Step over the drawbridge, if you will, Mr. Pip.

(Pip crosses over with Wemmick, who has grown very affable.)

WEMMICK: I must warn you, our little cannon fires at nine o'clock every evening, Greenwich time, so you won't be alarmed.

PIP: It's wonderfully…original here.

(The Aged Parent enters, pulling a small cannon on wheels.)

WEMMICK: Ah, here's the Aged. *(Very loud.)* Well, Aged Parent, how are you this evening?

AGED PARENT: All right, John, all right.

WEMMICK: Here's Mr. Pip, come to tea. *(To Pip.)* Nod at him, Mr. Pip, that's what he likes. He's deaf as a post, he is.

(Pip nods at the Aged, who nods back.)

AGED PARENT: This is a fine place my son's got, sir.

(Pip nods. Aged nods.)

WEMMICK: Proud as punch, ain't you, Aged?

(All three nod.)

WEMMICK: There's a nod for you, and there's another for you. *(To Pip.)* Mr. Jaggers knows nothing of all this. Never even heard of the Aged. I'll be grateful if you don't mention it—the office is one thing, private life's another. I speak now in my Walworth capacity.

PIP: Not a word, upon my honor.

WEMMICK: When I go to the office I leave the castle behind me, and vice versa. One minute to nine—gun-fire time. It's the Aged Parent's treat. Ready? Here we go!

(There is a big boom.)

AGED PARENT: It's fired! I heard it!

(All three nod happily.)

NARRATION: A few weeks later, Pip was invited, along with Herbert and Bentley Drummle, to dine at Mr. Jaggers'.

(Jaggers' home. A dining table.)
JAGGERS: *(Aside, to Pip.)* I like your friend Drummle, he reminds me of a spider.
PIP: He's not my friend, we merely study together. He's a poor scholar, and he is incredibly rude.
JAGGERS: Good. You keep clear of him, he's trouble. But I like such fellows. Yes, he's a real spider.
(Molly appears. Jaggers turns to her.)
JAGGERS: Molly, Molly, Molly, Molly, may we sit down?
(She nods. He turns to the others.)
JAGGERS: Ah, dinner is served, gentlemen.
(They sit, she serves.)
NARRATION: Pip studied her carefully. The night before, he had been to the theater to see *Macbeth*. The woman's face resembled those he had seen rise out of the witches' cauldron. She was humble and silent…but there was something about her…
JAGGERS: So, Mr. Drummle, in addition to conjugating the past conditional tense of French verbs, you gentlemen also go rowing for exercise?
DRUMMLE: We do. And your Mr. Pip's rowing is better than his French—
HERBERT: —I say, Drummle!
DRUMMLE: But I'm stronger with an oar than either of these fellows.
JAGGERS: Really? You talk of strength? I'll show you strength. Molly, show them your wrists.
MOLLY: *(Cringes.)* Master, don't—
JAGGERS: Show them, Molly! *(He grabs her arm, runs his finger up and down her wrist delicately.)* There's power, here. Few men have the sinews Molly has, see? Remarkable force, beautiful power. Beautiful. That'll do, Molly, you've been admired, now you may go.
(She goes.)
JAGGERS: To your health, gentlemen.
(Darkness.)

BIDDY: My dear Mr. Pip: I write at the request of Mr. Gargery, for to let you know he is coming up to London and would be glad to see you. He will call at Barnard's Hotel next Tuesday morning at nine. Your sister continues to linger. Your ever obedient servant, Biddy. P.S. He wishes me most particular to write "what larks!" He says you will understand. I hope you will see him, even though you *are* a gentleman now, for you had ever a good heart and he is so worthy. He asks me again to write "what larks!" Biddy.

NARRATION: With what feelings did Pip look forward to Joe's visit? With pleasure? No, with considerable disturbance and mortification. What would Bently Drummle think of someone like Joe? And what would Joe think of Pip's expensive and rather aimless new life?

(Barnard's Inn. A knock at the door. Joe enters, awkwardly dressed in a suit.)

PIP: Joe!

(Joe holds his arms out to embrace Pip, Pip sticks out his right hand. They shake.)

JOE: Pip, old chap.

PIP: I'm glad to see you, Joe. Come in, give me your hat!

(Joe remembers he has one, removes it from his head, but holds fast to it.)

JOE: Which you have that grow'd and that swelled with the gentlefolk!

PIP: And you look wonderfully well, Joe. Shall I take your hat?

(Joe continues to clutch it.)

JOE: Your poor sister's no worse nor no better than she was. And Biddy is ever right and ready, that girl.

(Herbert enters from bedroom.)

PIP: Here's my friend, Herbert Pocket. Joe.

(Herbert extends his hand, Joe drops his hat.)

HERBERT: Your servant, sir.

JOE: Yours, yours. *(He picks up the hat.)*

HERBERT: Well. Have you seen anything of London, yet?

JOE: Why, yes, sir. Soon as I left the coach, I went straight off to look at the Blacking Factory warehouse.

HERBERT: Really? What did you think?

JOE: It don't come near to its likeness on the labels.

HERBERT: Is that so?

JOE: See, on the labels it is drawn too architectooralooral.

(Herbert nods. Pip covers his face in mortification. Joe drops his hat.)

HERBERT: You're quite right about that, Mr. Gargery—he is, Pip. Well, I must be off to work. It's good to have met you.

(He offers his hand. Joe reaches, drops his hat. Herbert goes out.)

JOE: We two being alone, sir—

PIP: —Joe, how can you call me "sir"?!

JOE: Us two being alone, Pip, and me having the intention to stay not many minutes more—

PIP: —Joe!—

JOE: I will now conclude—leastways begin—what led up to my having the present honor, sir. Miss Havisham has a message for you, Pip, sir. She says to tell you Miss Estella has come home from abroad and will be happy to see you.

PIP: Estella!

JOE: I tried to get Biddy to write the message to you, sir, but she says, "I know Pip will be glad to have that message by word of mouth." Which I have now concluded. *(He starts to go.)* And so, Pip, I wish you ever well and ever prospering to greater height, sir—

PIP: —You're not leaving?!

JOE: Which I am.

PIP: But surely you're coming back for dinner?

JOE: Pip, old chap, life is made of ever-so-many partings welded together, and one man's a blacksmith, and one's a whitesmith, and one's a goldsmith. Diwisions among such must be met as they come. You and me is not two figures to be seen together in London. I'm wrong in these clothes. I'm wrong out of the forge. You won't find half so much fault in me if you think of me in my forge clothes, with my hammer in my hand. And so, ever the best of friends, Pip. God bless you, dear old chap, God bless you, sir.

NARRATION: And he was gone. After the first guilty flow of repentence, Pip thought better of such feelings. He dried his eyes, and did not follow Joe into the street to bring him back. The next day Pip took the coach down from London. He did not bother to call in at the forge.

(Miss Havisham's. Estella waits in the shadows. Pip enters.)

HAVISHAM: So, you kiss my hand as if I were a queen?

PIP: I heard you wished to see me, so I came directly.

HAVISHAM: Well?

(Estella turns, smiles at him.)

HAVISHAM: Do you find her much changed?

PIP: I…

HAVISHAM: And is he changed, Estella?

ESTELLA: Very much.

HAVISHAM: Less coarse and common?

(Estella laughs.)

HAVISHAM: Go into the garden, you two, and give me some peace until tea time.

(Estella takes his arm, they wander out.)

PIP: Look, it's all still here.

ESTELLA: I must have been a singular little creature. I hid over there and watched you fight that strange boy. I enjoyed that battle very much.

PIP: You rewarded me very much.

ESTELLA: Did I? *(She picks up a clay pot of primroses, smells them, picks one, and puts it in Pip's buttonhole.)*

PIP: He and I are great friends, now. It was there you made me cry, that first day.

ESTELLA: Did I? I don't remember. *(She notices his hurt.)* You must understand, I have no heart. That may have something to do with my poor memory.

PIP: I know better, Estella.

ESTELLA: Oh, I've a heart to be stabbed in or shot at, no doubt. But I've no softness there, no…sympathy. If we're to be thrown together often—and it seems we shall be—you'd better believe that of me. What's wrong, is Pip scared? Will he cry? Come, come, tea's ready. You shall not shed tears for my cruelty today. Give me your arm, I must deliver you safely back to Miss Havisham.

(They return to Miss Havisham, who takes Estella's hand and kisses it with ravenous intensity. Estella goes out.)

HAVISHAM: Is she not beautiful, Pip? Graceful? Do you admire her?

PIP: Everyone who sees her must.

HAVISHAM: Love her, love her, love her! If she favors you, love her! If she wounds you, love her! If she tears your heart to pieces, love her, love her, love her!

PIP: You make that word sound like a curse.

HAVISHAM: You know what love is? I do. It is blind devotion, unquestioning self-humiliation, utter submission. It is giving up your whole heart and soul to the one who smites you, as I did. That is love.

(Darkness.)

NARRATION: Love her! Love her! Love her! The words rang triumphantly in his ears all the way back to London. That Estella was destined for him, once a blacksmith's boy! And if she were not yet rapturously grateful for that destiny, he would somehow awaken her sleeping heart!

(Barnard's Inn.)

PIP: I've got something particular to tell you.

HERBERT: That's odd, I've something to tell you.

PIP: It concerns myself—and one other person.

HERBERT: That's odd, too.

PIP: Herbert, I love—I adore Estella!

HERBERT: Oh, I know that. My dear Handel, you brought your adoration along with your valise the day you came to London.

PIP: She's come home—I saw her yesterday. I do love her so!

HERBERT: What are the young lady's sentiments?

PIP: Alas, she is miles and miles away from me.

HERBERT: If that's so, can you not detach yourself from her?

(Pip turns away.)

HERBERT: Think of her upbringing—think of Miss Havisham! Given all that, your love could lead to misery.

PIP: I know, but I cannot help myself. I cannot "detach."

HERBERT: Well. But perhaps it doesn't matter—perhaps your feelings are justified. After all, it would seem you've been chosen for her. Yes, I'm sure it will work out!

PIP: What a hopeful disposition you have.

HERBERT: I must have—I've not got much else. But since the subject's come up, I want you to know first—I'm engaged.

PIP: My dear Herbert! May I ask the bride's name?

HERBERT: Name of Clara. Clara Barley.

PIP: And does Clara Barley live in London?

HERBERT: She does. Oh Pip, if you could see her—so lovely!

PIP: Is she rich?

HERBERT: Poorer than me—and as sweet as she is poor. I'm going to marry her—

PIP: That's wonderful, Herbert. When?

(Herbert's face falls.)

HERBERT: That's the trouble. A fellow can't marry while he's still looking about him, can he?

PIP: I don't suppose he can. But cheer up, it will all work out. Yes, I feel it…it *shall* work out!

ESTELLA: Dear Pip: I am coming to London the day after tomorrow, by midday coach. Miss Havisham insists that you are to meet me, and I write in obedience to her wishes. Yours, Estella.

NARRATION: And suddenly she was there, in London!

(Estella hands a valise and hatbox to Pip.)

PIP: I'm glad, so glad you've come.

ESTELLA: Yes. I'm to live here with a chaperone, at great— ridiculous expense, really. She is to take me about. She's to show people to me, and show me to people.

PIP: I wonder Miss Havisham could part with you.

ESTELLA: It's all part of her great plan. She wants me to write her constantly and report how I get on—

PIP: Get on? Get on? With what? With whom?

(Estella smiles.)

ESTELLA: Poor Pip. Dear Pip.

BIDDY: Dear Pip: I am writing to inform you that your sister died at peace the night before last. Her funeral was held this morning. We discussed whether to wait until you could attend it, but decided that as you are busy in your life as a gentleman we should go forward with the affair as we are. Yours, Biddy. P.S. Joe sends his fond wishes and sympathy.

NARRATION: As Pip got on, he became accustomed to the idea of his great expectations. He grew careless with his money, contracting a great quantity of debts. And Herbert's good nature combined with Pip's lavish spending, to lead them both into habits they could ill-afford. They moved their lodgings from the spartan Barnard's Inn to more luxurious quarters in the Temple, on the banks of the Thames.

(Herbert and Pip enter, each holding sheaves of bills.)

PIP: My dear Herbert, we are getting on very badly.

HERBERT: My dear Handel, those very words were on my lips! We must reform.

PIP: We must indeed.

(They look at each other, toss the bills up in the air, watch them float down.)

NARRATION: Their affairs went from bad to worse, so they began to look forward eagerly to Pip's twenty-first birthday— In the hope that Mr. Jaggers, by way of celebration, might give Pip some concrete evidence of his expectations.

(Jagger's office. Jaggers is washing his hands.)

WEMMICK: Happy birthday, Mr. Pip. *(To Jaggers.)* He's here.

JAGGERS: Well, well, twenty-one today, is that not the case?

PIP: Guilty, sir. I confess to being twenty-one.

JAGGERS: Tell me, Pip, what are you living at the rate of?

PIP: I…don't know, sir.

JAGGERS: I thought as much. Now it's your turn to ask me a question.

PIP: Have—have I anything to receive today?

JAGGERS: I thought we'd come to that! Take this piece of paper in your hand. Now unfold it. What is it?

PIP: It's a banknote…for five hundred pounds!

JAGGERS: And a handsome sum of money, too, you agree?

PIP: How could I do otherwise?

JAGGERS: It is yours. And at the rate of five hundred per year, *and no more,* you are to live until your benefactor chooses to appear.

PIP: Is my benefactor to be made known to me today?

JAGGERS: As to *when* that person decides to be identified, why, that's nothing to do with me, I'm only the agent—

PIP: But she—

JAGGERS: —She?—

PIP: —My patron——

JAGGERS: —Hah! You cannot trick me into giving evidence, young man. Now, excuse me, I'm off to court.

(He goes, followed by Wemmick. Pip stares at the banknote, holds it up, suddenly starts to smile.)

NARRATION: The following Sunday Pip made a pilgrimage down to Walworth to see Mr. Wemmick. For he had an idea about how he would like to spend at least part of his money.

(Walworth. Pip crosses over the little drawbridge. The Aged Parent greets him.)

AGED PARENT: Ah, my son will be home at any moment, young man.

(Pip nods.)

AGED PARENT: Make yourself at home. You made acquaintance with my son at his office?

(Pip nods.)

AGED PARENT: I hear he's a wonderful hand at his business.

(Pip nods.)

AGED PARENT: Now to be precise, I don't actually *hear* it, mind, for I'm hard of hearing.

PIP: Not really!

AGED PARENT: Oh, but I am! Look, here comes John, and Miss Skiffins with him. All right, John?

WEMMICK: All right, Aged P. So sorry I wasn't here to greet you, Mr. Pip. May I present Miss Skiffins, who is a friend of mine, and a neighbor. The Aged and Miss Skiffins will prepare tea, while we chat—

PIP: I wish to ask you—you are in your Walworth frame of mind, I presume?
(Wemmick nods, the Aged nods, they all nod.)

WEMMICK: I am. I shall speak in a private and personal capacity.
(Miss Skiffins leads the Aged away.)

PIP: I wish to do something for my friend, Herbert Pocket. He has been the soul of kindness and I've ill-repaid him by encouraging him to spend more than he has. He'd have been better off if I'd never come along, poor fellow, but as I have, I want to help him. Tell me, how can I set him up in a small partnership somewhere?

WEMMICK: That's devilish good of you, Mr. Pip.

PIP: Only he must never know I had any part in it. You know the extent of my resources, Wemmick. Can you help me?
(Wemmick thinks for a moment.)

WEMMICK: Perhaps…perhaps—yes! Yes, I like it. But it must be done by degrees. We'll go to work on it!
(Miss Skiffins appears.)

SKIFFINS: Mr. Wemmick, dear, the Aged is toasting.

PIP: I beg your pardon, but what did she say?

WEMMICK: Tea is served.
(They go off.)

NARRATION: Before a week had passed, Wemmick found a worthy young shipping broker named Clarriker—who wanted intelligent help—and who also wanted some capital—and who might eventually want a partner. Between this young merchant and Pip secret papers were signed, and half of Pip's five hundred pounds disappeared. The whole business was so cleverly managed that Herbert hadn't the least suspicion that Pip's hand was in it.
(Herbert races in to find Pip reading.)

HERBERT: Handel, Handel, I've the most mighty piece of news! I've just come from an interview in the City—man name of Clarriker—I'm to have a position there and—oh, Handel, I start next week, and I might, in time—

PIP: I'm happy for you, Herbert, so happy—

NARRATION: Pip went quickly into his room and wept with joy at the thought that his expectations had at last done some good to somebody. But what of Estella? She rapidly became the belle of London, seen and admired by all. Pip never had an hour's happiness in her society— Yet his mind, twenty-four hours a day, harped on the happiness of possessing her someday. On the occasion of Miss Havisham's birthday they were asked to come down from London together to visit.

(Miss Havisham's. Pip bows. Estella kisses her cheek. Miss Havisham clutches Estella's hand.)

HAVISHAM: How does she use you, Pip, how does she use you?

PIP: According to your designs, I fear.

NARRATION: And he suddenly saw his fate...In the cobwebs...In the decayed wedding cake...In the face of the clocks that had stopped...And his profound sadness communicated itself to Estella.

(Estella withdraws her hand from Miss Havisham.)

HAVISHAM: What, are you tired of me?

ESTELLA: Only a little tired of myself.

HAVISHAM: No, speak the truth, you're tired of me!

(Estella shivers, turns away.)

HAVISHAM: You cold, cold heart.

ESTELLA: What? You reproach me for being cold? I am what you made me—take all the credit or blame.

HAVISHAM: Look at her, so thankless. I took you to my heart when it was still bleeding from its wounds.

ESTELLA: Yes, yes, what would you have of me?

HAVISHAM: Love.

ESTELLA: Mother-by-adoption, how can I return to you what you never gave me?

HAVISHAM: Did I never give her love? You are so proud, so proud!

ESTELLA: Who taught me to be proud? Who praised me when I learned my lesson?

HAVISHAM: So hard, so hard!

ESTELLA: Who taught me to be hard?—

HAVISHAM: But to be proud and hard to me—to *me,* Estella!

ESTELLA: I cannot think what makes you so unreasonable, when Pip and I have ridden all the way down here for your birthday. I have never forgotten the wrongs done you. I've learned the lessons you taught me—God knows I wish I could unlearn them! *(Pause. Estella comes to her, kisses her.)*

NARRATION: And as soon as the quarrel began, it was over, and never referred to again.

(Estella leads Miss Havisham off.)

NARRATION: The following week, Herbert and Pip were dining at their club.

DRUMMLE: Gentlemen, raise your glasses. I give you Estella.

PIP: Estella who?

DRUMMLE: Estella of Havisham, a peerless beauty.

HERBERT: *(To Pip.)* Much he knows of beauty, the idiot.

PIP: I am acquainted with that lady you speak of. Why do you propose a toast to one of whom you know nothing?

DRUMMLE: Ah, but I do know her. I escorted her to the opera last night.

NARRATION: Now she was seen around the town with Drummle, at the theater, at a ball, at the races…But wasn't she destined for Pip? He took comfort in that thought, and in Herbert's happiness— For *he* had Clara Barley. And so, two years passed.

(The Temple apartment. Night. Pip sits reading.)

NARRATION: It was the night of Pip's twenty-third birthday. The weather was wretched, wet, and stormy. St. Paul's had just chimed eleven when—Pip thought he heard a footstep on the stair.

PIP: Who's there? *(He puts down his book, takes up a candle.)* Answer! There's someone down there, is there not?

MAGWITCH: *(In shadows.)* Yes.

PIP: What floor do you want?

MAGWITCH: The top. Mr. Pip.

PIP: That is my name. Pray, state your business.

(Magwitch slowly emerges from the shadows, warmly dressed in seafaring clothes. He holds out his hands to Pip.)

MAGWITCH: My business?

PIP: Who are you? Explain, please.

(Magwitch advances.)

PIP: I don't understand—keep away—!

MAGWITCH: It's disappointing to a man, arter having looked for'ard so distant

and come so far, but you're not to blame for that. *(He gazes at Pip admiringly.)* You're a game 'un. I'm glad you grow'd up a game 'un.
(He takes off his cap. Pip freezes.)

MAGWITCH: You acted nobly out on that marsh, my dear boy, and I never forgot it! And now I've come back to you! I've come back to you, Pip, dear boy!

(And to Pip's horror, Magwitch throws his arms around him and embraces him. Darkness.)

END OF ACT I

ACT II

The Temple. As it was at the end of Act I. Magwitch embraces the horrified Pip.

MAGWITCH: I've come back to you, Pip, dear boy!

PIP: I know you now, and if you're grateful for what I did on those marshes years ago, that's fine, but—

MAGWITCH: You look to have done well since then.

PIP: I have—please release me, I beg you.

(Magwitch lets go of Pip.)

MAGWITCH: May I make so bold as to ask *how* you have done well since you and me was out on those shiverin' marshes?

PIP: How? I've been chosen to succeed to some property.

MAGWITCH: Might a warmint ask *what* property?

PIP: *(Brief pause.)* I don't know.

MAGWITCH: Might a warmint ask *whose* property?

PIP: *(A long pause.)* I…don't know…

MAGWITCH: Might there be some kind of guardian in the picture, then; some lawyer, maybe? And the first letter of this lawyer's name, could it be…J? For Jaggers?!

PIP: My God—no! No, it can't be…you!

MAGWITCH: Yes, Pip, dear boy, I've made a gentleman of you—it's me wot done it! I'm your second father, lad, and I've come back to you, to see my fine gentleman— *(He embraces Pip again.)* Didn't you never think it could be me?

(Pip disengages with a wail.)

PIP: Never! Never, never, never!

HERBERT: *(Entering in his dressing gown.)* I say, Handel, you're making an awful racket—oh, I beg your pardon, I didn't know you had company…

(Magwitch takes a knife out.)

PIP: Herbert, this is…a visitor of mine. *(Pip sees the knife. To Magwitch.)* He's got every right to be here—he *lives* here! He is my friend.

MAGWITCH: *(Puts away knife, takes out a little Bible.)* Then it's all right, dear boy. Take the book in your hand, Pip's friend. Lord strike you dead if you ever split in any way sumever. Kiss the book.

(Herbert does so.)

PIP: Herbert, this is my…benefactor.

(Herbert gapes.)

HERBERT: Oh…I…how do you do, my name's Herbert Pocket. I hope you're quite well…?

MAGWITCH: How do you do, Pip's companion. And never believe me if Pip shan't make a gentleman on you, too!

HERBERT: I'll look forward to it. Ah…Pip?

(Pip shrugs at him, bewildered.)

PIP: Tell me, do you have a name? By what do I call you?

MAGWITCH: Name of Magwitch. Christened Abel.

HERBERT: Abel Magwitch, fancy…

MAGWITCH: I were born and raised to be a warmint, but now I'm Pip's second father, and he's my son. More to me than any son. Ever since I was transported to Australia, I swore that each time I earned a guinea, that guinea should go to Pip. And I swore that when I speculated and got rich, it'd all be for Pip. I lived rough so that he should live smooth. *(He admires Pip benevolently.)* How good-looking he have grow'd. There's a pair of bright eyes somewhere wot you love, eh, Pip? Those eyes shall be yourn, dear boy, if money can buy 'em. *(He beams at Pip, yawns.)* Now then, where shall I sleep tonight?

PIP: Pray, take my bedroom.

MAGWITCH: By your leave, I'll latch the door first. Caution is necessary. *(He does so.)*

HERBERT: Caution? How do you mean, caution?

MAGWITCH: *(Whispers.)* It's death.

HERBERT: *(Whispers.)* What's death?

MAGWITCH: If I'm caught. I was sent up for life, warn't I? It's death for me to come back to England; I'd be hang'd for it, if I was took.

PIP: *(An anguished explosion.)* Then why in God's name have you come?!!

MAGWITCH: To see my dear boy. To watch him be a fine gentleman.

(He nods, beams, exits into the bedroom. Pip buries his head in his hands.)

PIP: Estella, Estella…I am lost!

HERBERT: Hold steady—he mustn't hear you.

PIP: The shame of it, Herbert! I always thought Miss Havisham—I thought Estella was intended for me. Fool. Foolish dreamer! And now I awaken to find I owe my fortune to this man, this wretched…criminal!…who has risked his life to be with me! It's a terrible joke, isn't it? And you know what's the funniest part? I scorned my most faithful friend for these "expectations"! Joe, Joe…

HERBERT: Take hold of yourself, Handel. There are practical questions to answer. How are we to keep him out of danger? Where will he live? *(Dreamily.)*

There are disguises, I suppose…wigs, spectacles. Given his intimidating manner, we can hardly dress him up as a vicar but…I think some sort of prosperous farmer's disguise would be best. We shall cut his hair! *(He looks at the suffering Pip.)* Get some sleep, Handel. You'll need it when morning comes.

PIP: When morning comes, Mr. Jaggers had better have a good explanation!

(Mr. Jaggers's office.)

NARRATION: The moment Pip walked in, Mr. Jaggers could see from his face that the man had turned up. Jaggers immediately immersed himself in soap and water.

JAGGERS: Now Pip, be careful! Don't *tell* me anything—I don't want to be told a thing! I am not curious.

PIP: I merely wish to be sure that what *I've* been told is true.

JAGGERS: Did you say *told* or *informed?* Told would imply verbal communication, face-to-face. You cannot have verbal communication with a man who's still in Australia, can you?

PIP: Lawyers' games!

JAGGERS: Games? The difference between the two verbs could mean a man's safety—his life!

PIP: I shall say "informed," Mr. Jaggers.

JAGGERS: Good.

PIP: I have been informed by a man named Abel Magwitch that he is my benefactor.

JAGGERS: That is the man. In New South Wales, Australia.

PIP: And only he?

JAGGERS: Only he.

PIP: I don't wish to make you responsible for my mistaken conclusions, but I always supposed it was Miss Havisham.

JAGGERS: As you say, Pip, that's not my fault. Not a particle of evidence to support that conclusion.

(Pip leaves.)

JAGGERS: Never judge by appearances—irrefutable evidence, that's the rule. Evidence!

(The Temple.)

NARRATION: During the following days, Pip studied Magwitch as he napped in the chair, wondering what evils the man had committed, loading him with all the crimes in the calender!

(As Magwitch dozes in the chair, Pip studies him. Herbert enters, lays a sympathetic hand on Pip's shoulder.)

HERBERT: Dear Pip, what's to be done?

PIP: I'm too stunned to think. I could run away for a soldier.

HERBERT: Of course you can't. He's strongly attached to you.

PIP: He disgusts me—his look, his manners!

HERBERT: But you've got to get him out of England, to safety. And you'll have to go with him or else he won't leave.

PIP: You're right, of course. He's risked his life on my account; it's up to me to keep him from throwing it away altogether.

HERBERT: Well said! We'll see the matter through together—

(Pip seizes his hand in gratitude. Magwitch wakes up, smiles.)

MAGWITCH: Ah, dear boy, and Pip's companion: I was napping.

PIP: Magwitch, I must ask you something. Do you remember that day long ago, on the marshes?

MAGWITCH: I do, dear boy.

PIP: You were fighting with another convict when the soldiers caught you—you recall?

MAGWITCH: I should think so! What of it?

HERBERT: If we're to help you, we must know more about that day…and about you.

MAGWITCH: You're still on your oath?

HERBERT: Assuredly.

(Magwitch takes out his pipe, the young men sit.)

MAGWITCH: Dear boy, and Pip's companion, I could tell you my life short and handy, if you like: in-jail and out-of-jail, in-jail and out-of-jail. I know'd my name to be Magwitch, christened Abel—but I've no notion of where I was born, or to who. I first came aware of myself down in Essex, stealing turnips for my food.

Thereafter there warn't a soul that seed young Abel Magwitch but wot took fright at him and drove him off. Or turned him in. I can see me, a pitiable ragged little creetur, who eveyone called "hardened." "This boy's a terrible hardened one." "This one spends his life in prisons." Then they'd preach at me about the devil and let me go. But wot the devil's a boy to do with no home and an empty stomach? So I'd steal food again, and be turned in again. Somehow I managed to grow up…tramping, begging, thieving…a bit of a laborer, a bit of a poacher. And so I got to be a man.

One day I was lounging about Epsom races, when I met a man. Him whose skull I'd crack wi' pleasure if I saw him now. His name was Compeyson. And that's the man you saw me a-pounding in the marshes that day long ago.

PIP: Compeyson.

MAGWITCH: Ay. Smooth and good-looking was Compeyson. He had book-learning, so he set hisself up as a gentleman. He found me, as I say, at the races. "To judge from appearances, you're out of luck," he says. "I've never been in it," I answers him. "Luck changes," he says. "What can you do?" "Eat and drink," says I.

So Compeyson took me on, to be his man and partner. And what was his business? Swindling, forgery, stolen banknote passing; suchlike. He had no more heart than an iron file. There was another man in the game with Compeyson—as was called Arthur.

(Pip and Herbert glance at each other.)

MAGWITCH: Mister Arthur. Poor fellow was in a sad state of decline. Him and Compeyson had been in some wicked business together—they'd made a pot of money off some rich lady a few years before.

(Herbert and Pip look at each other.)

MAGWITCH: But Compeyson had gambled it all away long since. Mr. Arthur had the look of a dying man when I first took up wi' them—from which I should have took warning. Soon after I came, Mr. Arthur took very ill and began crying, delirious-like, that he was haunted. "She's coming for me—I can't get rid of her. She's all dressed in white, wi' white flowers in her hair." And Compeyson says to poor Mr. Arthur, "She's alive, you fool. She's living in her wreck of a house in the country." And Mr. Arthur says, "No, she's here, in her white dress; and over her heart there are drops of blood—you broke her heart! And now she's coming to hang a shroud on me!"

And so he died. Compeyson took it as good riddance. Next day him and me started work. I won't tell you what we did. I'll simply say the man got me into such nets and traps as made me his slave. He were smarter than me. He used his head and he used my legs to keep his own self out of trouble. He had no mercy! My missus—no, wait, I don't meanter bring my missus in— *(He looks about him, confused.)* No need to go into that. But Compeyson! When we two was finally caught and put on trial, I noticed what a gentleman he looked wi' his curly hair and his pocket handker-chief, and what a common wretch I looked. Judge and jury thought so too, and even the great Mr. Jaggers couldn't get me justice that day. For when it's time for sentencing, it's him wot gets seven years and me wot gets fourteen!

After the trial, we was on the same prison ship—I paid him back—I smashed his face in. You seed the scar, dear boy. Then I found a way to escape, and I swam to shore, where I first saw you, in among those old graves.

HERBERT: What an astonishing tale!

MAGWITCH: And true. Little Pip gave me to understand that Compeyson had escaped too, and was out on them marshes. And I vowed then and there, whatever the cost to me, I would drag that scoundrel back to the prison ship. And I did, too. I did.

PIP: Is Compeyson dead?

MAGWITCH: He hopes I am, if he's still alive. Well, I've talked myself near to death. Good night, dear boy. Good night, Pip's companion. *(He exits into the bedroom.)*

(Pause.)

HERBERT: Handel?

PIP: Yes, I know. Miss Havisham's brother was named Arthur.

HERBERT: Compeyson is the man who broke her heart.

PIP: Herbert, before I get Magwitch out of the country, I must try to speak with Estella. I must see her once more.

NARRATION: Pip set off by the early morning coach, and was into open country when the day came creeping on. The fields were hung about with mists. At length the coach stopped at the Blue Boar Inn, which was in the neighborhood of Miss Havisham's house. When Pip alighted, he was amazed to see a familiar figure lounging by the Inn door.

PIP: Bentley Drummle!

DRUMMLE: You've just come down?

(Pip nods.)

DRUMMLE: Beastly place. Your part of the country, I think?

PIP: I'm told it's very like your Shropshire.

DRUMMLE: Not in the least like it.

PIP: Have you been here long?

DRUMMLE: Long enough to be tired of it.

PIP: Do you stay here long?

DRUMMLE: Can't say. And you?

PIP: Can't say.

(Drummle gives a brief, unpleasant laugh.)

PIP: Are you amused, Mr. Drummle?

DRUMMLE: Not very. I'm about to go riding…to explore the marshes. Out-of-the-way villages, here, I'm told, quaint little public houses. Smithies, too. Boy!

(A stable boy appears.)

BOY: Yes, sir.

DRUMMLE: Is my horse ready?

BOY: Waiting in the yard, sir.

DRUMMLE: The young lady won't ride today, the weather is too foul. And boy—

BOY: Yes, sir?

DRUMMLE: Tell the innkeeper I plan to dine at the young lady's this evening.

BOY: Quite so, sir.

(Drummle goes. The boy turns to Pip.)

BOY: May I help you, sir?

(Pip, in a rage, shies his valise at him.)

(Miss Havisham's. Miss Havisham is in her bath chair. Estella sits a little apart, knitting.)

NARRATION: Pip found the two women seated by the fire. Their faces were lit by the candles that burned on the wall.

HAVISHAM: And what wind brings you down here, Pip?

PIP: I wished to see Estella, and hearing that some wind had blown her here, I followed.

HAVISHAM: Pray, sit down.

PIP: What I have to say to Estella, Miss Havisham, I shall say before you. It won't displease you to learn that I am as unhappy as you can ever have meant me to be.

(Miss Havisham says nothing. Estella knits.)

PIP: I have found out who my patron is. It's not a pleasant discovery. It's not likely to enrich my reputation.

HAVISHAM: Well?

PIP: When you first brought me here, when I still belonged to that village yonder that I wish I had never left, I suppose I was picked at random, as a kind of servant, to gratify a whim of yours?

HAVISHAM: Ay, Pip.

PIP: And Mr. Jaggers—

HAVISHAM: —Mr. Jaggers had nothing to do with it. His being my lawyer and the lawyer of your patron is coincidence.

PIP: Then why did you lead me on? Was that kind?

HAVISHAM: *(Striking her stick upon the ground.)* Who am I, for God's sake, that I should be kind?!

PIP: In encouraging my mistaken notion, you were also punishing some of your greedy relations?

HAVISHAM: Perhaps.

PIP: There is one branch of that family whom you deeply wrong. I speak of my former tutor, Mr. Matthew Pocket, and his son Herbert. If you think those two to be anything but generous, open, and upright, you are in error.

HAVISHAM: You say so because Herbert Pocket is your friend.

PIP: He made himself my friend even when he thought I had taken his place in your affections.

HAVISHAM: Yes, well?

PIP: Miss Havisham, I speak frankly: If you could spare the money to do Herbert a lasting service in life—secretly—I could show you how.

HAVISHAM: Why secretly?

PIP: Because I began the service myself, two years ago, secretly, and I don't wish to be betrayed. Why I cannot complete it myself is…it is part of another person's secret.

(Havisham stares into the fire. Estella knits.)

HAVISHAM: Well, well, well, what else have you to say?

PIP: Estella, you know I've loved you long and dearly. I'd have spoken sooner, but for my foolish hope that Miss Havisham intended us for one another. Whilst I believed you had no choice in the matter I refrained from speaking, but now…

(Estella shakes her head, knits on.)

PIP: I know, I know. I've no hope that I shall ever call you mine.

(Again, Estella shakes her head. She knits.)

PIP: If she'd have thought about it, she'd have seen how cruel it was to torture me with so vain a hope, but she couldn't see. Poor Miss Havisham: Enveloped in her own pain, she could not feel mine.

(Havisham clutches her heart.)

ESTELLA: It seems there are fancies…sentiments—I don't know what to call them—which I cannot comprehend. When you say you love me, I hear your words but they touch nothing here. I did try to warn you.

PIP: Yes.

ESTELLA: But you wouldn't be warned. I am more honest with you than with other men—I can do no more than that.

PIP: Bentley Drummle is here, pursuing you?

(She nods.)

PIP: Is it true you encourage him? Ride with him? Is it true he dines with you today?

ESTELLA: Quite true.

PIP: You cannot love him.

ESTELLA: What have I just told you? I cannot love!

PIP: You would never marry him?

ESTELLA: *(Pause.)* I am going to be married to him.

PIP: Dearest Estella, don't let Miss Havisham lead you into so fatal a step. Forget me—you've already done so, I know—but for the love of God, bestow yourself on a man worthier than Bentley Drummle!

ESTELLA: Wedding preparations have already begun. It is my own act, not hers.

PIP: Your own act, to fling yourself away on a brute?!

ESTELLA: Don't be afraid of my being a blessing to him!

(A pause. Miss Havisham moans.)

ESTELLA: As for you, Pip, I trust you'll get me out of your thoughts within a week.

PIP: Out of my thoughts! You have been in every prospect I've seen since I first met you—on the river, in the wind, on the city streets. To the last hour of my life you cannot choose but remain part of me. O, God bless you, God forgive you!

(Miss Havisham clutches at her heart again. Pip kisses Estella's hand, leaves.)

NARRATION: All done, all gone! Pip wandered through the lanes and bypaths around the house...Then he turned and walked all the way back to London.

NARRATION: It was past midnight when he crossed London Bridge, closer to one when he approached his lodgings. He was stopped by the night porter.

PORTER: Urgent message for you, Mr. Pip.

(Pip tears open an envelope, reads, as.)

WEMMICK: Dear Mr. Pip: Don't go home. Yours, J. Wemmick.

NARRATION: Pip turned hastily away. He spent the remainder of the night in an hotel in Covent Garden. Footsore and weary as he was, he could not sleep. And after an hour, those extraordinary voices with which silence teems began to make themselves audible. The closet whispered. The fire-place sighed. The washstand ticked. And they all spoke as if with one voice: Don't go home. Whatever night-fancies crowded in on him, they never ceased to murmur: Don't go home. When at last he dozed in sheer exhaustion, it became a vast shadowy verb he had to conjugate, imperative mood, present tense: Do not thou go home. Let him or her not go home. Let us not go home. Do not ye or you go home. Early the next morning Pip went to Walworth to consult Wemmick. This was obviously not a matter for the office.

(Walworth. Pip crosses over the drawbridge.)

WEMMICK: You got my note?

PIP: I did.

WEMMICK: I hope you destroyed it. It's never wise to leave documentary evidence if you can help it. *(He hands Pip a sausage speared on a toasting fork.)* Would you mind toasting a sausage for the Aged while we talk?

PIP: Delighted.

WEMMICK: You understand, we're in our private and personal capacities here?
(Pip nods.)

WEMMICK: I heard by accident yesterday that a certain person had recently disappeared from Australia, a person possessed of vast portable property. Yes? I also heard that your rooms were being watched, and might be watched again. All right, ain't you, Aged P? *(He takes the toasting fork from Pip, puts the sausage on a plate for the Aged.)*

AGED PARENT: All right, John, all right, my boy!
(They all nod.)

PIP: Tell me, the disappearance of this person from Australia and the watching of my rooms—are these two events connected?

WEMMICK: If they aren't yet, they will be.
(They all nod.)

PIP: Mr. Wemmick, have you ever heard of a man of bad character whose name is Compeyson?
(Wemmick nods.)

PIP: Is he living?
(Wemmick and the Aged nod.)

PIP: Is he in London?
(All three nod.)

WEMMICK: I see you've got the point. When I learned of it, I naturally came to your rooms, and not finding anyone at home—or answering the door, anyway—I went to Clarriker's office to see Mr. Herbert. And without mentioning any names I explained that if he was aware of any Tom, Dick, or Richard staying with you, he had better get him out of the way.

PIP: Herbert must have been mystified.

WEMMICK: Not for long. He conceived a plan. Seems he's courting a young lady who lives in Mill Pond Bank, right on the river. And *that's* where Mr. Herbert has lodged this person, this Tom, Dick, or Richard! It's a sound idea, because although *you're* being watched, Mr. Herbert isn't…And as he visits there often, he can act as go-between!

PIP: Good thinking.

WEMMICK: But there's an even better reason for the move. This house is *by the river.* You understand?

(Pip shakes his head.)

WEMMICK: When the right moment comes, you can slip your man aboard a foreign packet-boat unnoticed. Here is the young lady's address in Mill Pond Bank—Miss Barley's the name, and a very odd name it is. You may go there this evening, but do it *before* you go home, so they won't follow you.

PIP: I don't know how to thank you—

WEMMICK: —One last piece of advice. You must get hold of your man's portable property as soon as you can. For his sake as well as yours. It mustn't fall into the wrong hands, must it? Well, I'd better be off to the City. I suggest you stay here until dark—you look tired enough. Keep out of sight and spend a restful day with Aged. Ain't that right, Aged P?

AGED PARENT: All right, John.

WEMMICK: Good-bye then, Mr. Pip. *(He goes.)*

(Pip stares into the fire.)

NARRATION: Pip soon fell asleep before the fire. He and the Aged Parent enjoyed each other's society by falling asleep before the fire throughout the whole day. When it was dark, Pip prepared to leave. The Aged was readying tea, and Pip inferred from the number of cups, three, that a visitor was expected. Could it be that odd lady with the green gloves…Miss Skiffins? Pip made his way to Mill Pond Bank. It was an old house with a curious bow window in front.

(Mill Pond Bank.)

HERBERT: All's well so far, Handel. But he's anxious to see you.

(Clara enters.)

HERBERT: Ah, here's Clara, here she comes.

CLARA: Pip, is it?

PIP: And you're Clara, at last! Herbert's words fail to do you justice. *(He kisses her hand.)*

CLARA: Mr. Magwitch wants to know if he may come down. Let me go fetch him. *(She goes out.)*

PIP: Herbert, she's so lovely.

HERBERT: Isn't she? I know where my good fortune lies, money or no— *(Magwitch enters.)*

MAGWITCH: I've brought you nothing but trouble, dear boy.

PIP: You're safe, that's all that matters. You know you'll have to go away?

MAGWITCH: But how—?

HERBERT: Handel and I are both skilled oarsmen—

PIP: And I've just hired a rowboat—I keep it tied up at the Temple stairs, near our rooms.

HERBERT: When the time comes, we plan to row you downriver ourselves, and smuggle you aboard a foreign packet.

PIP: Starting tomorrow I'll go rowing every day. If they see me out on the river often enough, it'll be taken as habit. If I'm out there twenty-five times, no one will blink an eye when I appear the twenty-sixth.

HERBERT: A bit of practice in the evenings won't hurt me, either. I've grown soft, cooped up in that office.

MAGWITCH: Hah. Hah! I like it—I like your plan, lads.

(Throughout the following montage, Compeyson, carefully muffled, lurks here and there.)

NARRATION: Pip and Herbert went rowing the next day. The young men, it appeared, felt a sudden urge to exercise…And after the first few days, no one seemed to notice. Pip often rowed alone, in cold, rain, and sleet…But no one seemed to notice. At first he kept above Blackfriars Bridge, but as the hours of the tide changed, he rowed further, past the tricky currents around old London Bridge. Once he and Herbert rowed past Mill Pond Bank. They could see the house with the curious bow window from the river. Magwitch was safe inside that house. There seemed no cause for alarm. But Pip knew there was cause for alarm. He could not get rid of the notion he was being watched. Meanwhile, Pip's financial affairs began to wear a gloomy appearance, for he had vowed not to accept any more money from Magwitch, given his uncertain feelings about the man. And as the days passed, Pip continued to think of Estella, the impression settled heavily upon him that she was married. But he could not bear to seek out the truth of it, and clung to the last little rag of his hope.

(Compeyson appears directly behind him.)

NARRATION: He was miserable. And still, he could not get rid of the notion he was being watched.

(Pip turns around, but bumps into Mr. Jaggers, who is walking down the road.)

JAGGERS: Mr. Pip, is it?

PIP: Mr. Jaggers.

JAGGERS: Where are you bound?

PIP: Home, I think.

JAGGERS: Don't you know?

PIP: I...hadn't made up my mind.

JAGGERS: You *are* going to dine, you don't mind admitting that?

PIP: I confess it, guilty of dining.

JAGGERS: And you're not engaged?

PIP: I'm quite free.

JAGGERS: Come dine with me. *(Jaggers takes his arm decisively.)* Wemmick will be joining us, too.

(Wemmick falls in with them.)

(Jaggers' house. Molly is serving soup from a tureen.)

JAGGERS: By the way, Miss Havisham sent you a message. She'd like to see you, a little matter of business. Will you go down?

PIP: Certainly.

(The three men sit down. Molly stands behind Jaggers' chair, silently.)

JAGGERS: When?

(Pip glances at Wemmick, who silently mouths the word "soon.")

PIP: I...soon. At once. Tomorrow.

(Wemmick nods.)

JAGGERS: Splendid. So, Pip, your good friend, the Spider— *(To Wemmick.)*— I refer to one Bentley Drummle—appears to have played his cards well. He has won the pool, eh? *(To Wemmick.)* I refer to a young lady.

PIP: It would seem he has.

JAGGERS: Hah! He's a promising fellow in his own way, but he may not *have* it all his way. The stronger of the two will win in the end; but who is the stronger, he or she? *(He sips.)* What do you think, Wemmick?

WEMMICK: *(Shrugs)* Here's to the Spider—what's his name?

JAGGERS: *(Lifts his glass.)* Bentley Drummle: and may the question of supremacy be settled to the lady's satisfaction. To the satisfaction of both of 'em, it never can be. *(He drinks.)* Ah, Molly, the soup is delicious this evening.

MOLLY: Thank you, master.

JAGGERS: Our Molly doesn't like company, she prefers to keep her skills for my palate alone.

(She turns her head to one side, fidgets with an apron string. Pip suddenly stares at her. Jaggers notices.)

JAGGERS: What's the matter, young man?

PIP: Nothing—we were speaking of a subject that's painful to me.

(Pip and Molly lock eyes for a moment. Wemmick and Jaggers attack their soup.)

NARRATION: The action of her fingers was not unlike that of knitting. The look on her face was intent. Surely Pip had seen such hands, such eyes recently. They were fresh in his mind. He stared at Molly's hands, her eyes, her flowing hair, and compared them with hands, eyes, hair he knew too well. He thought what those dearer hands might be like after twenty years of a brutal, stormy life—and suddenly he felt absolutely certain that this woman was Estella's mother. Pip managed to get through the rest of his meal as best he could. At last, he and Wemmick thanked their host and took to the street.

(Pip and Wemmick stroll. They pass Compeyson without noticing him.)

PIP: Mr. Wemmick, we were speaking of Miss Havisham's adopted daughter at dinner. Have you ever seen her?

WEMMICK: Can't say I have. Something troubling you, Mr. Pip?

PIP: The first time I dined at Jaggers', do you recall telling me to notice the housekeeper. A wild beast tamed, you called her.

WEMMICK: I daresay I did.

PIP: How did Mr. Jaggers tame her?

WEMMICK: We're in our private and personal capacities?

(Pip nods.)

WEMMICK: About twenty years ago she was tried for murder at the Old Bailey, and was acquitted. Mr. Jaggers was her lawyer, of course, and I must say his defense was astonishing. The murdered person was another woman, older than Molly, and even stronger. It was a case of jealousy. Molly was married to some sort of tramping man, and he got too familiar with the other woman She was found dead in a barn near Hounslow Heath, all bruised and scratched—choked to death. There was no other candidate to do the murder but our Molly. You may be sure Mr. Jaggers never pointed out how strong Molly's wrists were then. He likes to, now.

PIP: Indeed he does. How did he get her off?

WEMMICK: Molly was also suspected of killing her own child by this man of hers, to revenge herself on him. Jaggers told the jury that they were really trying her for that crime and since there was no child, no body, no trace of a child or a body, they had no proof. I tell you, he got the jury so confused that they capitulated and acquitted her of killing her rival. She's been in his service ever since.

PIP: Do you remember the sex of the child?

WEMMICK: Said to have been a little girl, around three.

PIP: Good night, Mr. Wemmick, we part here.

(They go off separately. Compeyson follows Pip.)

(Havisham's.)

NARRATION: The following morning Pip journeyed down to Miss Havisham. There hung about her an air of utter desolation, an expression, almost, of fear.

HAVISHAM: Thank you for coming. I want to show you I'm not all made of stone. What do you wish me to do for Herbert Pocket?

PIP: I had hoped to buy him a partnership in the firm of Clarriker and Company. He's worked successfully there for the past year or so.

HAVISHAM: How much money do you need?

PIP: Nine hundred pounds.

HAVISHAM: If I give it to you, will you keep my part in it as secret as your own?

PIP: Faithfully. It would ease my mind about that, at any rate.

HAVISHAM: Are you so unhappy?

PIP: I'm far from happy—but I've got other causes of disquiet than any you know.

HAVISHAM: Pip? Is my only service to you to be this favor for young Pocket? Can I do nothing for you yourself?

PIP: Nothing, Miss Havisham.

(She takes pen, paper, writes a note.)

HAVISHAM: This is an authorization to Jaggers to pay Clarriker nine hundred pounds to advance your friend.

(He takes the paper.)

PIP: I thank you with all my heart.

(She takes another paper, writes.)

HAVISHAM: Pip, here is my name. If you can ever write "I forgive her" under it, even after my death, it would mean so much...

PIP: Oh, Miss Havisham, I can do that now. I want forgiveness myself too much to be bitter with you.

(He reaches for her hand, but she drops suddenly to her knees, sobbing.)

HAVISHAM: What have I done, what have I done?

PIP: I'd have loved her under any circumstances. Is she married?

HAVISHAM: She is. What have I done? What have I done?

PIP: I assure you, Miss Havisham, you may dismiss me from your conscience. Estella is a different case.

HAVISHAM: I meant to save her from a misery like my own! I stole her heart and put ice in its place.

PIP: Better to have left her a natural heart, even if it were to break.

HAVISHAM: What have I done, what have I done?

PIP: Whose child was she?

(She shakes her head.)

PIP: You don't know? But Mr. Jaggers brought her here?

HAVISHAM: I asked him to find me a little girl whom I could rear and love and save from my own fate. One night, a few months later, he brought her...she was fast asleep. I called her Estella. She was about three.

PIP: Good night, Miss Havisham. And thank you for your kindness to Herbert.

(He kisses her hand, goes.)

NARRATION: Twilight was closing in. Pip went into the ruined garden, and roamed past the place where he and Herbert had had their fight...Past the spot where she had kissed him...Past the little pot of flowers whose fragrance she had once inhaled...He turned to look at the old house once more— When suddenly he saw a great, towering flame spring up by Miss Havisham's window, And he saw her running shrieking, with a whirl of flame blazing all about her, soaring high above her head.

(Screams. Fire.)

NARRATION: Pip raced back into the house tore off his greatcoat, and wrapped her in it, Beating out the flames with his bare hands.

(Screams. Then they subside. Silence.)

HAVISHAM: What have I done...what have I done...Pip, Pip...forgive me... please, God forgive me...

(Darkness.)

(The Temple. Pip lies on the sofa, Herbert is dressing his burnt hands.)

HERBERT: Steady, Handel, dear boy.

PIP: You are the best of nurses.

HERBERT: The right hand's much better today. The left was pretty badly burned, it will take more time—

PIP: Time.

HERBERT: Steady on! I saw Magwitch last evening. He sends his love.

PIP: And how is Clara?

HERBERT: Taking good care of him. She calls him Abel—she'll miss him when he goes.

PIP: She's such a darling. You'll be marrying soon, won't you?

HERBERT: *(Grins.)* How can I respectably care for her otherwise? Now, this bandage will have to come off gradually, so you won't feel it. *(He works on it.)* You know what, Handel? Old Magwitch has actually begun to grow on me.

PIP: Yes. I used to loathe him, but that's gone. Don't you think he's become more gentle?

(Herbert nods.)

HERBERT: He told me the story of his "missus" the other night, and a wild, dark tale it is. Ah, the bandage is off most charmingly. Now for the clean, cool one.

PIP: Tell me about his woman.

HERBERT: She was a jealous one, vengeful to the last degree.

PIP: What last degree?

HERBERT: Murder—am I hurting you?

(Pip shakes his head.)

HERBERT: She was tried and acquitted. Jaggers defended her, that's how Magwitch first came to learn of him. Is the bandage too tight?

PIP: It is impossible to be gentler. Pray, go on.

HERBERT: This woman had a child by Magwitch, on whom he doted. After she killed her rival, she told Magwitch she would also kill their child. There, the arm's nicely done up. You're sure you're all right? You look so pale.

PIP: Did she kill the child?

HERBERT: She did.

PIP: Magwitch thinks she did. Herbert, look at me.

HERBERT: I do look at you, dear boy.

PIP: Touch me—I've no fever? I'm not delirious?

HERBERT: You seem rather excited, but you're quite yourself.

PIP: I know I'm myself. And the man we have been hiding in Mill Pond Bank, Abel Magwitch, is Estella's father!

(Jaggers' office.)

NARRATION: Pip was seized with a feverish need to verify the truth of it. As soon as he was able to leave his bed he visited Mr. Jaggers.

(Jaggers and Wemmick are busy with paperwork. Pip walks in, hands Jaggers a note.)

JAGGERS: And the next item, Wemmick, will be— *(He sees Pip.)* What's this? *(Reads.)* An authorization signed by the late Miss Havisham…nine hundred pounds, payable to the firm of Clarriker and Company, Ltd., on behalf of…Herbert Pocket? This must be your doing, Pip. I'm sorry we do nothing for you.

PIP: She was kind enough to ask. I told her no.

JAGGERS: I shouldn't have told her that, but every man knows his own business.

WEMMICK: Every man's business is portable property.

PIP: I did ask her for information, however…regarding her adopted daughter. She obliged, and I now know more about Estella than she does herself. I know her mother.

JAGGERS: Her mother?

PIP: And so do you—she cooked your breakfast this morning.

JAGGERS: *(Unperturbed.)* Did she?

PIP: But I know more, perhaps, than even you do. I also know Estella's father.

(Jaggers looks up, surprised.)

JAGGERS: You know her father?

PIP: His name is Magwitch. He…lives in Australia.

JAGGERS: On what evidence does he make this claim?

PIP: He doesn't make it at all—he doesn't even know his daughter is alive.

NARRATION: Then Pip told Jaggers all he knew, and how he knew it. For once the lawyer was at a loss for words.

JAGGERS: *(Pause.)* Hah!—Where were we, Wemmick?

PIP: You cannot get rid of me so easily. I must confirm the truth from you. Please.

(Jaggers doesn't respond.)

PIP: Wemmick, you are a man with a gentle heart. I've seen your pleasant home and your old father; I know your kind and playful ways. Please, on my behalf, beg him to be more open with me—

JAGGERS: What's this?! Pleasant home? Old father?!

WEMMICK: So long as I leave 'em at home, what's it to you, sir?

JAGGERS: Playful ways?!! *(To Pip.)* This man must be the most cunning impostor in London.

WEMMICK: It don't interfere with business, does it? I shouldn't be surprised if, when you're finally tired of all this work, you plan a pleasant home of your own!

JAGGERS: Me?!

PIP: The truth, I beg you—

JAGGERS: Well, well, Pip, let me put a case to you. Mind, I admit nothing.

PIP: I understand.

JAGGERS: Put the case that a woman under such circumstances as you have named hid her child away, and only her lawyer knew where. Put the case that, at the same time, this lawyer held a trust to find a child for an eccentric, rich client, a lady, to adopt.

PIP: Yes, yes.

JAGGERS: Put the case that this lawyer lived in an atmosphere of evil. He saw small children earmarked for destruction, he saw children whipped, imprisoned, transported, neglected, hounded, cast out—qualified in all ways for the hangman. And he saw them grow up and be hanged. And always, always, he was helpless to intervene.

Put the case that here was one pretty little child out of the heap that he could save. Put the case that the child grew up and married for money. That the natural mother was still living. That the father and mother, unknown to each other, were living within so many miles, furlongs, yards, if you will, of one another. That the secret was still a secret...until one day *you* got hold of it. Now tell me, for whose sake would you reveal the secret?

(Pause. Pip shakes his head.)

JAGGERS: Now, Wemmick, where were we when Mr. Pip came barging in?

(The Temple.)

NARRATION: The next evening, Herbert came home from the office bubbling with joy, for Clarriker had offered him—

HERBERT: *(Rushing in.)*—A partnership! Think of it! We're establishing a branch office in the East Indies and I—I am to go out and take charge of it! I'll be able to take Clara and—it's a miracle! Are you surprised? No, of course not, you've always had more faith in me than I had in myself. But my dear Handel, after your commitment to Magwitch is over, perhaps…have you given any thought to your own future?

PIP: I'm afraid to think further than our project.

HERBERT: You might think of a future with me—I mean with Clarriker's, for in the East Indies we'll need a—

PIP: —A clerk?

HERBERT: Yes, a clerk. But Handel, you could expand into a partnership soon enough—look at me! Clara and I have talked it over—she worries about you too, the darling. You're to live with us. We get along so well, Handel…
(Pip, deeply moved, hugs him.)

PIP: Not yet. Not for a while. After we've seen our project through there are some other things I must settle.

HERBERT: When you are ready, then?

PIP: When I am ready. And thank you.

NARRATION: That same evening, Pip received a message.

WEMMICK: Burn this as soon as you read it. Be ready to move your cargo out on Wednesday morning. J. Wemmick.

HERBERT: Wednesday!

PIP: We can be ready. Will you warn Magwitch?

HERBERT: I'll visit Clara tonight. But your burns haven't healed yet—I can tell your arm still hurts.

PIP: I shall be ready.

NARRATION: Tuesday. One of those March mornings when the sun shines hot and the wind blows cold…summer in the sun, winter in the shade. The plan:
(Pip and Herbert pore over a map.)

PIP: The tide turns at nine tomorrow morning—it's with us until three.

HERBERT: Just six hours.

PIP: We'll have to row into the night, anyway.

HERBERT: Where do we board the big ship?

PIP: Below Gravesend—here. See, the river's wide, there, and quite deserted. The packet ship to Hamburg passes at midnight.

HERBERT: Wemmick has booked two passages to Hamburg. The two passengers are expected to make an…unconventional boarding, to say the least.
(They smile at each other. Compeyson lurks on the sidelines.)

NARRATION: Wednesday. The relief of putting the plan into action was enormous. The two young men set out in their boat as was their habit. Pip felt sure they went undetected. They soon passed old London Bridge, then Billingsgate Market, with its oyster-boats. The White Tower. Traitor's Gate. Now they were among the big steamers from Glasgow and Aberdeen. Here, at their moorings, were tomorrow's ships for Rotterdam and Le Havre. And there stood the packet scheduled to leave for Hamburg later that evening. Pip and Herbert rowed past it with pounding hearts. Finally they touched the little dock at Mill Pond Bank, Where a man dressed as a river pilot was waiting. He climbed into the boat.

MAGWITCH: Dear boy, faithful boy, thankee. And thankee, Pip's companion.

NARRATION: Herbert and Pip rowed their cargo back out on the river.

MAGWITCH: If you know'd, dear boy, what it is to sit alonger my boy in the open air, arter having been kept betwixt four walls…

PIP: I think I know the delights of freedom.

MAGWITCH: No, you'd have to have been under lock and key to know it equal to me.

PIP: If all goes well, you'll be free again within a few hours.

MAGWITCH: I hope so. But we can no more see to the bottom of the next few hours than we can to the bottom of this river. Nor yet can we hold back time's tide than I can hold this water…see how it runs through my fingers and is gone?

NARRATION: The air felt cold and damp. Pip's hands throbbed with pain. In mid-afternoon the tide began to run strong against them, but they rowed and rowed until the sun set. Night. They passed Gravesend at last, and pulled into a little cove. They waited. Magwitch smoked his pipe. They spoke very little. Once Pip thought he heard the lapping of oars upon the water, and the murmur of voices—but then there was nothing. He credited it to exhaustion and the pain in his hands. They continued to wait silently by the river bank. Then—they heard an engine! The packet for Hamburg was coming round the bend—even in the dark Pip thought he could see the smoke from her stacks!

PIP: Yes, here she comes!

HERBERT: She's slowing down—start rowing!

NARRATION: They eased out on the river again, and headed toward the packet steamer—when suddenly, a four-oared galley shot out from the bank, toward them—on board were four oarsmen and two other figures. One held the rudder lines, and seemed to be in charge—the other figure sat idle: He was cloaked and hidden. The galley began pulling up fast toward Pip's boat—while Pip and Herbert rowed furiously toward the packet.

VOICE FROM GALLEY You have a returned convict there—that man in the pilot's coat. His name is Abel Magwitch. I call upon him to surrender, and you others to assist!

NARRATION: With a mighty thrust, the galley rammed Pip's small boat.

(Sound of wood on wood, cries, water.)

NARRATION: Magwitch stood in the boat and leaned across, yanking the cloak from the other man's face.

MAGWITCH: Compeyson!

COMPEYSON: Yes, it's Compeyson.

VOICE FROM GALLEY Surrender!

MAGWITCH: You shan't get away with it, not again, not this time!

VOICE FROM GALLEY To starboard, to starboard—look out—

COMPEYSON: Help, he's got hold of me—he's pulling me—overboard...help!—

VOICE FROM GALLEY We're going to capsize—watch—

(Screaming. The packet sounds its horn, thrashing in water.)

VOICE FROM GALLEY My God, the steamer! The steamer's upon us! Help—the steamer—headed toward us—

(The packet horn blows with increasing insistence. Shouts, cries, screams, splintering wood.)

PIP: Magwitch...!

(Then silence. The lapping of water.)

NARRATION: As the confusion abated, they saw Magwitch swimming ahead. He was hauled on board and manacled at the wrists and ankles. He had sustained severe injuries to the chest and head. There was no sign of Compeyson. Magwitch told his captors they had gone down together, locked in each other's arms. After a fierce underwater struggle, only Magwitch had found the strength to swim to the surface. Pip, shivering and wet, took his place beside the wounded, shackled creature.

MAGWITCH: Dear boy...I'm quite content. I've seen my boy. Now he can...be a gentleman without me...

PIP: I will never stir from your side. Please God, I will be as true to you as you have been to me.

NARRATION: Magwitch was removed to the prison hospital, but was too ill to be committed for immediate trial. Pip tried to think what peace of mind he could bring to the wounded man.

PIP: His money—his property—

JAGGERS: —It will all be forfeit to the crown, Pip. I'm sorry.

PIP: I don't care, for myself. But for mercy's sake, don't let him know it's lost. It would break his heart if he thought I weren't to have it.

JAGGERS: You let it slip through your fingers. Poor Pip.

WEMMICK When I think of the sacrifice of so much portable property! Your creditors will be after you now, I fear.

JAGGERS: However, I'll say nothing to Magwitch. Poor Pip. I'm late to court.

NARRATION: *(Voices echo.)* Late to court. Late to court. Late to court.

(The prison hospital. Magwitch lies on a mattress. Pip enters.)

MAGWITCH: Dear boy, I thought you was late.

PIP: It's only just time. I waited by the gate.

MAGWITCH: Thankee, dear boy. You never desert me.

PIP: Are you in much pain today?

MAGWITCH: I don't complain of none.

PIP: You never do complain.

(A prison doctor looks at Magwitch, shakes his head.)

PIP: Magwitch, I must tell you now, at last—can you understand what I say?
(Magwitch nods.)

PIP: You had a child once, whom you loved and lost?
(Magwitch nods.)

PIP: She lived. She lives, and has powerful friends. She is a lady, and very beautiful. And I love her!
(Magwitch kisses Pip's hand. He dies.)

PIP: Oh Lord, be merciful to him, a sinner.
(Darkness.)

(The Temple. Pip lies sleeping on a sofa.)

NARRATION: Now Pip was all alone. Miss Havisham and Magwitch were dead. And Herbert had left for the Far East. Pip should have been alarmed by the state of his financial affairs, for he was heavily in debt—but that he scarcely had the strength to notice. For he was ill, very ill with fever. He dreamed he was rowing, endlessly rowing. He dreamed that Miss Havisham called to him from inside a great furnace.

(Creditors begin carrying off the rug, a chair, and so on. In the end there is only the sofa and one chair.)

NARRATION: He dreamed he was a brick in the wall—the steel beam of a vast engine. He dreamed that the creditors had carried off all his furniture but a bed and a chair—and that Joe was seated in the chair. He dreamed he asked for a cooling drink, and that the beloved hand that gave it to him was Joe's. He dreamed he smelled Joe's pipe. And finally, one day he took courage and woke up.

PIP: Is it…Joe?

JOE: Which it are, old chap.

PIP: Oh, Joe, you break my heart.

JOE: Which, dear old Pip, you and me was ever the best of friends. And when you're better—wot larks!

(Pip covers his eyes for a moment.)

PIP: How long, dear Joe?

JOE: Which you meantersay, how long have you been ill? It's the end of May.

PIP: And you've been here all this time?

JOE: Pretty nigh. For Biddy said, "Go to him, he needs you!" And I do what she tells me. Now rest, Pip. I must write a letter to Biddy, else she'll worry.

PIP: You can write?

JOE: Biddy taught me.

NARRATION: Pip was like a child in the hands of Joe, who cared for him so tenderly that Pip half-believed he *was* a child again, and that everything that had happened to him since he left the forge was a dream. Finally the fever was gone. But as Pip grew stronger, Joe seemed to grow less comfortable.

JOE: Dear old Pip, old chap, you're almost come round, sir.

PIP: Ay. We've had a time together I shall never forget. I know for a while I *did* forget the old days, but—

JOE: Dear Pip…dear sir…what have been betwixt us—have been. You're better now.

PIP: Yes, Joe.

JOE: Then good night, Pip. *(He tiptoes out.)*

NARRATION: And when he awoke the next morning, Joe was gone.

(Pip finds a note on Joe's chair.)

PIP: *(Reads.)* Sir: Not wishful to intrude, I have departed. For you are well again, dear Pip, and will do better without Joe. P.S. Ever the best of friends.

NARRATION: Enclosed with the note was a receipt for Pip's outstanding debts. Joe had paid them.

(Pip puts on his jacket, takes his hat.)

PIP: I'll go to him—to the forge. Biddy was right, he has such pride, such honor. And Biddy—Biddy is there too. Perhaps she'll find me worthier of her than I once was. Perhaps— *(He rushes off.)*

NARRATION: The first person he encountered when he climbed off the coach was his old mentor, Mr. Pumblechook.

PUMBLECHOOK: So, young man, I am sorry to see you brought so low. Look at you, skin and bones. But I knew it! You were ever pigheaded and ungrateful. I always knew it would end badly. Lo, how the mighty are fallen! How the mighty are—

NARRATION: —But Pip could not wait to hear the conclusion of the greeting. He headed down a country lane to the forge. The June weather was delicious. The sky was blue, and larks soared over the green corn. He felt like a pilgrim, toiling homeward from a distant land.

BIDDY: It's Pip! Dear Pip—Joe, Joe, Pip's come home! Look at you, so pale and thin.

PIP: Biddy, dear girl.

BIDDY: How did you know to come today?

PIP: Today?

BIDDY: It's our wedding day. Joe and I were married this morning!

(Pip's face falls for an instant, then he brightens. Joe appears.)

PIP: Married. Married!

JOE: Which he warn't strong enough fur to be surprised, my dear.

BIDDY: I ought to have thought, but I was so happy—

PIP: —And so am I! It's the sweetest tonic of all. Biddy, you have the best husband in the world; and you, Joe, the best wife. She'll make you as happy as you deserve to be. *(He kisses her.)* And now, although I know you've already done it in your hearts, please tell me you forgive me.

JOE: Dear old Pip, God knows as I forgive you, if I have anything to forgive.

BIDDY: Amen.

(He embraces them both.)

PIP: And now, I must be off, to catch the coach to London.

(Joe and Biddy watch him go. For a moment, they look after him, arms around each other.)

WEMMICK: Mr. Pip? I know it's a trying time to turn your mind to other matters, but—

PIP: —What? Anything, Wemmick.

WEMMICK: Tomorrow is only Tuesday...still, I'm thinking of taking a holiday.

PIP: Are you? That's very nice...?

WEMMICK: I'd like you to take a walk with me in the morning, if you don't object.

PIP: Of course not. Delighted.

NARRATION: The next morning early, after fortifying themselves with rum-and-milk and biscuits, they did take a walk, to Camberwell Green. Pip was puzzled.

WEMMICK: Halloa! Here's a nice little church. Let's go in.

NARRATION: And they went in.

WEMMICK: Halloa! Here's a couple of pairs of nice gloves. Let's put them on.

(They do so. The Aged Parent and Miss Skiffins (still in her green gloves) appear with a clergyman.)

WEMMICK: Halloa! Here is Miss Skiffins. Let's have a wedding. All right, Aged P?

AGED PARENT: All right, John!

CLERGYMAN Who giveth this woman to be married to this man?

(No response.)

CLERGYMAN Who giveth this woman to be married to this man?

WEMMICK: *(Shouts.)* Now, Aged P. You know, "who giveth."

AGED PARENT: I do! I do! I do! All right, John?

NARRATION: And so Mr. Wemmick and Miss Skiffins were wed, with Pip as witness.

(All kiss the bride.)

WEMMICK: *(To Pip.)* Altogether a Walworth sentiment, you understand?

PIP: I understand. Private and personal, not to be mentioned in the office.

WEMMICK: If Mr. Jaggers knew of this, he might think my brain was softening.

(The Aged nods. They all nod.)

NARRATION: Within a month Pip had left England. Within two he was a clerk in the Far Eastern branch of Clarriker and Pocket. Three years later he was promoted to associate director of that branch. For many years Pip lived happily with Herbert and Clara Pocket. When at last he returned to England, he hurried to the little village and the forge.

(The forge kitchen. Joe sits smoking. Biddy sews. There is a small boy with a slate on Pip's old stool. Pip gazes for a moment, then enters. They embrace him. He picks up the child.)

JOE: We giv' him the name of Pip for your sake, dear old boy, and hope he may grow a little like you.

PIP: You must lend him to me, once I get settled.

BIDDY: No, you must marry and get your own boy.

PIP: So Clara tells me, but I don't think so…

BIDDY: *(Pause.)* You haven't forgotten her.

PIP: I've forgotten nothing that ever meant anything to me. But that poor dream has all gone by, dear Biddy, all gone by.

(Miss Havisham's garden.)

NARRATION: The next evening Pip's steps led him to Miss Havisham's gate. There was no house left, only ruins and a garden overgrown by weeds. *(A figure moves from the shadows toward him.)*

PIP: Estella!

ESTELLA: I wonder you know me, Pip. I've changed.

PIP: How is—

ESTELLA: My husband is dead.

PIP: I'm sorry.

ESTELLA: Don't be. He used me with great cruelty. It is over.

PIP: How strange we should meet here, where we first met.

ESTELLA: *(Pause.)* You do well?

PIP: I work pretty hard, so I do well enough. I want so little.

ESTELLA: I have often thought of you. Once you said to me, "God bless you, God forgive you." Suffering has taught me what your heart used to be—

PIP: God has forgiven you, my dear.

ESTELLA: Ay. I have been bent and broken but, I hope, into a better shape. Tell me we are friends, Pip.

PIP: We are friends.

ESTELLA: And shall continue friends apart?

(He starts to speak, hesitates, nods. He bends and kisses her hand.)

PIP: God bless you, Estella.

(She leaves through the garden gate. Pip looks around the old place. He sees the little pot of flowers, now broken and charred, but with a few blooms still growing. He picks it up, smells them, picks one and folds it into his breast pocket. He sits on the old garden bench. As he does, voices of the past rise up. They begin slow, but speed up, overlapping.)

NARRATION: Philip Pirrip, late of this parish.

And then, Pip, wot larks!

Stop, thief, stop that boy!

Be grateful, boy, for them what has brought you up by hand.

Love her, love her, love her!

Wot larks.

Coarse little monster, why don't you cry. Cry. Cry.

This young man has...great expectations
Wouldn't you be happier as you are?
Did you never think it could be me?
Portable property
My dear Handel
You've the arm of a blacksmith
Love her, love her, love her!
I cannot love
I've come back to you, Pip, dear boy
A wild beast tamed
Name of Magwitch
What have I done? What have I done?
Going to be a gentleman
Great expectations.
(Pip rises.)
Great expectations.
(He strides out the garden door. Darkness.)

THE END

THE BOOK OF RUTH

by Deborah Lynn Frockt

THE AUTHOR

Deborah Lynn Frockt is in her sixth season as resident dramaturg and literary manager at Seattle Children's Theatre. Three of her plays have premiered at SCT: *Winnie-the-Pooh, Alice's Adventures in Wonderland,* and *The Book of Ruth,* which was the recipient of a 1999 AT&T *OnStage®* Award. Her plays have also been seen at Actors Theatre of Louisville and the Alabama Shakespeare Festival. Ms. Frockt was the literary associate at Actors Theatre Louisville where she was a dramaturg for the Humana Festival of New American Plays. She has been the dramaturg for three dozen new plays and her freelance work includes work at A Contemporary Theatre and the Empty Space Theatre. She holds masters degrees from Stanford University and the University of London.

ORIGINAL PRODUCTION

The Book of Ruth was originally produced by Seattle Children's Theatre on February 26, 1999. It was directed by Steven E. Alter. Liz Engleman and Tobin A. Maheras were the dramaturgs. Renée Roub* and Lisa Schaible* were the stage managers. The cast was:

David . . . . Jacob Fishel
Avram . . . . Gene Freedman*
Ruth . . . . Jennifer Sue Johnson*
Hannah . . . . Marjorie Nelson*
Mr. Stein/Cook . . . . R. Hamilton Wright* and Randy Hoffmeyer*

Understudies—Sharva Maynard*, David Silverman*, Rebecca Osman, Orion Taraban
* Members of Actors' Equity Association, the union for stage professionals

The Book of Ruth was commissioned and premiered by Seattle Children's Theatre, with the support of AT&T *OnStage®*, a project of the AT&T Foundation.

CHARACTERS

RUTH: Jewish girl, early teens. Doubles as Young Hannah (Ruth's granddaughter) in the final scene

HANNAH: Ruth's grandmother, sixties. Doubles as Old Ruth in the final scene

DAVID: Jewish boy, early teens

AVRAM: Jewish man, sixties

MR. STEIN/COOK: Jewish man, thirties or forties

TIME AND PLACE

The spring of 1944 in Terezín and, briefly, the present in America.

PLAYWRIGHT'S NOTE

After my grandparents died I took three things from their house: a picture taken soon after their marriage that I had loved since childhood; a *menorah* for Chanukah; and all of my grandmother's recipes. They were scattered in no particular order in two kitchen drawers. They reveal someone who was a cook for life. The recipes aren't even really that. They are more like refreshers for someone far too experienced to ever need formal instruction. To this day, it strikes me that multiplication problems abound on these index cards. Strudel times three; cake times two; tradition times infinity.

My grandmother and grandfather had two *seders* in their home, every year, until they died. Every spring at Passover, around thirty members of this extended family would gather in their modest home. Many of the relatives had bigger houses where you might think the family would be more comfortable, but this house is where everyone was at home.

Rectangular folding tables would be added to the mahogany dining table, extending it the length of the dining room and living room. Passover tablecloths would be pulled out for their yearly appearance, then sheathed in plastic to protect them from wine, children, and people hungry after long prayers. The men always sat at the head of the table in the living room. The older men, the younger men, then near the kitchen, the women; and with the women, the children. My grandmother sat closest to the swinging door that led to the kitchen, but I don't think anyone ever saw her actually sit during a *seder*.

My grandfather would lead the ceremony, with the help of the other family elders. We'd all participate by sharing in the reading of the *Haggadah*, usually in English. And of course, the youngest child would be called upon to chant in Hebrew the Four Questions.

It would take my grandmother endless weeks to prepare for *seder* and the week-long festival during which no leavened food was eaten. Her kitchen would be divided, with *homitz* (the leavened food of fifty-one weeks of the year) and *pesadichy* (for Passover) separated. Counters were made *pesadichy* when they were covered with linoleum. Separate dishes for milk and meat, necessary for a kosher kitchen year around, were stored away; and *pesadichy* milk and meat dishes took their place.

And then she would cook. And cook. And cook. Each *seder* would consist of chopped liver, matzah bagels, matzah ball soup, gefilte fish, meat blintzes, *kishke*, roast chicken, stuffed cabbage and was there ever a green vegetable in sight? Not in a southern Jewish home with Russian roots. I've heard that some families have fruit as their *seder* dessert, since the food is traditionally heavy and the baking choices so restricted. Unheard of at my grandma's house. She made *pesadichy* sponge cakes leavened with only whipped egg whites, then soaked in Manishevitz wine. And jelly rolls. And macaroons. A full sit-down dinner for thirty, two nights in a row—until she was seventy-seven.

But cooking for sixty wasn't the end of it. Uncle Harry liked the matzah balls, so he was sent home with a week's worth. Uncle Sam liked the gefilte fish, so likewise for him.

Anyone with children went home with something sweet to put in the lunch box alongside the ubiquitous matzah sandwiches.

When I was growing up, I adored my grandmother; but I had my questions. Why did she make everything from scratch? Why were there so many dishes? Why not simplify? Why spend endless hours, shopping, cleaning, chopping, boiling, baking, cooking? Why did she want to work in the kitchen until two in the morning after having worked a full day outside of the house? Why did she do all this?

Like my grandma, Hannah is a cook certain in her way of doing things. Like me, Ruth wonders why. In the midst of a prison camp starving nearly to death, why should she learn recipes for strudel, for matzah balls, for anything? Ruth learns her grandmother's lessons in depravation and terror. I am more fortunate; I learned my lessons right over an ordinary kitchen counter.

Now, I am grown-up with a family of my own. In the home I make with my husband, there is a son who bears his great grandfather's name. There is a brother who will help him light the *menorah* when he is old enough. There is a box of recipes from which I cook and learn and feed my family. And now I know why.

ACT I

In a very tight pool of light, an old woman and a young woman are together. They are Hannah and Ruth. Objects that might be kitchen utensils surround them. Note: " / " indicates overlapping speech.

HANNAH: Do we have everything?
   (Ruth does not respond.)
HANNAH: Do we have everything?
RUTH: Why do we have to/
HANNAH: Let's check before we start.
RUTH: We have everything.
HANNAH: What did I tell you about stopping in the middle?
RUTH: Don't.
HANNAH: Flour, baking powder, salt, eggs and… *(Urging Ruth.)* and…
RUTH: *(Grudgingly.)* Oil.
HANNAH: Now I can show you. I can show you how to make Bubbe's strudel.
   You like Bubbe's strudel, don't you?
RUTH: Everyone likes your strudel.
HANNAH: It's good?
RUTH: The best.
HANNAH: Then let me show you. You crack the eggs.
   (Ruth does nothing.)
HANNAH: Go on.
   (Ruth cracks an egg.)
HANNAH: Be careful. Make sure no shell goes in. Now the salt.
RUTH: With the eggs?
HANNAH: That's right.
RUTH: Why does everything take salt—even the sweet things?
HANNAH: Because a little salt brings out the sweet and makes it all the sweeter.
   Are the eggs well mixed?
RUTH: They're mixed.
HANNAH: Well mixed?
RUTH: My arm gets tired.
HANNAH: It's not easy, but it's worth it.
RUTH: *(Overlapping with Hannah.)* …but it's worth it.
HANNAH: That's right. Now you mix the eggs with the flour and you get a
   nice dough.
RUTH: Nice?

HANNAH: You don't want it too wet and you don't want it too dry.

RUTH: How can you tell?

HANNAH: Experience.

RUTH: I don't have any.

HANNAH: But we're working together so you have the benefit of my experience. Mix it together well. *(Hannah pats her hands in the bowl.)*

RUTH: With our hands?

HANNAH: Get messy. It tastes better. When it's good and mixed, you roll it out. Go on.

(Ruth starts to roll out the dough.)

HANNAH: Make a rectangle because after you fill it, you're going to want to roll it like a jellyroll.

RUTH: I've never rolled a jellyroll.

HANNAH: I'll show you. Don't worry. *(Hannah adjusts Ruth's style.)* Now, the filling. Apples, cherries, nuts.

(Ruth is still.)

HANNAH: You spread it on, and roll it up.

RUTH: This is the hard part.

HANNAH: No. You can't think it's hard. If you think that, you'll be nervous. And if you're nervous, then the nerves at the tips of your fingers will stand on end. And if the nerves are standing on end, you'll be shaky and you won't be able to roll straight. And then you won't have strudel. So, you relax and enjoy and you roll.

RUTH: Relax and enjoy?

HANNAH: And roll.

(Hannah moves Ruth's arms to roll strudel, and Ruth begins.)

RUTH: I'm rolling. I'm rolling. I'm rolling.

HANNAH: There you go.

RUTH: I'm rolling. I'm almost done. I'm rolling. I'm done.

HANNAH: You did it.

RUTH: I rolled strudel. *(Unsure of herself.)* It looks/

HANNAH: Like Bubbe's strudel.

RUTH: You think so?

HANNAH: You did it *mamala*. You did the hard part.

RUTH: You said it wasn't hard.

HANNAH: I said you can't *think* it's hard, or you'll never make it. A little cinnamon, a little sugar and into a hot oven/

RUTH: And into my stomach!

(A harsh German voice interrupts them.)

GERMAN VOICE: *Raus! Raus! Alle Kinder zu den Kinderbaracken. Alle zuruck zu den eigenen Baracken. Ausgeh Verbot gielt absofort.* [*Raus, raus!* Children to the *kinderholm.* Everyone to his own barracks. Curfew will begin immediately.]

(The lights expand to reveal that Ruth and Hannah are in the women's barracks in Terezín and not their comfortable kitchen. We now see that all the ingredients, utensils, and most importantly the strudel, were either fiction or makeshift mockeries of the real items.)

RUTH: Never even a taste.

HANNAH: Next time, we'll be faster. We'll smell the apples and sweet dough. Next time, Ruthala. You'll get three pieces at least.

(The announcement comes through again, and Hannah helps Ruth put her coat on, revealing a Jewish star. Lights up on Mr. Stein. He addresses the audience.)

MR. STEIN: At last. At last. The weapons have arrived. Blades of steel that will strike at the heart of our enemy. Swords that will cut to the quick. Sabers to rattle. Sabers that cut. Sabers that I entrust to each of you.

(Ruth and David enter. Mr. Stein is a teacher of sorts and this is the Terezín "school." Mr. Stein pauses and reveals a pair of scissors with one hand. With the other he pulls out paper. Through the following, he is cutting the paper.)

MR. STEIN: Some of you are skeptical, but you needn't be. In the right hands, this weapon is as deadly as guns on the battlefield, tanks in the trenches, or bombs from the sky. And these are not all. Pencils today. Paper today. Fight with these. And voila… *(He puts down a row of paper cut-out dolls.)* an army!

(Mr. Stein hands Ruth paper with a great flourish. He finds a nub of a pencil for her. She sits down alone to work. Mr. Stein then goes to David.)

MR. STEIN: David, try these.

DAVID: No thank you.

MR. STEIN: You don't know yet what a scarce commodity these are. I can't remember when we last saw scissors.

DAVID: Thank you, but I'm not artistic.

MR. STEIN: What does that matter? David, listen to me. Here, there are rules for everything. Rules even prohibiting teaching of children.

DAVID: I understand.

MR. STEIN: I don't think you do. People are risking things, David. For you to be educated, for you to learn, the community takes enormous risks. Imprisonment. Deportation. Execution. People risk these things for the future. For you. *(Mr. Stein hands paper and scissors to David.)* Try. *(Mr. Stein exits.)*

(Ruth is engrossed in her drawing. David helplessly considers his tools. He goes to Ruth.)

DAVID: What are you making?

(Ruth doesn't look up.)

DAVID: I said, "What are you making?"

RUTH: *(Without looking up.)* I heard you.

DAVID: I'm not good at drawing.

RUTH: Then make a collage.

DAVID: Not very good at cutting or pasting either. Sketching. Painting. Etching, shaping, coloring. You name an artistic technique and chances are, I can't do it.

RUTH: Everyone has something they're good at.

DAVID: Oh, I have lots of things I'm good at. But none of them are art things.

RUTH: Fortunately for you, we rarely get supplies. *(Ruth continues to draw.)*

DAVID: If you won't show me what you're making, tell me.

RUTH: Tell you about my picture?

DAVID: You look like you must be good at drawing. Drawing, coloring, cutting/

RUTH: And pasting. Yes. I do all of those things.

DAVID: If you won't tell me everything in detail, give me an idea of its theme. Is it historical, futuristic, realistic/

RUTH: I can't work with you watching and talking.

(He picks up the scissors and paper, contemplates using them, puts them down.)

DAVID: I have a secret.

RUTH: There are no secrets in Terezín. There's no place to keep them.

DAVID: Maybe I have news about the war. Maybe I'm really an American spy watching the Germans' every move. Perhaps I have a stash of gold, or I'm really the son of a king or a movie star or/

RUTH: *(To stop him.)* What is your secret?

DAVID: If you can't trust me with your picture, I can't trust you with my secret.

(Ruth turns back to her picture.)

DAVID: I'll tell you just this much. I know a place.

RUTH: You know a place?

DAVID: Yes.

RUTH: I know a place too. In fact, I know several: the courtyard, the barracks. The morgue.

DAVID: A *secret* place.

RUTH: A secret place?

(David nods.)

RUTH: A secret place in the camp?

DAVID: That's what I said.

RUTH: Here? Where we sleep one hundred to a room?

DAVID: You don't believe me.

RUTH: No.

(Mr. Stein re-enters. He picks up the unused scissors and paper. Seeing Mr. Stein's disappointment, David tries to encourage him.)

DAVID: Maybe another day.

MR. STEIN: Luxuries are rare and necessities are even rarer. Have you been assigned a work detail yet?

DAVID: Yes, sir.

MR. STEIN: Then it's time to go to it.

(David exits. Ruth starts to go, but Mr. Stein stops her.)

MR. STEIN: (Indicates scissors.) You think we'll win the war with these or merely a battle?

RUTH: I didn't know we were in the fight.

MR. STEIN: Every day. May I see what you've made?

RUTH: It's not finished yet.

MR. STEIN: Then let me see a work-in-progress.

RUTH: It doesn't look right.

(Mr. Stein gently takes the picture.)

MR. STEIN: A magical place.

RUTH: I suppose.

MR. STEIN: Do you have a favorite place, Ruth?

RUTH: Here?

MR. STEIN: Here? That hardly seems possible. No. At home.

RUTH: No.

MR. STEIN: Think about it.

RUTH: If I ever did have one, how would I remember it after all this time?

MR. STEIN: Mine was Wencelas Square. Anyone could go there and everyone did. A place for all the people. A place to be a Czech, first and always.

RUTH: My bubbe and zeyde's flat.

MR. STEIN: Some place private.

RUTH: It had a smell…

MR. STEIN: Sweet?

RUTH: Sometimes. Other times onions. But it always smelled…warm.

MR. STEIN: You know, I'm not a teacher by training. I've learned on my feet—

as we all have. I never imagined I'd be with children all day—and like it. We—my wife and I—we never had any. I wonder if we might have one day. *(He considers the picture again. He takes a sketching pencil from his pocket.)* This seems the simplest thing in the world, doesn't it? An implement. A means to an end. Not even the thing itself. It shouldn't be of any value, but how precious it has become. *(He gives her the pencil.)*

RUTH: To keep?

MR. STEIN: Just between us. So you can finish your picture. *(Mr. Stein exits.)* *(Ruth stashes the pencil in her clothes. Shift to Hannah mending a stack of well-worn German uniforms. This is her work detail. When she is sure no one is looking, Hannah tears the inner pocket of one of the uniforms and pockets the cloth. After a moment, Ruth comes stealthily in and stands before Hannah.)*

HANNAH: *Got in himmel,* Ruth! Get under! *(Indicating the uniforms.)* Under here! If the shop elder sees you, God help us!
(Ruth gets down partially camouflaged by the clothes. Hannah continues her darning.)

HANNAH: You know the rules. In the barracks, only during family hours. Not while we work. You put yourself in harm's way/

RUTH: I needed to see you, Bubbe.

HANNAH: Are you sick?

RUTH: No/

HANNAH: When they're looking for another transport, when they're making the next list for the East, all they need is to see a little girl sneaking around, distracting others from orders. That's all they need. *(Referring to the presence of the shop elder.)* We'll wait until she turns the corner, then you'll go.

RUTH: I was very careful to make sure no one noticed.

HANNAH: You can't draw attention to yourself.

RUTH: I said I was careful.

HANNAH: *(About the shop elder.)* There she goes past Frieda. Careful means nothing.

RUTH: Maybe I'm special.

HANNAH: What?

RUTH: Maybe I'm special. Special so they won't see me.

HANNAH: You're not special. No one is. *(About the elder.)* There. Past Margot. Now Sophie.

RUTH: They shouldn't be making you do all this hard work.

HANNAH: This is old lady's work.

RUTH: You're not an old lady.

HANNAH: An old lady who sticks herself with the needle.

RUTH: Because they've taken your glasses. Because there's no light.

HANNAH: She's about to turn the corner.

RUTH: Bubbe, I needed to see you because/

HANNAH: Ruth. Pay attention.

RUTH: I wanted to show you/

(As Hannah interrupts her, Ruth starts to take out the picture. Ruth and Hannah overlap as they hurry to speak.)

HANNAH: We have only a minute before she turns back this way.

RUTH: In class/

HANNAH: Walk quickly, but don't run.

RUTH: Bubbe, today/

HANNAH: Look as if you are supposed to be here. Like someone sent you.

RUTH: I drew this picture.

HANNAH: Go now! Now, Ruth!

(Hannah shoves the picture back into Ruth's hands, then pushes Ruth out of the space, and returns to her work, surreptitiously watching to see that Ruth exits safely. Shift to the next day in class. David sits struggling with an art project. Ruth sits and begins drawing again. After a moment.)

RUTH: You decided to make something today?

DAVID: It's awful.

RUTH: I'm sure it's not.

(David shows her the picture.)

RUTH: It is awful. *(Pause.)* When did you get here?

DAVID: One week ago. How long have you been here?

RUTH: Long enough to know there are no secret places.

DAVID: Mr. Stein just told me this was…provocative. That's how he said it. As if he had to look hard for the word. *(Pause.)* I do know a secret place.

RUTH: Where is this place?

DAVID: You don't get something for nothing. I've learned that much already. Let me see your picture.

(Ruth considers carefully, decides to risk it and show him the picture.)

DAVID: What is it?

RUTH: Where's the place?

DAVID: Information for information.

RUTH: This is a castle.

DAVID: That's not enough.

RUTH: This is a castle in the sky.

DAVID: Mine's a real place. Not just a picture. You have to tell me more.

RUTH: If this is some trick/

DAVID: It's not.

(Ruth considers carefully.)

RUTH: This is a castle in the sky. But it's not an ordinary castle. Instead of a king or a queen or even a lord or a duke, bakers live here. Hundreds of bakers and bakers' helpers. And on each turret, there is a chimney because in each turret, there is an oven for baking the most delicious creations of the entire world...and beyond.

In some ovens, bakers are baking bread—dark, rich, hearty bread from Bohemia. And some of the bread is fluffy and white—from Paris. And in other parts of the castle, there are dozens of master bakers making *kuchen* or apple pastry or strudel. And some make teacakes and some make coffeecake and some make little cookies that only the smallest people are allowed to eat.

And all of this baking, this extraordinary, wonderful-smelling, fresh baking isn't for the bakers to eat and it isn't for the people on Earth. No. This castle baking is for the angels. They come from all over the heavens to do their shopping everyday. And the angels love this baking so much that they sing the bakers' praises throughout the heavens and the earth.

DAVID: Doesn't God get jealous or angry that the angels are spending their time singing the praises of ordinary bakers when they could be singing His praises?

RUTH: God is never angry with the angels because the bakers make the heavens smell so sweet that sometimes God even joins the angels and sings praises for the bakers.

DAVID: Do you think there could really be a place like that?

RUTH: They must still be baking fresh bread, real bread somewhere.

DAVID: Just not here.

RUTH: No, not here. (Beat.) I gave you a picture. You owe me a place.

DAVID: It's not easy to find.

RUTH: You said this was no trick.

DAVID: I'd have to show it to you.

RUTH: When?

DAVID: Today. After class.

RUTH: During family hours?

DAVID: It's the perfect time because everyone is in the barracks pretending they're at home.

RUTH: Won't we be missed?

DAVID: Not me. I've no one to pretend with. Do you?

RUTH: *(Pause.)* No. No one. Just like you.

DAVID: All right then. During family hours. We go as soon as class ends.

RUTH: We can't go together. Everyone would notice.

DAVID: Then how will you get there?

RUTH: We'll meet behind the hospital. Do you know it?

DAVID: The building no one goes near.

RUTH: The hearses come and go there. Avoid the courtyard. The cooks are always there sneaking a cigarette that time of day. Don't let anyone see you waiting around. From there, no one will notice us together.

DAVID: You know all the rules.

RUTH: Soon, you will too.

(Shift to Hannah standing in line for food. She holds a pathetic ration bowl, and slowly advances as she gets closer to the soup pot, perhaps bending over to pick up a potato peel. Lights shift to David and Ruth entering the secret place. Ruth is impressed.)

RUTH: How could you find this place?

DAVID: I told you I was good at things. Just not art things.

RUTH: Nobody knows of it but you?

DAVID: Not until now.

RUTH: It's so quiet.

DAVID: Private.

RUTH: Why didn't you keep this secret to yourself?

DAVID: I felt alone up here. Which was the idea—at first. To be alone. To breathe alone. But then it became too alone, and all I could think of is that there's no one down there for me and no one up here either—and it was too alone.

RUTH: Why did you pick me to tell?

DAVID: Maybe you're special.

RUTH: I'm not.

DAVID: You drew that picture.

RUTH: It was just something I thought of.

DAVID: If you can think it, it could be.

RUTH: Thinking something doesn't make it so.

DAVID: Yes it does. I wanted to find this place. I wanted to find a place where I didn't have to share every inch and suffocate every moment, and as I was thinking just that thought, I stopped and saw this building and I decided to go in. And I came five flights up to a floor that barely exists.

RUTH: It's high, isn't it? Probably higher than any place here.

DAVID: We're so close to your sky castle, we could smell the baking from here.

RUTH: There is no baking to smell.

DAVID: If we could smell it, we could taste it.

RUTH: What are you talking about?

DAVID: And if we tasted it, it would fill us.

(David closes his eyes.)

DAVID: Close your eyes.

(Ruth does not close her eyes. With his eyes still closed.)

DAVID: Close your eyes.

(Ruth closes her eyes.)

DAVID: Now see if you can smell baking.

(They sit in silence, straining to smell. Ruth opens her eyes.)

RUTH: I don't smell anything.

DAVID: Then try harder. Think about your sky bakery.

(Ruth closes her eyes. They strain to smell again. Ruth opens her eyes.)

RUTH: I still don't smell anything—let alone fresh bread.

(David reluctantly opens his eyes.)

RUTH: It was just a picture.

DAVID: But we're in the sky.

RUTH: We're not in the sky. We're in a *kumbal.*

DAVID: We're in the sky.

RUTH: In a building.

DAVID: We're in the sky.

RUTH: In a fortress.

DAVID: We're in the sky.

RUTH: In the middle of a war.

DAVID: We're in the sky.

RUTH: You can make yourself believe that?

DAVID: It's true.

RUTH: All right. We're in the sky.

DAVID: So, if we're in the sky, all our sky needs is a bakery.

RUTH: A bakery?

DAVID: A bakery. We make a bakery.

RUTH: I suppose we'll just start by putting an oven up here.

DAVID: No. We'll have to make one.

RUTH: We just make an oven?

DAVID: Yes. We just make an oven.

RUTH: With what?

DAVID: Iron, steel.

RUTH: Iron and steel that you smuggled in past guards and thieves?

DAVID: Then rocks, stones, bricks, sticks. Whatever we can find. We'll make an oven, and in our oven we'll make bread. We'll make so much bread that there will be crumbs to give to the birds and extra to make a pudding and some even for tea.

RUTH: Bread?

DAVID: Fresh bread! If it began to look just a little stale, we'd throw the whole loaf out.

RUTH: Dark brown bread from Bohemia and fluffy white bread from Paris.

DAVID: Real bread.

RUTH: If there were real bread/

DAVID: There'd be real school.

RUTH: Real houses.

DAVID: Real games.

RUTH: Real rules.

DAVID: Real life. (*David picks up a stone.*) We've got work to do.

RUTH: You think we can do this?

DAVID: Are you hungry?

RUTH: Always.

DAVID: Then we don't have a choice. Now. How do you make an oven?

RUTH: I thought you'd know.

DAVID: I told you.

DAVID AND RUTH: I'm no good at art.

RUTH: Then I will be the oven architect.

DAVID: And I will be the oven architect assistant.

RUTH: We should start right here.

(*Ruth puts her foot down, but notices something odd.*)

RUTH: This board is loose.

DAVID: Then do it here.

(*David moves here and Ruth gestures for him to lay the cornerstone. She straightens it slightly.*)

DAVID: We should say something.

RUTH: To who?

DAVID: To us. To mark what we've started.

RUTH: You say something.

DAVID: Today marks the first day of our building. We hope to complete our oven quickly, so that we can begin baking without delay. Now you.

RUTH: And when we bake, the bread will smell so sweet. Our noses and stomachs will be full of this bread, and we'll leave our rations far behind.

DAVID: This is *our* secret now. Both of ours.

(David offers his hand to Ruth to seal the pact. They shake and Ruth exits. David fiddles with the loose floor board. Shift to Mr. Stein in class.)

MR. STEIN: I know that you all have heard the talk about another transport. The younger children hear, but they don't know. But you children are just old enough to know. You deserve an explanation, a reason why one thousand are sent East whenever an order comes. A teacher should provide a lesson for his pupils. He should do that. But when the teacher cannot understand, how can he explain it to his students? I ask myself, what can I give you? And the only answer I find is another day of our secret learning.

(Shift to Hannah. She has a half loaf of stale bread in a linen napkin from home. She carefully unwraps it and slices two minuscule pieces. She then arranges them on the napkin as if it were a meal and waits. Ruth enters then sits, the bread between them. After a moment, Hannah pushes the bread toward Ruth and nods, indicating she should eat.)

HANNAH: I have nothing to put on it today.

RUTH: It doesn't matter.

HANNAH: It's better when it has some spread. The spread gives it some taste. It goes down better.

(Ruth eats a few bites.)

HANNAH: What did you eat yesterday?

RUTH: I had my rations.

HANNAH: Just what they usually give the children?

RUTH: It's enough.

HANNAH: You need this extra bit. You need it every day.

RUTH: *(Indicating the second slice.)* You should eat yours.

HANNAH: This isn't mine. It's yesterday's.

RUTH: You saved it for me even though I didn't come?

HANNAH: It's yours.

(Ruth picks up the second slice but does not eat it. She studies Hannah.)

RUTH: Your clothes are getting bigger on you.

HANNAH: Nonsense.

RUTH: It's true. Your clothes get bigger and mine seem to be shrinking by the minute.

HANNAH: Two years in the same dress. *(Regarding Ruth's dress.)* There's no more hem to let out.

(Ruth pushes the bread toward Hannah.)

RUTH: Eat some of it, since I have double today.

HANNAH: I've had mine already.

(Ruth picks up the loaf and sees that Hannah has not eaten today.)

RUTH: You couldn't have. Look how much is left. You're giving it all to me. You're not eating any of it, are you?

HANNAH: I said that I have already had mine today.

RUTH: Bubbe, if you don't eat/

HANNAH: Are we going to spend our time arguing about stale bread?

(Ruth sits silently, then continues eating.)

RUTH: What was that dish you used to have on the Sabbath, when you were little?

HANNAH: When I was a girl like you?

RUTH: In Kolin.

HANNAH: The *soulet*.

RUTH: That's it. Tell me about the *soulet*.

HANNAH: Every Friday morning, my mama, the first thing she would do with our Liesel, she would make the *soulet*. The barley, the beans, the potatoes, the meat. All into the pot, layered. Liesel would chop and mama would layer, and my job was to go to the *soulethaus,* to Mr. Sachel with the pot. The oven there was so big, he had room for all the *Shabbas* pots from all the Jewish families. Side by side they'd go, cooking in the slowest heat in an old stone oven. Rich and poor pots next to one another, and when Mr. Sachel got older, he'd mix up the pots and the poor families would have extra meat and the rich families would have extra potatoes. That was how we did it when I was a girl.

RUTH: What kind of stones were they?

HANNAH: What?

RUTH: The stones for the oven, were they big or small, evenly shaped or all different?

HANNAH: What's so interesting about stones?

RUTH: It was stone and not brick?

HANNAH: You don't ask me anything about how to make the *soulet*. What goes in. How much of this, how much of that. You don't want to know those things?

RUTH: What good will ingredients I don't have do me?

HANNAH: What good will the size and shapes of stones from the past do you?

(Ruth finishes the bread. They sit in silence. Ruth hesitantly takes out the pencil.)

HANNAH: How in the world did you get that?

RUTH: I just did.

HANNAH: Did you take it from/

RUTH: I just got it, that's all.

HANNAH: What are you going to do with it?

RUTH: Mama. Let's use it to write Mama a postcard.

(No response from Hannah.)

RUTH: We'll write her together.

HANNAH: They haven't let us send anything for so long, Ruthala.

RUTH: That must mean they'll let us send something soon. Maybe we'll hear back from her this time.

(Hannah pulls out the stolen cloth.)

HANNAH: You write on this for now.

RUTH: How did you get this?

HANNAH: I just did.

(Ruth takes the cloth and writes.)

RUTH: "Dearest Mama. We miss you so much, but Bubbe and I are taking care of each other. Who is taking care of you? Have you any word of Papa or Zeyde? We think of you always. Your loving daughter, Ruth." Your turn now, Bubbe.

(Ruth tries to hand the cloth and pencil to Hannah. Hannah won't take them.)

HANNAH: I don't know what to write.

RUTH: What do you mean?

HANNAH: I need to gather my thoughts.

RUTH: It's mama, Bubbe. You just write.

HANNAH: I can't think now.

(Ruth insistently puts the cloth before her, then breaks the pencil in two, laying half of it before Hannah.)

RUTH: You write her, Bubbe.

(Lights shift to David in the secret place. There is a partially constructed oven. He is placing and repositioning scraggly rocks. He hears a noise and gets panicked. Ruth enters with rocks hidden under her coat.)

RUTH: Did I scare you?

DAVID: *(Obviously scared.)* No. *(Beat.)* What do you have?

(Ruth pulls out three rocks.)

DAVID: That's all?

RUTH: It took all morning to find these. What about you?

(David points to his contribution.)

RUTH: They're not very big.

DAVID: Do you expect me to haul huge stones across the courtyard?

RUTH: This isn't going to work.

DAVID: Yes it will.

RUTH: It's too slow this way, one rock at a time.

DAVID: We can only carry what we can carry.

RUTH: Then we have to carry more.

DAVID: How?

RUTH: With a cart or a wheelbarrow.

DAVID: We'll just walk past guards and thieves with a cart full of stones, in full view of everyone?

RUTH: No. *(Long beat.)* Or maybe we should.

DAVID: What?

RUTH: If we walk in front of everyone with a cart full of stone and rock/

DAVID: They'll put us on the next transport.

RUTH: No. If we walk in front of everyone with a cart full of stone and rock in the middle of the day; if the cart is filled to the brim and we're confident and innocent, they'll think we're just two more children diligently working. And no one will say a word.

DAVID: That's crazy.

RUTH: No it's not.

DAVID: It's dangerous.

RUTH: Not any more than this is.

DAVID: If they hang us—oven or not—I won't be your friend anymore.

(Ruth and David exit the kumbal. *During Mr. Stein's following speech, they gather stones and rocks; return to the kumbal; then build the oven with them.)*

MR. STEIN: With winter changing to spring, the teachers took a vote—nearly unanimous—and decided that our lessons should now include Passover. Passover—the ancient story of a time when God remembered his chosen people. As I myself am not a believer in God, this lesson perplexes me. Perhaps we may decipher its meaning together.

Let us begin by telling the story as it has been handed down through the ages. For centuries, scores of Hebrew generations toiled for the pharaohs of Egypt. These ancient Jews hoisted stones upon their backs to raise magnificent structures in honor of their captors. One day, so the story goes, the Hebrew God saw fit to intervene through his prophet Moses. This Moses said to Pharaoh, "Let my people go." But Pharoah would not listen. A man's plea was not enough to soften Pharaoh's hard heart. Not in this story. In this story, it took God to bring freedom to a people. Moses led them, but it was God who brought them through the sea and through the desert. In this story, it was God who brought them freedom.

(Ruth and David complete their building. Scene shifts to Hannah in the barracks, reading the cloth letter. Ruth enters, surprising her.)

RUTH: You did write her. "Potatoes, onions, oil, vinegar, salt, pepper." What is this?

HANNAH: You've already given your mama the news. I thought she might need some help making do with whatever rations there might be.

RUTH: Our first letter in months, and you write a recipe?

HANNAH: This is what I want to tell her.

RUTH: You want to tell her potato salad?

HANNAH: Yes.

RUTH: A recipe for potato salad?

HANNAH: Yes.

RUTH: Potato salad is easy. You don't need a recipe for it.

HANNAH: You think so, *greysen maidela* (smart girl)? Then tell me how you do it. *(Hannah snatches the cloth away, so Ruth can't read from it.)*

RUTH: You boil the potatoes. Then, when they're cool enough just to hold, you slice them and mix with the onions. Then add the oil, vinegar, maybe some mustard. Then the seasoning. Oh yes. Then you taste it. Or if I'm there, I taste it.

HANNAH: How do you know all this?

RUTH: I've watched you do it so many times, I guess I just know it.

HANNAH: Your mama needs my help. She never paid attention in the kitchen. You're looking more and more like her, *shaynala.*

RUTH: No. She's beautiful.

HANNAH: More every day. I tried to show her how to make so many things. Dumplings and cakes, soups and roasts. Just like my mama showed me.

RUTH: Your mama was a good cook?

HANNAH: Such a cook.

RUTH: Not better than you.

HANNAH: My mama taught me everything I know. The bread she would make. *Zey get!* [So good] Even after all these years, my bread doesn't taste like hers.

RUTH: I want to show you something. *(Ruth takes out the castle drawing.)*

HANNAH: You made this?

RUTH: Yes.

HANNAH: Ruthala, may I keep it with me?

RUTH: Do you like it?

HANNAH: It is beautiful. I can look at it in the long nights after curfew, when I miss you the most.

RUTH: You miss me?

HANNAH: Every night.

(Ruth folds the picture, and gives it to Hannah, who puts it in her pocket.)

RUTH: Maybe tonight I could stay here. Then you wouldn't have to miss me.

HANNAH: The safest place for the *kinder* is in the *kinderholm.*

RUTH: Not tonight.

HANNAH: Where the other children are.

RUTH: Just not tonight.

HANNAH: Not with sick people and old people.

RUTH: I'm lonesome for you, for our home, for mama and papa and/

(The sound of a harsh voice, a German voice interrupts her.)

VOICE: *Raus, Raus!*

HANNAH: It's curfew already?

RUTH: Not yet. It's too early.

VOICE: *Raus, raus! Juden! Appell! Der Herr Kommandant hat einer Appen befohlen. Juden mussen sich am Hof melden und werden darn einer nach dem anderen aus Theresienstadt abtransportieren.* [Raus, raus! Herr commandant orders a Juden roll call. All Jews will file out of Theresienstadt.]

RUTH: Why are they counting us again?

(Hannah puts on her coat.)

RUTH: They counted just this morning.

HANNAH: Come, Ruth.

RUTH: It's already dark. *(Beat.)* We should run away, Bubbe. When we're outside the walls, in the dark, we'll run and/

HANNAH: Ruth.

RUTH: And no one will see us in the night. We'll run home.

HANNAH: Ruth. I am too old to run.

VOICE: *Raus, raus! Juden! Appell! Der Herr Kommandant hat einer Appell befohlen. Juden mussen sich am Hof melden und werden darn einer nach dem anderen aus Theresienstadt abtransportieren.* [Raus, raus! Herr commandant orders a Juden roll call. All Jews will file out of Theresienstadt.]

(Hannah takes Ruth's hand. A transition brings Ruth and Hannah outside the gates of Terezín. Every occupant of the camp is standing outside with them [unseen by the audience]. Throughout the remainder of the scene, there is the sound of German voices counting, yelling, silence: "Vortretten, zwei acht-funf eins sieben [Step forward, 28517]; In der Reihe bleiben [Stay in line]; Ruhe! [Quiet!]; Still gestanden! [Stand still!] The orders come and go but give no indication that the end of the roll call is near. It was twilight when they were called from the barracks, but it is clearly now the middle of the night. Through the scene, time shifts from late night to the first light of dawn.

As Hannah speaks, she grows increasingly exhausted. As lights come up, Ruth is collapsing into Hannah, who pushes her up.)

HANNAH: Ruth. Ruth, listen to me. You have to stand up so they don't see you looking weak. You have to look strong.

RUTH: I am weak. Tired and weak. Let them put me on the list.

HANNAH: No transport. You and I stay together. Here. Stand up!

RUTH: I can't

HANNAH: You have to. *(Pause.)* Do you remember the secret of the *knaidela?*

RUTH: There is no secret to matzah balls.

HANNAH: There is. Didn't you see it the last time I made them at home? Tell me the first thing I did.

RUTH: I don't remember matzah balls.

HANNAH: You've seen me make them a hundred times. I'll tell you this time, but pay attention because who knows when we'll have another chance to cook all night. First you have to take the matzah meal and you mix it with the eggs and the *schmaltz* (chicken fat). You remember?
(Ruth does not answer.)

HANNAH: If you want the good flavor, you add some *schmaltz* when you mix up the meal. And don't be skimpy, but don't use too much. Are you listening?

RUTH: Bubbe/

HANNAH: Good. I wanted to make sure you were listening. I don't give my recipes to just anyone. So after you've put everything in, you want to mix it up with your hands. You have to make the *knaidela* with your fingers because that's where the recipe really rests—in your fingertips. If you don't get your hands messy, how are you going to know if it's any good? Ruth?

RUTH: Bubbe/

HANNAH: Good. You're still listening. Then you add your salt and pepper. Don't worry about measuring. You just *sht and sht and sht and sht* (shake and shake and shake and shake). You have to taste it. That's the only way you can really tell. Tell me what it needs. Ruth, taste it for me.

RUTH: I can't taste it. There's nothing to taste.

HANNAH: A little more salt. A little more pepper. A little more this. A little more that. Now you make the *knaidela.* Don't make them too big, but don't make them skimpy. You want everyone to have a nice bowl of soup. Now the secret. You've got to put the *knaidela* in the icebox for a good long time. If they're not good and cold, you know what happens?
(Ruth does not answer.)

HANNAH: They'll sink, and they'll be hard as rocks. But if they're good and cold/

(An order comes from somewhere as the sun begins to rise.)

GERMAN VOICE: *Der Aufruf is beendet. Achtung! Juden mussen sich sofort bei der morgenlichen Arbeits Einteilung melden.* [The roll call is complete. Attention. The roll call is complete. Juden report to morning work detail. The roll call is complete. Report to work detail, immediately.]

HANNAH: …if they're good and cold when you start—if they're good and cold— then you'll know you've got a *knaidela* that will always make them come back to your table. *(Hannah collapses against Ruth.)*

RUTH: Bubbe?

(No response.)

RUTH: It's time to go. We have to go back in for work now.

(Hannah passes out.)

RUTH: Bubbe, get up! You've got to get up. They'll see. They'll see that you're old and weak. They'll send you away. Get up.

(Ruth sees it's futile and begins to sob, slumped over next to Hannah. Mr. Stein comes on, zombie-like after the roll call. At first it seems as if he will go right past the sobbing girl.)

MR. STEIN: Ruth? Is that you, Ruth?

(Ruth remains sobbing. Mr. Stein tries to get her up, to move her to safety.)

MR. STEIN: Ruth, we must go now. You've got to stop this sobbing and come back in the gates.

RUTH: I can't leave her.

MR. STEIN: She's old, Ruth. It may be for the best.

RUTH: No, I can't leave her. She's all I have.

MR. STEIN: You know her?

(Ruth nods.)

MR. STEIN: Who is she?

RUTH: She is my grandmother.

(His callousness registers on him.)

MR. STEIN: Your grandmother? Ruth, Ruth, stop crying. Stop crying. I will help you. We'll carry her in. We each take an arm over our shoulder. Like this. You see? Now lift her. That's right. It's all right. I'm going to help you. *(Ruth and Mr. Stein carry Hannah off. Shift to David in the secret space. He is asleep next to a hodgepodge of stones that only resembles an oven if you use your imagination. Ruth enters decisively, with a stone in hand. David does not hear her. She sees David sleeping and places a final stone in the oven.)*

RUTH: Now it's ready. Now I can cook. *(Ruth nudges him awake.)* David. David.

(He awakes startled.)

RUTH: It's done.

DAVID: What?

RUTH: *(Indicating oven.)* Look.

DAVID: You finished it.

(David closes his eyes in an action reminiscent of the earlier smell test. Ruth keeps her eyes open.)

DAVID: Fresh bread. Dark rich, hearty bread from Bohemia and/

RUTH: There's nothing to smell.

DAVID: If we try/

RUTH: It's an oven with nothing in it. But at least now we can get to the real work. We need food to make food. We have to find ingredients.

DAVID: Maybe a picture really is just a picture.

RUTH: That can't be true.

DAVID: Are you hungrier today than you were yesterday?

RUTH: When you get here, you think it can't get worse, but it does. You think you'll get used to it, but you don't. You just get hungrier. I'll be hungrier tomorrow than I am today. And so will you. So will everyone.

(Ruth steps on the loose floorboard. She bends down and lifts it, removing a tiny, folded paper tied with an old shoelace. David quickly takes it from her. After a moment.)

DAVID: I have one more secret. *(David unties the lace and very delicately unfolds the paper. He lays it out before them, clearing the floor dirt away and smoothing the paper with his hands.)*

RUTH: It's old.

DAVID: Probably a hundred years. Right before my parents hid me, my papa took his two hands, and with one, he held the book firmly. With the other, he pulled the page, *this* page from its binding. He had to crack the spine. He had hundreds, maybe even thousands of books. He never did that before—not with any of them. He loves his books. He folded this page in half. Then half. And again. And again. And he pressed this small thing into my palm. And then it was time for me to go.

RUTH: He chose a page only in Hebrew? You read Hebrew?

DAVID: No.

RUTH: You speak Hebrew?

DAVID: No.

RUTH: You understand Hebrew when it's spoken?

DAVID: No.

RUTH: Why did he give it to you?

DAVID: I don't know. Every day, I ask myself, why didn't he give me something that I could make sense of?

RUTH: Does he read Hebrew?

DAVID: Once or twice a year. Maybe I would have learned for bar mitzvah.

RUTH: Why did you put it here? If I had something from my papa, I'd keep it near me always.

DAVID: It must have meant something to him; so whatever it says, whatever it means, it shouldn't be down there.

(There is a distinct noise of someone coming up the steps. The footsteps are labored and seem on the verge of stopping during the following dialogue.)

DAVID: Do you hear/

RUTH: Yes. Sshh!

DAVID: What if it's a guard? What if/

RUTH: Sshh. Sshh.

DAVID: If we're caught here/

RUTH: Hush. Sshh.

(Ruth pulls David to the far side of the space. They press themselves up against a wall, but there is really nowhere to hide. They have inadvertently left the Hebrew paper lying on the floor. They do not breathe. An old man, Avram, enters. It has obviously exhausted him coming up five flights of stairs. It appears that he does not see the kids. He sees the paper on the floor. He picks it up with respect. He sits down and squints to see the paper. He begins to read the Hebrew, moving his lips but making no sound. He chuckles, kisses the page gently, and lays it back down. He puts his glasses away. Ruth and David have not moved.)

AVRAM: So you're studying the old prayers up here, are you?

(Ruth and David are frozen.)

AVRAM: Speak up. Is she prepping you, Bar Mitzvah boy? A boy and a girl studying Hebrew in a Terezín *kumbal*, but these days, who knows? A Rabbi pulls a bread wagon that's really a hearse and old people who think they're on their way to a spa end up peeling potatoes. So a boy and a girl making a Hebrew lesson together shouldn't shock this *alter cocker* so much. You don't understand what I'm talking about. Not to worry. I don't quite know myself.

DAVID: You're not a guard.

AVRAM: Not a bit.

DAVID: You're just an old man.

AVRAM: And you're just a kid.

DAVID: You don't have any business being up here.

AVRAM: My business is this. I'm looking for a space in which to breathe.

DAVID: Breathe?

AVRAM: The transport.

RUTH: Has the list been made?

AVRAM: No, but the old woman says they're very close. And the old woman is never wrong.

RUTH: I'm going.

DAVID: Where?

AVRAM: You go back and forth from this place?

DAVID: What are you doing?

RUTH: I have to go. *(Ruth is exiting.)*

AVRAM: Young lady, someone will see you/
    (Ruth is gone.)

AVRAM: This is no way to keep a safe haven safe.

DAVID: Safe haven? Do you mean to *stay* here?

AVRAM: Just as you do.

DAVID: I don't stay here.

AVRAM: Then what are you doing?

DAVID: That's none of your business. All you need to know is that you can't stay.

AVRAM: Listen, it's not so good once you're no longer protected. At first I knew a man—really just a boy to me. He was on the Council. His father and I were close. I knew him since he was only… *(He indicates a height just to his knee.)* And he made sure I didn't end up on a list. But for all the good he did protecting me, they took him, too. And now I don't know a soul, and I don't know a soul who knows a soul. So…just until this transport goes.

DAVID: No. You can't. I'll tell the Council. I'll tell you're hiding here.

AVRAM: You won't.

DAVID: How do you know?

AVRAM: It would be needlessly cruel. And then they'd know your secret. *(Avram has him here.)*

DAVID: I am the rightful and sole owner of this *kumbal.*

AVRAM: Owner?

DAVID: If you are to be a tenant here/

AVRAM: Tenant?

DAVID: As a tenant, it's only fair you make some kind of payment to me.

AVRAM: Money?

DAVID: Something of value. Food.

AVRAM: Gone, except for what I can't live without.

DAVID: Diamonds?

AVRAM: Gone.

DAVID: Gold?

AVRAM: Gone.

DAVID: Silver?

AVRAM: Long gone. I am bankrupt. My young entrepreneur, if I had anything of value, I would pay it to the Council.

DAVID: *(Beat.)* Hebrew.

AVRAM: What?

DAVID: You read Hebrew?

AVRAM: For a long time.

DAVID: And you know what it means?

AVRAM: Some of it I do. But I can read all of it.

DAVID: You pay me with Hebrew.

AVRAM: I don't understand.

DAVID: Teach me Hebrew.

AVRAM: Why Hebrew?

DAVID: That's my business.

AVRAM: Do you know your *aleph-bet?*

DAVID: My what?

AVRAM: Your letters, your alphabet.

DAVID: Not in Hebrew.

AVRAM: You don't know anything?

DAVID: We'll work with this page. You teach me to read it. To know what it means. In exchange, I'll keep your secret.

AVRAM: To read I can teach you. What it means—that's for you to learn on your own.

(Shift to Hannah lying absolutely still in a bed. Hannah looks dead. This is the Terezín hospital. Ruth enters.)

RUTH: Bubbe…Bubbe!

(Hannah wakes up.)

HANNAH: You see. I told you, I am an old woman.

RUTH: No one could stand in the cold damp like that all night.

HANNAH: What happened to me?

RUTH: You couldn't get up. And my teacher came, and we carried you here.

HANNAH: You carried me?

RUTH: Yes.

HANNAH: You had to carry me.

RUTH: We carried you here to get well. Have you eaten your food yet?

HANNAH: No.

RUTH: To get well, you need to eat. *(Ruth picks up the ration bowl.)* The hospital rations are supposed to be bigger.

HANNAH: It's the same as everyone gets.

RUTH: I'll go talk to a nurse or a doctor/

HANNAH: You don't have to talk for me.

RUTH: You need more food, better food.

HANNAH: You keep to yourself. The only way is to be as little noticed as possible.

RUTH: You can't be sick now, Bubbe.

HANNAH: I'll get better.

RUTH: They're making another list.

HANNAH: How many?

RUTH: The same. One thousand. *(Beat.)* They take from the hospital first. If I got you more food/

HANNAH: They take from the troublemakers first.

RUTH: Bubbe/

HANNAH: You listen to me, Ruth. *(Hannah eats the soup.)*

RUTH: Let me help you/

(Hannah turns away from Ruth and continues to eat.)

RUTH: Bubbe…

(Hannah eats. Ruth watches her.)

RUTH: Bubbe.

(Hannah will not respond. Ruth exits. Hannah pulls the picture and the pencil from her coat. She looks at it, then turns it over and furtively begins to write on it as the lights go down.)

END OF ACT I

ACT II

Lights come up on a cart of potatoes in a food-prep area. Ruth appears, skulking in the shadows. She is trying to get her nerve up and also figure out how it would be possible to steal an extra potato or two. She has obviously never done this before. Finally, she walks confidently out, takes two shabby potatoes from the pile, and quickly hides them beneath her garment. She straightens herself and is about to walk away.

COOK: What are you doing?

RUTH: I was just…

COOK: Just what? What exactly are you doing?

RUTH: I was just…I was hungry.

COOK: We're all hungry.

RUTH: I was hungry so I…I decided to see if maybe I came early…maybe I could get a little extra.

COOK: You thought you'd get a little extra just by being here earlier?

RUTH: You know, by getting in line before everything in the soup is all eaten up and it's just dirty water.

COOK: So, you weren't here to steal.

RUTH: No. I wouldn't do that.

COOK: You don't look like you're the kind who would.

RUTH: I wouldn't. I swear. I don't steal.

COOK: No. You wouldn't.

RUTH: No sir.

COOK: Not even two scrawny potatoes. *(The Cook removes the potatoes from Ruth's clothes and holds them up.)* You've never done this before.

RUTH: How do you know that?

COOK: Anyone who had done this before would not get caught. And anyone who'd done this before would not have swiped two such miserable looking potatoes. Did your parents put you up to this?

RUTH: My parents aren't here.

COOK: Oh, then you thought of it all by yourself.

RUTH: My grandmother/

COOK: So even the old people are telling the young to steal now.

RUTH: No. She doesn't know anything about this. You won't tell her, will you? Please don't tell her.

COOK: I'd have to know her to tell her. So, from your grandmother's wrath you're safe.

RUTH: I don't steal. The whole time I've been here, I haven't taken a thing. But I don't have any choice now. Could I just keep one of them?

COOK: If I let one take a potato here and another take a turnip there, then before you know it/

RUTH: Everyone might have some food to eat.

COOK: Before you know it, they'll have me on the next train East. Or maybe they'd just be done with me here.

RUTH: Sir, my grandmother needs something to make her strong again. She's sick and/

COOK: If she's sick then there's nothing you can do for her. Once the old ones get sick that way, nobody can do anything for them. *(Pause.)* What would you be willing to do to get a little extra food? And I don't mean very much extra at all. Just a little.

RUTH: I would do anything.

COOK: You would even steal?

RUTH: I would even steal.

COOK: Well, what I have in mind is worse. Maybe not morally worse, but worse nonetheless. Listen, in the flour we get—if you can call it that—it's full of weevils. There's no getting them all, but we've got to at least get some of them out. Personally, it's the one thing I cannot stomach. I get the bugs out of the flour, and then I can't eat the bread. And what's the point of being a baker here if you can't get a little extra in your own belly? I see them even when they aren't there. If you would come every day before we bake and get the weevils out, then I could see about making sure you get a little extra whenever we can spare it.

RUTH: I'll do it.

COOK: It means coming here in the dark and still doing your other work and/

RUTH: I said I'd do it. May I start right now?

COOK: It's done for today. You come back tomorrow. Listen, if I give you one of these, *(Indicates potato.)* will you promise me something?

RUTH: Anything.

COOK: Promise me that if I give you this potato, you won't waste it on your grandmother. You eat. You're young. You have to stay strong.

RUTH: I promise.

(Cook does not give her the potato.)

RUTH: I said that I promise.

(Cook tosses Ruth the potato. She runs off. He calls after her.)

COOK: You're a worse liar than you are a thief! *(Under his breath.)* It's a good thing you've got honest work now.

(Lights shift to the attic. Avram is inspecting the oven, perplexed. Ruth enters decisively, Avram backs away from the oven. There is a long moment.)

AVRAM: What's the news?

RUTH: Soon. The transport will be soon.

AVRAM: They try to keep the children here, so you and the boy/

RUTH: I'm not afraid of the transport.

AVRAM: *(Beat.)* The boy said this *kumbal* belonged to him.

RUTH: It does. But this *(Indicating the oven.)* belongs to both of us. I have private business here.

AVRAM: But no privacy.

RUTH: You could leave.

AVRAM: Unlike you, brave young woman, I am afraid of the transport.

(Another moment. Ruth begins to pull straw out of her coat. She stuffs it into the oven. She then hesitantly pulls out the potato.)

AVRAM: It's an oven?

RUTH: Yes.

AVRAM: A secret cooking society, you and the boy?

RUTH: I suppose so.

AVRAM: Brave and resourceful. Don't let me stop you. Cook.

(Realizing there's no way to light the fire.)

RUTH: Food, an oven, kindling, but no way to light a fire. I'll have to go down to find a match somewhere/

AVRAM: You'll attract too much attention going in and out like it's shopping day.

(Avram pulls a single match from his coat.)

RUTH: Is this your only one?

AVRAM: No. Of course not.

RUTH: You're sure?

AVRAM: Listen, it's not like I can light a candle to read by. The boy is getting payment. Let me pay you too.

(Avram offers the match. Ruth hesitates.)

AVRAM: Take it.

(Avram hands her the match. Ruth lights the straw.)

AVRAM: Put it in quickly. This fire won't last long.

(Ruth puts the potato in the oven.)

RUTH: This is the first thing I've ever cooked for my grandmother.

AVRAM: Your grandmother is here?

RUTH: In the hospital.

AVRAM: You have to have something to bring her.

RUTH: She's the cook. She's the best cook I know. There's nothing that doesn't taste good after she's cooked it.

AVRAM: I knew a cook like that once.

RUTH: Who was that?

AVRAM: My mama. My mama could take a whole lot of nothing—and that was all we ever had—and she could make the sweetest smells come out of her kitchen. You could smell it down the block. And at *Pesach!* Oh at *Pesach,* she cooked and cooked.

RUTH: For *seder.*

AVRAM: A *seder* like you've never seen. So many people and so much food. Sometimes it felt like the whole point was the food. My mama would say to my papa, "They're hungry, Mendel. Pray faster!"

RUTH: We had *seder*…before my papa and zeyde were sent to Dachau. That was the last one we had. Bubbe would cook so many things. Everybody had a favorite, and she'd make that favorite special for each person. And Zeyde would say the prayers. He hardly looked at the book, the…

AVRAM: The *Haggadah.* You know why we have *seder?*

RUTH: To ask the questions.

AVRAM: To ask the questions. Maybe to find the answers, but definitely to ask the questions. *(Pause.)* The fire's gone out.

RUTH: The straw didn't last long.

AVRAM: See what it's done.

(Ruth removes the potato.)

RUTH: It doesn't look very good.

AVRAM: It will be nourishing.

RUTH: She'd know what to do with a plain old potato—even here. *(Impulsively.)* You have some.

AVRAM: I can't take your food.

RUTH: But what are you eating up here?

AVRAM: You've got your grandmother to worry about. Don't start worrying about a stranger.

RUTH: It's payment. Without your match, I couldn't have cooked it. If I had a knife, I'd cut you a piece, but I don't. Please take a bite.

(He won't.)

RUTH: Take it.

(Avram takes a small bite.)

RUTH: Is it all right to give her?

AVRAM: She'll dine like a queen tonight.

(Avram hands the potato back to Ruth. She starts to go, then turns back.)

RUTH: My name is Ruth.

AVRAM: I am Avram. It's a pleasure to make your acquaintance, Ruth.

(Ruth exits as lights shift to Hannah, still in the hospital. Ruth enters the hospital. Ruth puts the napkin from the barrack down.)

HANNAH: What are you doing?

RUTH: You can't have a meal without a tablecloth. It doesn't look very good… *(Furtively takes out the potato.)* But it's not rotten.

HANNAH: A whole potato?

RUTH: It's not potato salad, but it is cooked. Go ahead. Eat it, Bubbe.

HANNAH: Me?

RUTH: You.

HANNAH: It's part of *your* rations.

RUTH: No.

HANNAH: You can't save your food to feed me.

RUTH: I eat everything that's mine.

HANNAH: Who did you talk to to get this?

RUTH: No one.

HANNAH: Then how?

RUTH: It's a whole, cooked potato. Eat it.

HANNAH: How fortunate I am this whole, cooked potato found its way to you.

RUTH: Eat.

HANNAH: There is stealing here. Some call it "organizing." *(With contempt.)* "Organizing." Stealing. *(Hannah pushes the potato to Ruth.)* You want to bring me something, bring me one of your pictures.

RUTH: You want pictures instead of potatoes?

HANNAH: Yes.

RUTH: Pictures won't get you out of here.

HANNAH: I'm hungry for your pictures.

RUTH: If you eat this potato—the whole thing—tomorrow I will bring you a picture.

HANNAH: You eat with me.

RUTH: I already did. I was so hungry coming here, I couldn't help myself. I hid in a corner and took that bite. *(Ruth points to the bite Avram took.)*

HANNAH: One bite?

(Ruth pushes the potato to Hannah.)

RUTH: The whole thing.

(Hannah takes a bite.)

RUTH: Is it alright?

HANNAH: *Zey get. Zey get.*

(The lights shift to the Cook entering with a sack of potatoes and a bowl of flour. It's full of weevils. He looks at in disgust.)

COOK: *Oy veys mere!* Today it's moving!

(Ruth enters)

COOK: Just in time.

(Cook hands Ruth the bowl. She patiently begins picking weevils out of the flour.)

COOK: You're very good at this. The best one I've seen yet. Doesn't it disgust you?

RUTH: They're harmless enough creatures. We just don't want them in our bread. Out of the bread, they don't bother me.

COOK: Did you eat your potato?

RUTH: All of it.

COOK: You don't look any fatter.

RUTH: It was one potato.

COOK: I can't give you more. If anyone knew that I paid for this, they'd move me right out of the bakery into the mines. *(Beat.)* Don't think about taking anything on the side.

RUTH: I've got honest work. I don't have to.

(Cook watches her.)

RUTH: They're thick in here.

COOK: I know.

(During the following, the Cook becomes more repulsed.)

RUTH: The whole bowl is moving like a living ocean. It's really quite amazing the way they nestle in there so comfortably, just like they belong in the flour and they won't leave it, even when its headed down your throat as bread. They're so black and crawly and/

COOK: *Oy veys mere. (He tosses her one potato as payment.)* Just bring me the bowl when you're done.

(The Cook beats a hasty retreat. Ruth regards the potato he gave her. She notices the sack of potatoes. She looks to make sure he is long gone. She takes a potato from the sack, then another, then another. She pockets them. Lights shift to David and Avram in the kumbal. *They have been at the Hebrew for a while and it shows. Their voices are getting louder and louder. Avram is pointing out letters, and David is struggling to identify them.)*

DAVID: *Aleph.*

(Avram points.)

DAVID: *Bet.*

(Avram points.)

DAVID: *Vet.*

(*Avram points.*)

DAVID: *Gimmel.*

AVRAM: (*Correcting him.*) *Nuhn.*

DAVID: You're purposely trying to trick me.

AVRAM: Not trick you. Teach you.

DAVID: When did you start learning?

AVRAM: At the old-fashioned age—when I was three.

DAVID: I'm never going to get anywhere at this rate! Instead of single letters, teach me whole words.

AVRAM: That's not how you learn.

DAVID: It may not be how you learned…

(*Ruth enters.*)

DAVID: …but it's the only way I'm going to.

RUTH: (*To David.*) What are you doing here now?

DAVID: Collecting my rent.

RUTH: What?

AVRAM: I pay him with Hebrew lessons.

RUTH: Hebrew lessons, David?

AVRAM: Ah ha! David! Of course you're a David. Just look at you.

DAVID: Did anyone see you?

RUTH: No.

AVRAM: You have more business?

RUTH: (*Because David is there.*) I don't have any right now.

DAVID: What are *you* doing here?

RUTH: Looking for privacy. (*Ruth takes out paper and pencil.*) I have a picture to draw.

DAVID: And I have Hebrew to learn.

RUTH: I won't disturb you.

(*Ruth sits to draw, and David returns to his work.*)

AVRAM: Again. *Aleph, bet, vet, gimmel/*

DAVID: Whole words.

AVRAM: David/

DAVID: I'm not three. Whole words.

AVRAM: You're a radical, David.

DAVID: Whole words.

AVRAM: (*Seeing his persistence.*) Fine. Whole words. (*Avram searches for a word to begin with.*) You see this? *Ka-dosh.*

DAVID: *Ka-dosh.*

AVRAM: *Koof, dalled, vav, shin, Kadosh, kadosh, kadosh* "Holy, holy, holy."

DAVID: Three times the same word.

AVRAM: In the middle of the private prayer, when each individual stands alone, whispering right in God's ear, we say "holy."

DAVID: So *kadosh* is the most important word?

AVRAM: Most important?

DAVID: I don't have time for every word. I need to know the most important ones.

AVRAM: *Rebbe* upon *rebbe* has organized and studied the *siddur*…and studied and studied and studied…and even they, all of those thousands of *rebbes* through the millennia, not one of them has really been able to say what is most important to God.

DAVID: I don't need to know what's most important to God, I need to know what's most important to my father.

(Avram looks carefully at David. He silently moves through the prayers. His eyes are downcast on the page and his lips move soundlessly through the words. His finger goes over a point in the writing. He silently mouths the same words several times. He looks up.)

AVRAM: I've been saying these prayers all my life and never have I asked myself what is most important. You're a better pupil than I first thought, David.

(Ruth goes to look over their shoulders.)

AVRAM: You want lessons now too?

(Ruth nods.)

AVRAM: *(Indicating three separate passages.)* Here, here and here.

RUTH: They're all the same.

DAVID: Three times on this one page.

AVRAM: Very good. I'll say it first. *L'dor va'dor. (He prompts them to repeat.)*

ALL OF THEM: *L'dor va'dor.*

DAVID: What does it mean?

AVRAM: The language of prayer has many meanings but simply put: from generation to generation.

DAVID: How many generations before me?

AVRAM: I can't count them.

DAVID: How many after me?

AVRAM: I don't know.

DAVID: From one to the next. *L'dor va'dor. L'dor va'dor.*

(Avram chants an old pro's Hebrew)

AVRAM: *Meemkomcha, molkeynu sofeeya, veseemloch, alaynu kee mechakeem anachnu lach. Masai teem loch betseeyon, bekarov beyamaynu, leolam vaed tishkon. Titgadal vesikadash besoch yerushalayeem eercha ledor vador ulnet-sach netsachim.* [Throughout Your universe reveal Yourself, our King, and reign over us, for we await You. When will you reign in Zion? Let it be soon, in our time and throughout all time. May Your glory and holiness be apparent to all in Jerusalem Your city, from generation to generation, eternally.]

RUTH: What does it mean?

AVRAM: More or less it's how we ask the Almighty to let the world know He is here. We're asking Him to let us know soon.

(Shift to Hannah in the barracks. She is putting her possessions back in order. She has the napkin, the pencil, the pocket. She considers the napkin, then begins to write on it. As Ruth enters, she hides the napkin.)

HANNAH: It's good you came to the barracks.

RUTH: It's good you're in the barracks.

HANNAH: I ate your potato—the whole, cooked potato.

(Ruth takes out the picture she drew in the kumbal. *She gives it to Hannah. Hannah is overwhelmed.)*

RUTH: Do you like it?

HANNAH: Oh, Ruthala.

RUTH: Your hunger for pictures is satisfied?

HANNAH: Very satisfied.

RUTH: Now I can take care of your hunger for food. *(Ruth takes out one potato.)* I wasn't able to cook this one. Not yet, but I will.

HANNAH: Ruth!

RUTH: And I've got more, Bubbe. *(She indicates her pockets.)* I will get as many as you need.

HANNAH: Get? Where you can get such things is only from trouble.

RUTH: They're good for you. They help you. The potato got you out of the hospital.

HANNAH: Yes. I am out of the hospital. So now there is no need to/

RUTH: You're still not better. You need more to get better.

HANNAH: You put yourself in harm's way/

RUTH: No. I am careful!

HANNAH: Careful like when you came to the shop? Ruth, listen to me. If something were to happen to you, if they took you… my child/

RUTH: I'm not a child anymore. I've had two birthdays in Terezín.

HANNAH: You're still my child.

RUTH: I keep growing.

HANNAH: My only child.

RUTH: I'm grown-up. I am grown-up enough to care for you.

HANNAH: It's not your place to care for me.

RUTH: Then who's is it? Who else is there to care for you? I have potatoes to give you. Take them!

HANNAH: It is my place to care for you.

RUTH: But you have nothing to give me.

(Hannah is at first stunned, then steely.)

HANNAH: Take your potatoes.

(Ruth does not.)

HANNAH: Take them away.

(Ruth runs off, without the potatoes. Shift to Mr. Stein, David, and Ruth at school.)

MR. STEIN: Today, boys and girls…we have ended our discussion of the Exodus, the flight from Egypt. We have grappled together to understand the meanings of this story, with belief and without it. I wish that you may look to this story and find possibility, even if you cannot find promise.

And as we come to the end of class today, it is time…I must tell you…this secret, this quiet education must end. Today is our last lesson. Tomorrow will be the list. And after the list, will be the train. Tomorrow will be another transport from Terezín. I am hopeful…I hope that we will one day gather together again to learn from each other.

(Mr. Stein exits, leaving David and Ruth on stage.)

DAVID: He's afraid. Everyone is afraid.

RUTH: Are you?

DAVID: No. Are you?

RUTH: No.

DAVID: Those with families will have to worry about each other all night long.

RUTH: Yes.

DAVID: We won't have that worry.

RUTH: No.

(Shift to Ruth and the Cook. He is waiting for her with neither flour nor potatoes.)

RUTH: Where is the flour?

COOK: Have you noticed the weather? It's a little warmer. Not in the air but in the trees. The earth is warming up for spring. This time last year, there was a little *pesach matzah*. Not enough for eight days. Just enough to know the time of year. Not this year. First *seder* and only the usual stale loaves of *homitz*. Even for the bakers. I suppose I'll know it's spring just by looking over the walls at the buds on the trees.

RUTH: I won't finish on time if I don't get started.

COOK: There isn't any.

RUTH: Then I'll come back later.

COOK: I can't employ you any longer. It's too risky.

RUTH: But who will prepare the flour?

COOK: If they're taking two thousand, who's to say/

RUTH: Two thousand?

COOK: Who's to say it won't be me? Who's to say it won't be you?
(Ruth is stunned. Realizing what he's said to a child, the Cook pulls out an almost whole, almost fresh, almost generous loaf of bread.)

COOK: Whatever happens tomorrow, bread is bread.
(She looks at him.)

COOK: Go ahead and take it before I change my mind. Try and make it last.
(Ruth takes the bread.)

COOK: *Gut yuntev.*

RUTH: *Gut yuntev.*
(Shift to Hannah—stooped, old, and starving. With her pitiful bowl in hand, she resignedly waits on line.)

RUTH: Bubbe, what will they put in here tonight?

HANNAH: It will be soup.

RUTH: Filthy, cold water…scraps of peelings.

HANNAH: Soup.

RUTH: It's a lie to call that soup. Soup is something else. Soup is something that feeds you. Come with me!

HANNAH: What?

RUTH: Leave this line, and come with me.

HANNAH: Ruth, these games must stop.

RUTH: They're not games. Trust me, Bubbe. Come with me.

HANNAH: There's nowhere to go.

RUTH: The transport is tomorrow, Bubbe.

HANNAH: You know already?

RUTH: Two thousand.

HANNAH: Two thousand?

RUTH: Two thousand will go. *(Beat.)* Come with me.
(No response from Hannah.)

RUTH: Bubbe, if tomorrow/

HANNAH: Shah! Don't say it!

RUTH: There is tonight. So tonight, we don't stand in line, and tonight, we don't eat this lie. *(A quiet plea.)* I can take care of you, Bubbe. Let me take care of you.

(Hannah reaches out for Ruth. They exit together. Lights shift to the kumbal *where we see David and Avram.)*

DAVID: Was it difficult to learn all that Hebrew?

AVRAM: It's taken my whole life.

DAVID: I can never learn like you have.

AVRAM: We'll study now. Whole words.

DAVID: It's too late. I need to talk to you. Man to man.

AVRAM: Then I'll try to uphold my end of the bargain and listen like a man.

DAVID: Tomorrow is the day.

(Ruth enters alone.)

RUTH: *(To David.)* I knew you'd be here. *(Looking at Avram.)* I knew he'd come to tell you. *(Ruth pulls Hannah into the* kumbal. *Silence.)*

DAVID: Who is she?

AVRAM: You bring her here now of all times?

DAVID: *(To Avram.)* You know her?

AVRAM: This is Ruth's grandmother.

DAVID: Your grandmother?

RUTH: *(She nods.)* This is Hannah.

DAVID: You said you had no one here.

RUTH: I didn't know how to tell you that I wasn't by myself.

DAVID: You lie, then you betray our secret!

RUTH: David, on this night, in our homes, we would set a long table. On this table, we would put candlesticks and a wine cup. On this table, we would put a special plate, with special things on it. *(To Avram.)* I need to know what things go on this plate.

DAVID: You jeopardize Avram's safety to come and talk nonsense?

AVRAM: *(To Hannah.)* It seems I have gained a young protector in Terezín.

HANNAH: This one thinks it has become her job to care for me, her own grandmother. Such times we live in/

AVRAM: When the young, not yet grown, must care for the old, not yet gone.

HANNAH: Such times.

AVRAM: Hannah, your granddaughter is reminding us that it's the first night of *Pesach.*

HANNAH: *Pesach* in Terezín?

RUTH: Bubbe, what goes on the *seder* plate?

HANNAH: I could have told you down there.

RUTH: We can't just talk about it. We have to make it. We have to make *seder*. Here. Now.

HANNAH: There are too many things we need to make *seder*. Not the least of which is food. Everything about *seder* is food—wine, eggs, matzah/

(Ruth takes out the bread from her coat, then lays it down on her coat, a makeshift tablecloth.)

RUTH: *(To Avram.)* It's not matzah. There is no matzah this year, but I thought that for this *seder,* for this Pesach, God might make an exception.

(There is silence as Avram considers making this unconventional seder.)

AVRAM: A *yuntev* must begin with blessing the light. *(Avram pulls a match from his coat.)*

DAVID: Where did you get that?

RUTH: He has more.

AVRAM: On the contrary, Ruth. It is my last one. On *yuntev*...on *yuntev,* women *bench licht.*

(Avram gives the match to Ruth. Ruth strikes the match against the floorboard, then holds it before Hannah. Hannah hesitates a moment then, moves her hands from the flame to her face in a circle three times and then covers her eyes. In a private voice.)

HANNAH: *Barukh attah hashem elokeinu melekh ha-olam, asher kid'shanu b'mitzvosav v'tzivanu l'hadlik ner shel yuntuv.* Amen. [Praised are You, Lord our God, King of the universe whose *mitzvot* add holiness to our lives and who gave us the mitzvah to kindle light for the Festival.]

AVRAM: Being that this is an exceptional circumstance, in every way, I think we should address with the Almighty our alternate choice for matzah. *(Avram searches for the right words as he improvises this prayer.) Got in himmel,* do you know our desire to do your will, to celebrate *Pesach* only with matzah and no leavened food? But in bondage, we struggle as best we can to fulfill the *mitzvah,* to keep the commandment. Keep us alive to see the time when we once again observe your *mitzvot* and do your will. Amen.

HANNAH AND RUTH: Amen.

AVRAM: Now the man of the house would raise the wineglass and make the first of four *kiddushim* we have on *Pesach.* David. David. A man must know how to make *kiddush.*

(Avram raises an imaginary wine goblet in the air. Halfway through the prayer, David follows his motion.)

AVRAM: *Barukh attah hashem elokeinu melekh ha-olam, bo-re p'ri ha'gafen.* [Praised are You, Lord our God, King of the universe who creates fruit of the vine.]

DAVID AND AVRAM: Amen.

DAVID: *(To Hannah.)* Tell us what goes on the *seder* plate.

HANNAH: You don't make dozens of *seders* in your life without feeling those six things in your hands. Bitter herbs.

AVRAM: For suffering.

HANNAH: Salt water.

AVRAM: For tears in bondage.

HANNAH: Greens.

AVRAM: For spring.

HANNAH: A roasted shankbone.

AVRAM: For a time when God spared us.

HANNAH: An egg.

AVRAM: For *chaim.*

HANNAH: For life.

DAVID: That's only five. You said there were six things on the plate.

HANNAH: And *charoset. (Realizing what the oven is.)* Mortar—for bricks and stones.

RUTH: Sweet apples, red ones with nuts and cinnamon and wine. *Charoset* that you chop—with my help.

AVRAM: Ruth, you remember what we talked about before?

RUTH: The questions.

AVRAM: Yes.

DAVID: We ask four of them.

AVRAM: Two excellent pupils. For the first three questions, we are in need of things we don't have. But for the fourth question, we need only what we have here. So, I propose that is the only question we will ask tonight. As the youngest, it is incumbent upon you—both of you—to ask this question.

(Avram prompts the children to repeat after him.)

AVRAM: *Shebechol ha-leylot Ah-nu ochlin*

RUTH AND DAVID: *Shebechol ha-leylot Ah-nu ochlin*

AVRAM: *Bayn yoshvin Ooh vayn misoobin*

RUTH AND DAVID: *Bayn yoshvin Ooh vayn misoobin*

AVRAM: *Ha-lai-lah hazeh Koolahnu missobin.*

RUTH AND DAVID: *Ha-lai-lah hazeh Koolahnu missobin.*

AVRAM: "On all other nights we eat either sitting or reclining. Why on this night do we recline?" On this night, we recline with the luxury of free human beings. Because on this night, we are free human beings. On this night, we are free.

HANNAH: At our age, we are free. Here.

AVRAM: *(Lifting up the bread.) Baruch atah hashem elokeynu melech haolam, hamotzi lechem min ha'aretz.* [Praised are You, Lord our God, King of the universe who brings forth bread from the earth.]

ALL: Amen.

(Ruth distributes the bread and the four eat as the lights come down on them. Lights change as we hear a voice-over of an interminable list of names being read in a German voice. David is revealed standing in front of a wall with an enormous list of names posted on it. He is unmoving, his face hidden. Avram enters.)

DAVID: What are you doing here?

AVRAM: I gave it some thought last night and decided that a free man must see for himself.

DAVID: Your name's not here. I've checked the whole list twice. I was on my way to tell you. You're safe.

(Seeing that there is no joy in David's face, Avram looks at the list, where David had been looking.)

AVRAM: Frankel…David. Of course, you are a David Frankel. I should have known.

(Ruth enters.)

RUTH: *(To Avram.)* You've come down?

DAVID: The news was good for Avram.

RUTH: For us too. It's good news.

(There is silence.)

RUTH: David, it's good news, isn't it?

(David slowly points to his name on the wall.)

RUTH: It can't be right.

DAVID: The list is always right. *(Looking at their glum faces around him.)* It's called the family camp. Maybe I'll find my family there. Perhaps it will be better.

AVRAM: Then we shall see together.

DAVID: What?

AVRAM: We will see if it's better—together.

DAVID: You can't. You can't just/

AVRAM: Man to man. We will go together.

DAVID: Avram, it may not be better where they are sending us.

AVRAM: You've still got Hebrew to learn. We go together. *(Avram turns to say farewell to Ruth.)*

AVRAM: You're a *ballabuse*, Ruth. A real *ballabuse*.

(Avram kisses the top of Ruth's head, then steps aside for Ruth to say good-bye to David.)

RUTH: When we closed our eyes, I could smell the angel bread.

DAVID: I could smell it too.

(They embrace. Then, Avram puts his arm around David. They walk off, slowly with their heads erect. Lights shift to Hannah in the attic. Ruth enters. They sit in silence a moment.)

HANNAH: A sailboat is flying through the night sky. On this night, there are more stars than exist and a moon to match their brilliance. The sailboat is flying above our home, above our street, above the lights of our city. And we are in the boat, you and I, each maneuvering a sail. We're making progress on our journey, headed to the warmth of the candle we left lit at home.

RUTH: My picture.

HANNAH: Your beautiful picture.

RUTH: You see it exactly.

HANNAH: Because our journeys have never been as different as either of us may have thought. *(Beat.)* How did you think to build an oven here?

RUTH: We thought we would cook for the world.

HANNAH: So you're ready to be a cook?

RUTH: When people are hungry, someone must cook their supper.

HANNAH: I know your secrets, it's time that you knew mine. Look in your oven.

(Ruth goes to the oven and pulls out a book, the covers of which are clearly her drawings. It is bound together with darning thread.)

RUTH: My pictures.

HANNAH: Open it.

(Ruth looks through the book. Hannah closes her eyes.)

HANNAH: Tell me what you see there.

RUTH: Strudel, bread, chicken, honey cake, cabbage soup, apple dumplings… potato salad—the letter to Mama…

HANNAH: We have no address for your mama now, so I said to myself, "Hannah, put it with the others for Ruth. It's good for her to have it, in case she forgets even a simple recipe like potato salad." I thought it was finished, but I needed your *seder* to make it complete. I sewed it together last night. It's ready for you now. It's time for you to take it, Ruth.

RUTH: No, Bubbe.

HANNAH: How will you know what to do without it?

RUTH: I have you to tell me what ingredients I need and how to do.

HANNAH: You are growing up Ruth. You have to be able to do things by yourself.

RUTH: You keep it for now. You can give it to me later. After/

HANNAH: You're getting taller everyday, and I am getting shorter. Not later. Now. You must take it now. You keep it here, and when the world once again welcomes cooks, you cook.

(Hannah slowly rises and kisses the top of Ruth's head. Ruth remains seated with the book. Two pools of light isolate Ruth and Hannah. Hannah watches Ruth, as the light slowly fades on the older woman. Ruth picks up the page from David's siddur, and just as Avram did in the first act, she kisses the page. She holds it up and then begins to write on it. She speaks aloud as she writes.)

RUTH: Do you remember the secret of the *knaidela?* I'll tell you this time, but pay attention because who knows when we'll have another chance to cook all night. First you have to take the matzah meal and you mix it with the eggs and the *schmaltz*. You remember? If you want the good flavor, you add some *schmaltz* when you mix up the meal. And don't be skimpy, but don't use too much. Are you listening?

(Old Ruth enters in contemporary clothing. She carries the same cookbook that Ruth holds. Old Ruth watches her younger self writing. The light fades on Ruth as Old Ruth approaches a counter top in an American home. Old Ruth places the book on the counter and reads from it.)

OLD RUTH: You're still listening. I don't give my recipes to just anyone. So after you've put everything in, you want to mix it up with your hands. You have to make the *knaidela* with your fingers because that's where the recipe really rests—in your fingertips. If you don't get your hands good and messy, how are you going to know if it's any good? That's the only way you can really tell. You have to taste it…then you'll know you've got a *knaidela* that will always make them come back to your table.

(Old Ruth starts to pull out bowls to mix, a stockpot, a mixing spoon. She wipes her hand on a towel and readies the kitchen to cook. The actor who has played Ruth enters in the clothing of a contemporary American girl. This is Young Hannah, Ruth's granddaughter.)

YOUNG HANNAH: Bubbe, what are you doing?

OLD RUTH: Just checking my recipe before we start.

YOUNG HANNAH: Checking a recipe? I've never seen you use a recipe before. You know everything by heart.

OLD RUTH: This *Pesach*, I needed a little help.

YOUNG HANNAH: This isn't even a cookbook. It's all drawings…and one page of a prayer book?

OLD RUTH: Look closely.

(Young Hannah gently takes the cookbook from Old Ruth's hands.)

YOUNG HANNAH: Wow. Wow. They're not in English.

OLD RUTH: I didn't always speak English.

YOUNG HANNAH: Who drew these?

OLD RUTH: A *klaiyna maidela* [young girl].

YOUNG HANNAH: You?

(Old Ruth nods.)

YOUNG HANNAH: I've never seen you draw before. But the writing doesn't look like yours.

OLD RUTH: It is my grandmother's.

YOUNG HANNAH: Hannah's. Was she a good cook, Bubbe?

OLD RUTH: You think I cook good?

YOUNG HANNAH: The best.

OLD RUTH: The things my grandmother could make, *zey get!*

YOUNG HANNAH: That good?

OLD RUTH: The best. Now, Hannahla, are you here to help me cook for *Pesach,* or are you here to talk?

YOUNG HANNAH: Both.

OLD RUTH: Then let's get started. Do we have everything?

YOUNG HANNAH: We have everything.

OLD RUTH: Let's check before we start.

YOUNG HANNAH: Bubbe, we have everything.

OLD RUTH: What did I tell you about stopping in the middle?

YOUNG HANNAH: Don't. *(A big breath.)* Matzah meal, eggs, oil, water, sugar, salt, pepper…and schmaltz. Everything. Let's cook.

OLD RUTH: Let's cook.

(The lights fade to black.)

THE END

CYRANO

Adapted by Jo Roets
Translated into English by Audrey Van Tuyckom
from the play by Edmond Rostand

ORIGINAL PRODUCTION

Cyrano was originally produced by Blauw Vier at the Monty Theatre in Antwerp, Belgium on September 12, 1996. It was directed by Jo Roets. *Cyrano* made its United States premiere at Seattle Children's Theatre on October 16, 1998. The English translation was by Audrey Van Tuyckom. It was directed by Jo Roets. Tamara Schlief* was the stage manager. The cast was:

Christian/De Guiche/Ensemble . . . . Alban Dennis*
Roxane . . . . Kari McGee*
Cyrano . . . . Todd Jefferson Moore*

Understudies—Christopher Guilmet, Rebecca Castelli*
*Members of Actors' Equity Association, the union for stage professionals

CHARACTERS

This adaptation was originally made for a cast of two actors and one actress. The roles were divided as follows:

ACTOR ONE: Cyrano
ACTOR TWO: De Guiche, Le Bret, Ragueneau, Christian, monk, narrator, soldier
ACTRESS: Duenna, Roxane, narrator

Of course, this text can be used for a cast of more than three.

INTRODUCTION and ACT I

ACTOR ONE: *(To the audience.)* Tell me why you're staring at my nose. Is something wrong with it? Is it not put on straight? Does it swing like an elephant's trunk? Is it curved, like a beak? Do you see a wart on it? Is it unusual? Is it like something you've never seen before? Do you think it's ugly? Grotesque? Does it have a sickly color?

ACTOR TWO: It's just big.

ACTOR ONE: Yes, indeed. It's big. Is that it? That's a rather uninspired way of putting it. Especially as there is scope for so many variations. Aggressive: If I had to go around with a nose like that, I'd hide my whole face under a hat. Friendly: Well, here we are, just the three of us. Descriptive: It's a rock, a hill, a mountain top! I'd love to rest on your magnificent Mount Everest!

ACTOR TWO: Considerate:

ACTOR ONE: Be careful sir, keep your head straight or you might topple over with all that weight.

ACTRESS: Gracious:

ACTOR ONE: Are you fond of birds? How sweet—a Gothic perch to rest their tiny feet. Insolent: Quite a useful gadget, that, you hold it high and then you hang up your hat.

ACTOR TWO: Pedantic:

ACTOR ONE: Only Aristophanes' hippocamelelephunt had an appendage of that size in front.

ACTOR TWO: Awestruck:

ACTOR ONE: Good grief. You must use a sheet for a handkerchief! Rustic: Sir, you've got to draw a number, if you want to go in for the biggest cucumber.

ACTRESS: Naive:

ACTOR ONE: When can we visit the monument? Speculative: Tell me sir, what is the rent? See there how a spiritual man is capable of phrasing it. You see, I enjoy making fun of myself, but I won't take it from anyone else. *(Exit.)*

DE GUICHE: Roxane! Roxane!

ROXANE: Monsieur De Guiche!

DE GUICHE: My heart is all aflame for you
I love you to distraction
You are so fair and so divine,
you are my one attraction.
And if you will accept my ring,
you will inherit everything.

CYRANO: Well said, monsieur De Guiche! Nicely put! And all that off the top of your head! With Madame here to watch, it seems your stage fright has fled!

DE GUICHE: Sir, this is none of your business.

CYRANO: This lady is my cousin and see, I am a little worried about the quality of your poetry.

DE GUICHE: You arrogant clod—a squire without gloves, without frills, without bows, without gold braid.

CYRANO: No gloves, you say? I did have one a while ago. But now it's vanished without a trace, I think I left it in some viscount's face.

DE GUICHE: Braggart! Bloody fool!

CYRANO: Pleased to meet you. Hercule Savinien Cyrano de Bergerac. Ouch!

DE GUICHE: What's the matter?

CYRANO: It's gone all stiff. Ouch!

DE GUICHE: But what's the matter with you?

CYRANO: My rapier is tingling.

DE GUICHE: All right then. En garde!

CYRANO: Good. Now here's what I propose: While we are crossing swords, I will compose a poem to remember it. And when the poem ends, I hit. "The Ballad of a Fencing Bout between Cyrano de Bergerac and a Foppish Lout."

DE GUICHE: What's that?

CYRANO: The title. Dedicated to Madeleine Robin, also known as Roxane.
    I swiftly toss away my hat,
    and then, more slowly, I untie
    my trailing cloak to follow that.
    Then from the scabbard on my thigh,
    I draw my sword and raise it high.
    And now the blade begins to flit,
    And when the poem ends, I hit.

    Come and be burst, you purple grape,
    spurt out the juice beneath your peel,
    Quiver and quake, you ribboned ape,
    the rolls of fat your silks conceal.
    Let's ring your bells, a pretty peal!
    Is that a fly? I'll see to it.
    And when the poem ends, I hit.
    I need a rhyme for one more verse.

You've gone as pale as winter sky,
courage beginning to disperse?
Your stroke went wide, I wonder why?
Your vision blurs? Your mouth is dry?

I see it's time to finish it,
so as the poem ends, I hit!
(Floors him, exit De Guiche.)

LE BRET: *(On.)* You make too many enemies, Cyrano. De Guiche is a powerful man. I've heard that he's looking for young talent. He could make you a famous writer.

CYRANO: Never!

LE BRET: You're exaggerating, Cyrano. If you'd just stop playing the hero, you could...

CYRANO: Become rich and powerful...Is that what you mean? Never.

LE BRET: You're exaggerating, Cyrano.

CYRANO: De Guiche...That lump of fat thinks he's God's gift to women. I hate him, especially since that night when I saw him slobbering all over her. Ugh! Like a slug leaving its trail of slime on a lily.

LE BRET: Her? You aren't...

CYRANO: In love? Yes, I am.

LE BRET: But with who then?

CYRANO: I love, who else, the most beautiful woman on earth. The cleverest, the most intelligent, the kindest.

LE BRET: I know! It's your cousin, Madeleine Robin. But why don't you tell her? You were her hero today.

CYRANO: Honestly, do you think she'll even look at me, with this grotesque thing here? I cherish no illusions. When I see a couple walking in the moonlight on a balmy summer's night, I often dream of strolling there too, with my arm around the waist of Roxane. Sometimes I feel so ugly.

LE BRET: Roxane was there when you were dueling today. She went white with fear.

CYRANO: She went white?

LE BRET: Cyrano, tell her. She's not indifferent to you.

CYRANO: But what if she laughs at me? Nothing could be worse.

DUENNA: *(On.)* My mistress Roxane requests the pleasure of meeting you, in secret.

CYRANO: Me?

LE BRET: You. She wants to see you.

DUENNA: Tomorrow, at the break of day, she will be going to the church of
   Saint-Germain. She sent me to ask where she could meet you after mass.

CYRANO: Oh my God! At...at...

LE BRET: *(Whispers.)* At Ragueneau's...

CYRANO: *(Shouts.)* At Ragueneau's, the master pastry-cook.

DUENNA: Who lives at...?

CYRANO: In...in...Oh, idiot!

DUENNA: Sorry, I didn't get that?

CYRANO: Excuse me...in...

LE BRET: On the corner of rue Saint Honoré!

DUENNA: I...She'll be there at seven. Will you be there?

LE BRET: He'll be there!

   (Exit Duenna.)

CYRANO: Me! And her! A rendezvous!

LE BRET: You're not sad anymore?

CYRANO: Why? I exist for her!

LE BRET: You see!

CYRANO: Arrhg! Roxane, Roxane, Roxane! I feel like howling and roaring like
   a wild man. I feel like taking on a whole army. Let them come! With ten
   hearts, twenty arms, my one nose, and my soul's defiance, I won't be fighting dwarfs anymore, but giants!

DE LIGNIERE: *(Drunk, on.)* Cyrano! I...I've been looking for you.

CYRANO: Monsieur De Ligniere, poet of poets in the streets of Paris!

DE LIGNIERE: Can you spare me a bed for the night? I can't go home. They're
   waiting for me at the Porte de Nesle. A hundred men, armed to the teeth,
   because of my little ditty about Count De Guiche...

CYRANO: A hundred men? You're going home! I'll tuck you in myself!

DE LIGNIERE: But a hundred men?

CYRANO: A hundred men? A nice round number, I'd say. Come on, follow me,
   but keep out of my way! A hundred men...! Marvellous! I can't wait to
   keep this rendezvous, let's go and teach them a lesson or two!

END OF ACT I

ACT II

NARRATOR: Act Two. Paris, 1640, the pastry shop of Mr Ragueneau, chef and master pastry-cook, on the corner of Saint Honoré.

CYRANO: What's the time?

RAGUENEAU: Six o'clock.

CYRANO: Another hour. I don't dare to speak to her. What's the time?

RAGUENEAU: Five past six!

CYRANO: I don't dare look her in the face. I'll write her a letter and then get out of here…What's the time?

RAGUENEAU: A quarter past…

CYRANO: I'll write it all down. I must have written that letter a hundred times. What's the time?

RAGUENEAU: Half past six.

CYRANO: I love you…Your eyes…Fear makes me tremble when you look at me. What's the time?

RAGUENEAU: Ten to…

CYRANO: The time?

RAGUENEAU: Five to…

CYRANO: The time?

(Roxane on.)

CYRANO: Blessed is the moment when you thought of me, when you remembered my existence. You wanted to see me. Here I am, your humble servant. What is it you wanted to tell me?

ROXANE: First of all, I want to thank you for your brilliant duel with that wretch.

CYRANO: Count De Guiche?

ROXANE: Yes. He's a powerful man and he wants to marry me.

CYRANO: So that means I fought, not for my honor, but for your bright blue eyes. So much the better.

ROXANE: Still, I had another reason to come here. I…There's something I've got to tell you, but first I want to see in you again the brother you used to be, at the lake, in the park, in the meadows,…

CYRANO: In Bergerac. The summers there…You were still a girl.

ROXANE: When your rapier was a pine branch…

CYRANO: And you played with dolls…

ROXANE: When everything was still a game…

CYRANO: And the blackberries were sweeter…

ROXANE: My wish was always your command…

CYRANO: And you wore short skirts, and people still called you Madeleine.

ROXANE: Was I pretty then?

CYRANO: Oh…You weren't Roxane yet…

ROXANE: You would come running to me, with a scratch on your hand from climbing trees, bleeding. I would say "Now how did you manage to get that?" sternly, like a mother who doesn't want to seem too concerned… *(Sees his wound.)* What's this?
(Cyrano pulls his hand away.)

ROXANE: Let me see! Now how did you manage to get that?

CYRANO: A bit of rough play with a few big boys, yesterday at the Porte de Nesle.

ROXANE: Were you in a fight?

CYRANO: Oh, it was a little skirmish.

ROXANE: How many of them were there?

CYRANO: Not even a hundred.

ROXANE: Tell me all about it!

CYRANO: No, some other time. You…What was it you didn't dare to tell me just then?

ROXANE: I can tell you know. The mild scent of the past has given me courage. I'm in love with someone…

CYRANO: Ah.

ROXANE: Someone who doesn't know, who doesn't suspect, not yet.

CYRANO: Ah.

ROXANE: But he will know soon.

CYRANO: Ah.

ROXANE: He loves me too, in silence. He's afraid of being turned down, so he hasn't said a word to me yet.

CYRANO: Ah.

ROXANE: But in his eyes, I read what his mouth does not dare to utter.

CYRANO: Ah.

ROXANE: He wears the colors of your regiment.

CYRANO: Ah.

ROXANE: What's more, he's even—what a small world this is!—in your company.

CYRANO: Ah.

ROXANE: He looks intelligent. He's proud, courageous, and noble.

CYRANO: Ah!

ROXANE: And he's good-looking.

CYRANO: *(Pulls his hand away.)* Good-looking?

ROXANE: What's the matter?

CYRANO: Nothing, nothing. My hand hurts a little.

ROXANE: I adore him. But I must admit, we've never spoken.

CYRANO: What's his name?

ROXANE: A beautiful name. Baron Christian de Neuvillette.

CYRANO: I don't know that name at all. He's not in the Guards.

ROXANE: He only just joined, this morning.

CYRANO: My dear, my poor dear child, think! Love is blind. You love beauty, fine words, wit. What if your great love turns out to be a nitwit?

ROXANE: He couldn't be. He has the curls of a Greek god.

CYRANO: The same curls grow on a sheep's head. What if he's an idiot?

ROXANE: Then I'd rather be dead.

CYRANO: *(Silence.)* So was this the sad news you came to tell me? I don't see what you want from me, so please explain…

ROXANE: I heard bad news. Somebody said that that company of yours is made up mainly of Gascons…

CYRANO: And that we haze the raw recruits? Is that what you heard?

ROXANE: Yes, I'm scared for him.

CYRANO: *(Aside.)* So you should be.

ROXANE: Give me your word that nothing will happen to him. I beg you. If he's under your protection, no one will dare to touch him.

CYRANO: All right then. I'll take that young man under my wing.

ROXANE: And defend him as much as you can? For my sake? We've always been friends, haven't we?

CYRANO: Always.

ROXANE: Are you willing to be his friend too?

CYRANO: Because you ask me.

ROXANE: And you'll never let him fight a duel?

CYRANO: I promise.

ROXANE: You're a very dear friend. I'd like to hear the story of the fight you were in last night. But not right now. I've got to go. Some other time. Will you ask him to write to me? Ah, I love you. I love you very much.

CYRANO: Yes, yes.

ROXANE: Tell him to write to me. A hundred men! *(Exit.)*

CHRISTIAN: *(On.)* We are the Gascony cadets,
    The men of Castel-Jaloux.
    We conquer hearts and wager bets,
    And all the blood in us is blue!

    We are the Gascony cadets,
    The men of Castel-Jaloux.

Our hats we wear for coronets
Have plumes to hide the holes from view!

We are the Gascony cadets,
The men of Castel-Jaloux.
We do not stop at empty threats,
But cook our enemies on brochettes!

CYRANO: One hundred men. Around midnight, I walked up to them. The silver bell of the moon was shining in the sky. A sombre cloud drifted by like a woolen shroud. It went dark, really pitch-black, and as there were no lamps lit on the quay, I couldn't see a hand in front of...

CHRISTIAN: your nose...

CYRANO: Who's this?

CHRISTIAN: I'm new here.

CYRANO: What's your name, rookie?

CHRISTIAN: Baron Christian de...

CYRANO: I see. I'm glad to know that...So I couldn't see a hand in front of my face. I thought to myself, if I go ahead with this, I might arouse the wrath of a powerful man, Count De Guiche, and he'll make me pay for it...

CHRISTIAN: through the nose...

CYRANO: dearly! I'm probably being reckless, sticking...

CHRISTIAN: my nose...

CYRANO: my hand into this hornet's nest. I'd better be careful not to get...

CHRISTIAN: up his nose...

CYRANO: ...his back up. Still, I didn't flinch, and I went on. Suddenly, I was...

CHRISTIAN: nose to nose...

CYRANO: face-to-face with a hundred ruffians, a foul stench...

CHRISTIAN: hit your nose...

CYRANO: of garlic, beer and cheese on their breath. I knocked two of them down, and a third I pierced with my...

CHRISTIAN: nose

CYRANO: rapier! You're a brave man. I like that. I'm her cousin.

CHRISTIAN: Her cousin? Whose cousin?

CYRANO: Hers! Roxane's! She told me everything.

CHRISTIAN: Does she love me?

CYRANO: Who knows. You really are good-looking. Roxane is expecting a letter from you tonight.

(Cyrano gives him pen and paper. Christian tries to write a few words, with great difficulty.)

CHRISTIAN: It's useless. I can never find the right words.

CYRANO: Nonsense. You were quite eloquent just then.

CHRISTIAN: That was nothing. It was simple soldier's talk. When I'm with a woman, I get tongue-tied. They like to look at me.

CYRANO: But that's it?

CHRISTIAN: I don't know the language of love.

CYRANO: I do, but it's of no use to me, with this... *(Taps his nose.)*

CHRISTIAN: You know Roxane. You know what she's like. Roxane is...

CYRANO: ...graceful.

CHRISTIAN: Graceful. Roxane is...

CYRANO: ...eloquent.

CHRISTIAN: Eloquent. She's...

CYRANO: ...poetic.

CHRISTIAN: Poetic. If only I could talk like you.

CYRANO: I'll lend you the words, and you'll lend me your charm, your looks. Together, we can be the perfect romantic hero.

CHRISTIAN: What?

CYRANO: I'll put the words into your mouth.

CHRISTIAN: You're proposing to...

CYRANO: Do you want to capture her heart or not? You don't understand why I would do such a thing? Well, I think it would be amusing. A challenge for a poet. You will fill in for me, and I for you. I'll be your voice, and you'll be my lips.

CHRISTIAN: But she's expecting a letter soon.

CYRANO: No problem. I've got one ready. All it needs is your signature and you can send it to her as it is. Don't worry, I was very inspired when I wrote it. It will go straight to her heart. I always carry a few love letters on me.

CHRISTIAN: But will the text suit Roxane?

CYRANO: Perfectly. In her vanity, she will think it was written for her.

CHRISTIAN: Thank you, my friend.

(Christian takes a series of letters to Roxane, who reads them avidly.)

ROXANE: "A hundred times I have written this letter in my mind. Now all I have to do is to lay my soul next to the paper and copy the words out."

"I am in your hands. This paper is my voice. This ink is my blood. This letter...is me."

"Dear, in your presence, such confusion grips
my heart that it grows wordless.
My pen brushes the paper like a kiss.

So read this letter, Madame; with your lips."

"Far from this dark, banal, deceitful world, there is a country where refined souls can meet each other. Far from this bitter, violent, and devious world, there is a country where lovers can be happy."

"I have lost my heart to you. Please send it back. I want to suffer as before."

CYRANO: Is Roxane's loved one still the most perfect man on earth?

ROXANE: Ah yes! He's so profound, so clever, witty, so…unexpectedly…

CYRANO: Brilliant?

ROXANE: Even more than you are! Never in my entire life have I met a man who is such a master of language as he is.

CYRANO: Really?

ROXANE: He turns sweet nothings into verbal jewels. Sometimes he falls silent for a while, as if his muse is refusing to sing for him. But then he says brilliant things again.

CYRANO: Really?

ROXANE: When you see him, then send him to me. I am longing to hear those brilliant words from his own mouth.

(De Guiche approaches.)

ROXANE: De Guiche! Go quickly! If he finds out about Christian and me, he'll put a stop to it right away.

(Exit Cyrano.)

DE GUICHE: *(On.)* Madame.

ROXANE: Monsieur De Guiche.

DE GUICHE: I have come to say good-bye.

ROXANE: You are leaving?

DE GUICHE: I am going to war. We are laying siege to Arras.

ROXANE: Are you really?

DE GUICHE: My departure seems to leave you cold.

ROXANE: Come, come. Cold? The sun shines sometimes even in Siberia, you know.

DE GUICHE: When will I see you again? I have been made commanding officer. At last, I'll be able to get back at that loud-mouthed cousin of yours.

ROXANE: Will the cadets be going too?

DE GUICHE: They belong to my regiment.

ROXANE: *(Aside.)* Christian!

DE GUICHE: What's that?

ROXANE: It hurts when someone who is dear to you goes to battle.

DE GUICHE: What sweet words, Madame. And that on the day of my departure!

ROXANE: So, do you want to get even with Cyrano?

DE GUICHE: I see far too much of him.

ROXANE: By sending him into battle, you'll be doing him a favor. Do you know how you could hurt him most? By leaving him, and his cadets, in Paris, while the war goes on in Arras. That would get him. Keep him out of the battle.

DE GUICHE: Women! Only a woman could be crafty enough to think of that.

ROXANE: Cyrano will be furious. And your revenge will be sweet.

DE GUICHE: So you love me? May I consider your help as a sign of your love?

ROXANE: Certainly.

DE GUICHE: These are the orders for all the companies. And here's the order for the Guards. I'll keep it. My dear Roxane, I am mad with love for you. Why do I have to leave now, just when you are warming to me? There's a Capuchin monastery nearby, where I can hide. And tonight, under the cover of a mask, I will come and see you, dear...May I? (*Moves to kiss her.*)

ROXANE: No, it's better you didn't. Go now. Fight like a hero, Antoine.

DE GUICHE: Wonderful. So you love...

ROXANE: The man who makes me tremble.

DE GUICHE: Those words are music to my ears. I'm leaving. Are you satisfied?

ROXANE: Yes, my dear friend.

(*Exit De Guiche.*)

END OF ACT II

ACT III

NARRATOR: Act Three. Roxane's Kiss. Old houses. A maze of narrow winding streets. There's the house where Roxane lives. Over the doorway there's a window with a balcony, and beside the door, there's a bench. Ivy creeps up against the wall, and a jasmine has wound itself around the window. Because of the bench and a few projecting stones, it is easy to climb up to the balcony.

CYRANO: Tonight you've got to prove yourself. She wants to talk to you. So learn this by heart.

CHRISTIAN: No. I'm not going to memorize anything. I'll do the talking myself.

CYRANO: Ah yes?

CHRISTIAN: Why not? I'm not a total idiot. I've learned a lot from you. And besides, I can always kiss her.

CYRANO: Suit yourself!

ROXANE: *(Whispers.)* Who's there?

CHRISTIAN: Me.

ROXANE: Who's me?

CHRISTIAN: Me, Christian.

ROXANE: Oh, it's you? I want you to talk to me.

(Christian wants to kiss her.)

ROXANE: No, wait. We're all alone. It's getting dark already. The evening air is soft. Come and sit here. Talk. I'm listening.

CHRISTIAN: I love you.

ROXANE: Yes, Christian, speak to me of love.

CHRISTIAN: I…love you.

ROXANE: That's the theme. Now for the variations. Embroider on it.

CHRISTIAN: I…I'm mad about you.

ROXANE: Very nice. And what else?

CHRISTIAN: I hope you love me too.

ROXANE: I was expecting champagne and all I get is water. How do you love me, HOW?

CHRISTIAN: A lot. Very much.

ROXANE: Unveil your feelings.

CHRISTIAN: I want to kiss your throat.

ROXANE: Not again!

CHRISTIAN: I don't love you…

ROXANE: Aha!

CHRISTIAN: I adore you.

ROXANE: Please stop it! My ears are in pain. What has happened to that brilliant oratorical talent of yours? Where are those finely wrought sentences, those well-chosen metaphors, those words that could only come out of your pen, your mouth, your heart?

CHRISTIAN: I…

ROXANE: Yes, you love me. Old hat! Adieu! Good night. *(Exit.)*

CYRANO: *(Claps his hands.)* Well done.

CHRISTIAN: Help me! Lend me your words just one more time…

CYRANO: Why should I?

(A lamp is lit on the balcony.)

CYRANO: Look! Start again…

CHRISTIAN: Roxane!

ROXANE: Is it you again?

CHRISTIAN: I have to talk to you!

ROXANE: No, your talk is too boring. Go away!

CHRISTIAN: Roxane, please!

ROXANE: No! You don't love me!

CHRISTIAN: *(Cyrano prompts him.)* How wrong, what abuse! I don't love you, you say? God knows my passion grows stronger day by day!

ROXANE: That's more like it.

CHRISTIAN: My love is so huge—how can you disdain it! It has such a force that my heart can't contain it!

ROXANE: Nice! But why do your words come out so slowly and haltingly?

CYRANO: Because they have to grope their way up to your ears in the dark.

ROXANE: But you can hear me alright, can't you?

CYRANO: Perfectly! Because I listen with a heart that beats for you. But your ears are hidden by your locks. Besides, your words descend, while mine must climb. Falling is swift, but rising takes up time!

ROXANE: I'm coming down!

CYRANO: No!

ROXANE: Come on, climb on the bench!

CYRANO: No!

ROXANE: Why not?

CYRANO: Let us enjoy this nightly visit for a little while longer. Let's talk softly…without seeing each other.

ROXANE: Without seeing each other?

CYRANO: Isn't it wonderful! All you see is this cloak in the night, while I see the white of a summer gown, I am a shadow, you are the sun's light.

ROXANE: Your voice sounds so different. Are you hoarse?

CYRANO: Yes, very different! Under the cloak of darkness, I finally dare to be myself…Everything I have always wanted to say, I can now blow up to you like a kiss. I love you, I am mad with love. I cannot forget a single little thing about you. I remember that, last year, on the twelfth of May, you changed your hair. Those beautiful locks of yours burnt themselves into my retina so fiercely they blinded me. If I look at you for too long, the whole world changes before my eyes into a maze of blondness!

ROXANE: Yes, that's true love.

CYRANO: Ah, this evening is a gift of heaven, far too dear ever to end. I speak to you—you hear! I, and you! Hope never ran so high. And nothing now remains except to die. Has the thought made you shiver as one who grieves? For you do tremble, a leaf among the leaves. I can feel the gentle tremor of your hand shaking the jasmine branches where I stand!

ROXANE: Yes, I'm trembling, I'm crying, I love you, I am transported by your words.

CYRANO: There's only one more thing I wish for…

CHRISTIAN: A kiss!

ROXANE: What?

CYRANO: Oh!

ROXANE: What was that you said?

CYRANO: I…er…You're going too fast! She's deeply touched. Do you want me to disappoint her?

ROXANE: You're not insisting anymore?

CYRANO: Of course I insist! Without insisting, I would ask you…not to grant this kiss!

CHRISTIAN: Why?

CYRANO: Shut up, Christian.

CHRISTIAN: What was that you said?

CYRANO: Nothing, I was angry with myself. I said: "Shut up, Christian."

CHRISTIAN: My kiss!

ROXANE: Where are you? You mentioned a…a…a…

CYRANO: A kiss!

ROXANE: Don't say that!

CYRANO: A kiss, the world's most priceless gem. Let your lips say it, it won't burn them! A kiss is such a noble thing, Madame, that the queen of France once gave one to the lucky Lord Buckingham.

ROXANE: He was handsome, just like you.

CYRANO: (Dejected.) Ah yes. I'd forgotten that for a moment.

ROXANE: Well then, come to me…

CYRANO: *(To Christian.)* Climb up!

ROXANE: Come, and pick this flower…

CYRANO: Climb up!

ROXANE: That tastes of my heart…

CYRANO: Climb up, you idiot!

ROXANE: That hums like a bee…

CHRISTIAN: Roxane!

(They kiss.)

CYRANO: *(To the audience.)* There's one crumb of comfort I can savor: She kisses, on his mouth, the words I gave her.

CYRANO: Roxane!

ROXANE: Who's there?

CYRANO: It's me, Cyrano.

(Christian slips away.)

CYRANO: Roxane, there's a monk at the door to see you.

ROXANE: At this time of night? Let him in.

MONK: *(On.)* Are you…Madeleine Robin?

ROXANE: Yes, brother.

MONK: This letter is for you. *(Hands her a letter.)*

ROXANE: De Guiche! *(Reads.)* "My dear Roxane. The drums are beating. I have to go to the front. But I have hidden in a monastery. I am writing this letter to let you know that I'm coming to see you. I want to marry you tonight. That is why I have sent this monk. He's a simple soul who has no idea of what it's all about. I will be with you in a quarter of an hour. Count De Guiche." *(To the monk.)* Brother, listen what it says here: "Mademoiselle, it is the high will of the Cardinal that you shall comply with his strict orders, without protest. That is why the bearer of this secret is a wise and discreet Capuchin. He is to perform the ceremony of holy matrimony tonight, in your house, between you and…"

CYRANO: And who?

ROXANE: "…and Baron Christian de Neuvillette, no matter how much you loathe him. Resign yourself to your fate. Count De Guiche." Argh! Terrible! I cannot escape from this marriage. Brother, how much time do you need?

MONK: …

ROXANE: Ah! *(Looks at letter.)* Postscript: Give the monk twenty gold pieces.

MONK: Fifteen minutes.

ROXANE: Quick! A cross…A veil. Christian!

CYRANO: Roxane, did you read the letter properly?

ROXANE: Certainly.

CYRANO: Are you sure?

ROXANE: I'm sure. Christian!

(De Guiche in the background.)

ROXANE: De Guiche! *(To Cyrano.)* Make sure he doesn't come in for at least fifteen minutes!

(De Guiche is walking through the woods, Christian and Roxane are married, Cyrano keeps De Guiche from arriving too early.)

DE GUICHE: Madame, as sweet as mountain dew,
It fills me with joy to think of you.

Madame, I come through wind and rain,
I long to be with you again.

Madame, the world is in your smile,
I'll be with you in a little while.

CYRANO: Roxane! How much more time do you need?

ROXANE: Another five minutes!

DE GUICHE: Madame, my love for you is strong,
I've had to miss you for so long.

Madame, tonight you'll wear my ring,
you'll be my queen, I'll be your king.

Madame, it is a pure delight
to think that we'll be wed tonight.

Madame? Madame? Roxane?
(Roxane on.)

DE GUICHE: Madame, where is the monk I sent you who was to join us in matrimony?

ROXANE: Alas, Count. I have just married Baron Christian de Neuvillette.

DE GUICHE: Madame, your wedding night is a long way off yet.

ROXANE: How's that?

DE GUICHE: Your husband will be leaving for Arras tonight.

ROXANE: To war?

DE GUICHE: To the front.

ROXANE: But Sir, the cadets will be staying here.

DE GUICHE: They're going. Here's the marching order. *(Throws the order on the floor, exits.)*

ROXANE: Cyrano, make sure his life is never in danger.

CYRANO: I'll try.

ROXANE: That he does not suffer from the cold.

CYRANO: I'll do my best.

ROXANE: See to it that he's faithful to me. And make sure he writes to me often.

CYRANO: I can promise you that.

END OF ACT III

ACT IV

NARRATOR: Act Four. At the front, just outside Arras. The camp of the company of Carbon de Castel-Jaloux. Early morning. The plain is strewn with military equipment. Tents, weapons, drums, a campfire. The soldiers are sleeping in each other's arms because of the cold.
(Night.)

SOLDIER ONE: Ssst!

SOLDIER TWO: My belly's rumbling. I haven't had anything to eat for two days.

SOLDIER ONE: Ssst!

(A horse gallops near, a gunshot.)

SOLDIER ONE: Don't shoot, it's Cyrano!

(Footsteps.)

LE BRET: Who goes there?

CYRANO: It's me, Cyrano.

LE BRET: I don't understand why you risk your life every day for a stupid letter.

CYRANO: I promised her.

LE BRET: Cyrano, where are you going?

CYRANO: To write another one.

(Day breaks.)

DE GUICHE: *(On.)* Gentlemen, ready for the roll call? The situation is getting untenable. The Spanish army has got us in a stranglehold. Even the rats are fleeing our army camp because of hunger. The regiment is going to try and get us some supplies today. But the cadets are to stay here to fend off the expected attack of the Spaniards. So gentlemen, your order for today is…To stop the Spaniards until we get back!

CYRANO: And how are we supposed to do that?

DE GUICHE: By fighting to the last man.

CYRANO: Is that your revenge?

DE GUICHE: My revenge? I am placing your unparalleled bravery in the service of the King. I will recommend you to him for a posthumous decoration.

CYRANO: I am much obliged.

DE GUICHE: I thought you enjoyed fighting a hundred men single-handed? Then this should be right up your alley. Adieu!

(Cyrano writes a letter.)

CHRISTIAN: What are you doing?

CYRANO: Nothing.

CHRISTIAN: You're lying. Show me that. *(No response.)* Show me.

CYRANO: I was writing your farewell letter.

CHRISTIAN: To Roxane?

CYRANO: Who else?

CHRISTIAN: And I suppose you're going to send it with a pigeon?

CYRANO: No, Vimy can be reached.

CHRISTIAN: Nonsense. We're surrounded.

CYRANO: I break through the enemy lines at night.

CHRISTIAN: You risk your life?

CYRANO: For you.

CHRISTIAN: No, for her. I see now.

CYRANO: You're wrong, Christian.

CHRISTIAN: And what about this spot then? That's a tearstain.

CYRANO: Yes, as I was composing the lines, I got a bit carried away. I was moved to tears. After all, I have…we have…you have…

(A carriage approaches in the distance.)

CYRANO: What's that?

SOLDIER: Movement of troops reported behind enemy lines.

CYRANO: How many vehicles?

SOLDIER: A total of one carriage.

CYRANO: A carriage!

SOLDIER: It comes from the enemy.

CYRANO: Shoot!

SOLDIER: No! The coachman is shouting something.

CYRANO: What's he shouting?

SOLDIER: "In the name of the King!"

CYRANO: Of the King?

SOLDIER: Attention…Salute! Make way for the King. Parade formation. Salute battery! Open the doors.

ROXANE: Hello!

CHRISTIAN: In the name of the King? You!

ROXANE: In the name of…King Cupid.

CYRANO: My God! Roxane, how did you find…?

ROXANE: My dear cousin…How did I find you? That was very easy. I followed the trace of death and destruction, always straight ahead. When I was asked about the purpose of my journey, I simply said: I am going to see my lover. And even the most bloodthirsty Spaniard closed the carriage doors with royal dignity, bowed to me like a comma, and said "Por favor, senorita."

CHRISTIAN: Roxane, you must leave.

ROXANE: Me?

CHRISTIAN: And hurry.

ROXANE: Why?

CHRISTIAN: This place spells death.

CYRANO: De Guiche has played a dirty trick on us.

CHRISTIAN: We are surrounded.

CYRANO: And the Spaniards can attack us any minute.

ROXANE: I'm staying. I have decided I want to witness a battle. This country air has made me hungry. Paté, a game dish, Burgundy.

CHRISTIAN: Roxane, we haven't got anything!

CYRANO: Our supplies have run out.

ROXANE: Take a look in my carriage.

(*Food is taken out of the carriage.*)

CYRANO: Christian! When you get to speak to Roxane in private, and she asks you about your letters, then don't be surprised. I've written to her more often than you think.

CHRISTIAN: How often have I written to her? Once a week?

CYRANO: More.

CHRISTIAN: Twice a week ?

CYRANO: More.

CHRISTIAN: Three times a week?

CYRANO: More. Much more.

CHRISTIAN: Every day?

CYRANO: Yes, every day. Twice.

CHRISTIAN: But that's crazy! No man is so passionate and risks his life like that, unless…

CYRANO: Quiet! She doesn't need to know…

CHRISTIAN: Roxane, why are you here? Because of a few love letters?

ROXANE: There were so many of them, and they were so beautiful, my God. I have loved you ever since you bared your soul to me, under the balcony. And in your letters, I kept hearing your voice again. I read your letters over and over again. Your love was burning inside me. Forgive me that I only loved your good looks at first.

CHRISTIAN: And now?

ROXANE: Now, I love your innermost being. I love your soul. Your looks are not important anymore. I would love you just the same if you were to lose them.

CHRISTIAN: If I were…ugly?

ROXANE: Yes. I swear.

CHRISTIAN: You love her. You love her. You love her.

CYRANO: Yes, I do. With heart and soul.

CHRISTIAN: Then tell her.

CYRANO: No, my…

CHRISTIAN: Even if I were ugly, she would love me.

CYRANO: Did she say that?

CHRISTIAN: Yes.

CYRANO: That's nonsense. She doesn't mean that.

CHRISTIAN: Tell her. I want to know whom she prefers.

CYRANO: You.

CHRISTIAN: Roxane! Cyrano has something very important to tell you. *(Exit.)*

ROXANE: Why did he run off like that? What did he tell you? Maybe he didn't believe me.

CYRANO: Were you telling the truth?

ROXANE: Of course. I love him. Even if he were…

CYRANO: Go ahead. You won't hurt me. Even if he were ugly?

ROXANE: Yes.

CYRANO: Terribly ugly?

ROXANE: Even then.

CYRANO: Deformed?

ROXANE: Then I would love him even more.

CYRANO: Ridiculous?

ROXANE: He could never be ridiculous.

CYRANO: *(Aside.)* My happiness is near.

ROXANE: What did you say?

CYRANO: I…Roxane…I want to…listen…

ROXANE: Dear cousin, there is something on your mind.

CYRANO: Yes, you could say that again.

> *(A gunshot in the distance.)*

SOLDIER: Cyrano!

> *(They whisper, the soldier gives Cyrano a letter.)*

CYRANO: Now?

ROXANE: My dear cousin, what did you want to tell me?

CYRANO: Nothing, nothing…I swear. Roxane, I assure you that Christian's thoughts were with you all the time.

ROXANE: "Were?"

CYRANO: It's over. He was the first to attack. *(Hesitates.)* This letter was found on him.

ROXANE: Christian! *(To Christian.)* My dear, my sweetheart. Your cheek grows cold against my lips. *(To Cyrano.)* Stay with me. Your were the only one who knew his letters. Wasn't he a unique and brilliant man?

CYRANO: Yes, Roxane.

ROXANE: A fine poet?

CYRANO: Yes, Roxane.

ROXANE: So warm-hearted. And so pure.

CYRANO: Yes, Roxane.

END OF ACT IV

ACT V

NARRATOR: Act Five. Cyrano's chronicle of the week. Fifteen years later. 1655. The convent garden of the Sisters of the Cross in Paris. There is a huge chestnut tree in the middle. The park is dark. Above it, there's the sky.

DE GUICHE: *(On.)* Still in mourning? Will you keep your beauty hidden like this forever?

ROXANE: I'm still in mourning.

DE GUICHE: And still faithful?

ROXANE: Still faithful.

DE GUICHE: And do you still wear his last letter on your heart?

ROXANE: I do.

DE GUICHE: Does Cyrano still come and visit you often?

ROXANE: He visits me every Saturday. On the stroke of seven, I hear his walking stick on the porch. Then they put his armchair ready underneath that tree. I'll let you out.

DE GUICHE: *(To the audience.)* Maybe it's better for her not to know. I have just paid a visit to Cyrano. I saw him leave the house, and so I ran, he turned the corner, and then, I saw a servant—by accident or on purpose, who shall say?, drop a log out of the window, just as he was passing by. I ran over to him, Cyrano was on the ground. He'd been knocked out, and he had a great gash in his head.
(Cyrano on.)

ROXANE: You're very late today. For the first time in fourteen years.

CYRANO: Forgive me. I was detained.

ROXANE: What detained you?

CYRANO: An unexpected visitor.

ROXANE: Was it a tiresome visitor?

CYRANO: Painfully so.

ROXANE: Did you send him away?

CYRANO: I said "Excuse me Sir, I cannot see you right now. This is Saturday, and I always have an appointment to keep at this time on Saturdays. Someone's expecting me. Come back in an hour."

ROXANE: He'll have to wait for a long time then. I shan't let you go until much later this evening.

CYRANO: I'm afraid I might have to leave earlier. My chronicle of the week…On Saturday the nineteenth, the king was unwell after drinking eight bottles of Moselle. On Sunday, they burned seven hundred and sixty-three real beeswax candles, and at the Queen's ball, there were a few scandals. Our army made the Austrians tremble on Monday at five, and four witches were burnt too, so they're no longer alive.

ROXANE: And on Tuesday?

CYRANO: On Tuesday, Madame Arthis' little lapdog got altered.

ROXANE: That will do!

CYRANO: For Wednesday, no news. At least, none was reported. On Thursday, the whole court went to Fontainebleau. Madame Mancini became the queen of France, for the night. On Friday, the Countess De Guiche said no in the morning, and yes in the evening, at the dance. And on Saturday the twenty-sixth…argh…

ROXANE: What's the matter? Cyrano?

CYRANO: It's nothing. It's those old wounds from Arras.

ROXANE: *(Takes the letter out of her habit.)* His letter.

CYRANO: Didn't you say you'd let me read it one day?

ROXANE: Do you want to read it now?

CYRANO: Yes, very much. Tonight. *(Takes the letter, stares over it.)* "Good-bye Roxane, I'm going to die, Good-bye, my dearly beloved. My heart is heavy with so much unspoken love and I am going to die. Never, never again, will my enchanted eyes enjoy…"

ROXANE: You read with such sensitivity.

CYRANO: "…your gracious movements. I can bring your smallest gesture to mind. My heart wants to cry out."

ROXANE: The way you read that letter…

CYRANO: "I cry out: Good-bye, my dearest, my love."

ROXANE: That voice…it's not the first time I've heard that voice!

CYRANO: "…My heart was always with you, and in the next world too, I will always love you."

ROXANE: How can you possibly read now? It's dark. It was you.

CYRANO: No, Roxane, no.

ROXANE: I should have recognized your voice.

CYRANO: It wasn't me. I swear.

ROXANE: Now I see: It was you who wrote those letters. All those sweet words. That voice in the night. It was your soul. You loved me.

CYRANO: No, I didn't love you.

ROXANE: You loved me.

CYRANO: No, it was the other one who loved you.

ROXANE: Your voice is getting fainter.

CYRANO: No, my dear, I did not love you.

ROXANE: Why did you keep silent for fourteen years? The tearstains on that letter were yours.

CYRANO: But the bloodstains are his. *(Dies.)*

ROXANE: I love you.

NARRATOR: *(To the audience.)* Excuse me, he has interrupted his chronicle. On Saturday the twenty-sixth, so we have heard, shortly before dinner, Monsieur De Bergerac spoke his last word.

THE END

THE KING OF IRELAND'S SON

by Paula Wing

ORIGINAL PRODUCTION

The King of Ireland's Son was originally produced by Seattle Children's Theatre on April 30, 1999. It was directed by Linda Hartzell. Deborah Lynn Frockt was the dramaturg. Kara L. Mullen* was the stage manager. The cast was:

Sean	Alban Dennis*
Widow/Auburn Mary	Katie Forgette*
Shaking Head	Allen Galli*
Druid/King of the Western World	Paul Klein*
Second Shanachie	Jerry McGarity*
King of Ireland/Shanachie	J. Christopher O'Connor*
Trembling	Wendy Saver*
Caer/ Finola	Stephanie Shine*

Understudies—Hans Altwies*, Mary Kae Irvin*
*Members of Actors' Equity Association, the union for stage professionals

A NOTE ON CASTING

The play is intended for a cast of eight actors, with some doubling required. The first production, at Seattle Children's Theatre, Spring 1999, had the following cast/character breakdown:

Sean Ruadh
Shaking-Head/Mourner
Widow Woman/Auburn Mary
Caer/Princess Finola/Mourner
The King of Ireland/ "Our" Shanachie/Mourner
The Old Druid/The King of the Western World/Mourner
The Second Shanachie/Mourner/Hound of the Hallows/Giant
Trembling/Mourner/Other Faery Girl

GAELIC GLOSSARY

Sean Ruadh	Shawn Ro	Sean the Red
Cuchulainn	Koo-cullen	Mythic Irish Hero
Shanachie	Shunna-key	Bardic Itinerant Storyteller
Gallous	Gal-us	Wild, exciting, brave
Fionn MacCumhaill	Finn MacCool	Mythic Irish Hero
Inish Kea	Inish Kay	The Island of Kea
Diachbha	Dee-ach-va	Fate or Destiny
Tir-ta-fonn	Tear-ta-fawn	Land of Enchantment
Quid	Kwid	dollars, money
Geisa	Guessa	holy laws or taboos
Musha	Moosh-ah	exclamation as in for heaven's sake
Whisht	Wished	exclamation meaning Shhhh!
Urfeist	Ur-fay-st	malignant sea serpent
Lugh	Loo	one of the old Irish Pagan gods
Caer	Ky-er	old Celtic name
Si sios	See shis	sit down
A'chuin	Och hone	cry of lamentation
Boreen	Boar-een	laneway, road
Fomorian		ancient race of Giants who lived in Ireland
Ogham	Ohmm	an old alphabet made up of horizontal lines carved into stone or wood
Omadhaun	Ahma-dawn	fool, misfortune person
Manky		dirty, filthy, smelly
Tirrah	Tear-ah	good-bye
Bodhran	Bod-rahn	drum shaped like a tambourine
Slaun latt	Slawn lat	farewell
Cara mo chroi	Currah ma chree	friend of my heart

ACT I

Dusk outside the Castle of the King of Ireland. The Chief Court Advisor, the Old Druid sits with Sean Ruadh, the King of Ireland's son, who is practicing his fancy moves with a broadsword. The Old Druid has sticks, like kindling, that he's putting into a particular shape, as though for a fire.

SEAN RUADH: I can face anybody now. Any swordsman in the Known World!

THE OLD DRUID: It takes more than fine swordplay to make a great fighter.

SEAN RUADH: I can ride a horse, I'm not afraid of anything at all at all, and I can fight like Cuchulainn. I'm ready, Master, you know I am.

THE OLD DRUID: Would you ever sit down? You're making me legs hurt watching you.

SEAN RUADH: All my brothers left to meet their Fate when they were thirteen. It's not fair! Why do I have to wait so long?

THE OLD DRUID: Every day the same question. It's enough to give you a pain in your face.

SEAN RUADH: "The *Shanachies* will make ballads about his *gallous* deeds," that's what you said when I was born.

THE OLD DRUID: I didn't. 'Twas an old time *Shanachie* itself said that over your cradle. He saw great things in you, he said. That fella now, he could talk the light to dark and the stars themselves would come out to hear him.

SEAN RUADH: Let me fight somebody and you'll see he was right.

THE OLD DRUID: The last time we saw him, it'd be years ago now. We watched him go, like we always did, but somethin' about it was …It wasn't 'til after that we realized.

SEAN RUADH: He'd left his harp behind.

THE OLD DRUID: Aye, so. That was the day the story famine began for true, though we didn't know it then.

SEAN RUADH: What started it? Why did he leave his harp? Will you ever tell me?

THE OLD DRUID: When the time is right.

SEAN RUADH: The time is never right for anything! I'm going to spend my whole life waiting.

THE OLD DRUID: Aach, there's not a particle of me that doesn't ache!

SEAN RUADH: *(Rubs the old man's shoulders.)* Master. I'm only wanting what's due to me, sure. I'm needed in the Great World, haven't you said so yourself?

THE OLD DRUID: By the hawthorn! Your day is coming, Sean Ruadh.

SEAN RUADH: That's what you always say.

THE OLD DRUID: No, that's what you always say I always say. Not so hard! I'm brittle as an old stick.

(A Blue Bird with a great wingspan appears. Five more people, common folk enter as well, following the Bird.)

SEAN RUADH: Look! Isn't he something?

THE OLD DRUID: Oh, Old Spirit. It's the Lonely Crane of *Inish Kea*.

THE PEOPLE: *(As one at a half-whisper.)* The Lonely Crane!

SEAN RUADH: Why is he lonely? *(To the Bird.)* Don't be lonesome!

THE OLD DRUID: He's brought something for you: your *Diachbha*.

(Upon the utterance of this great word, the grouping of sticks begins to glow: It has become a magical fire. The Bird wheels and flies off.)

SEAN RUADH: My Fate? Now? My day is today?

THE OLD DRUID: Sit down.

SEAN RUADH: Where did he go? I should follow him.

THE OLD DRUID: I have a story to tell you.

SEAN RUADH: Is it a long story, Master?

THE OLD DRUID: It is. What's the point of a short one?

SEAN RUADH: Just tell me first: Is my Bird coming back?

THE OLD DRUID: *(In the Voice of Power.)* A long time ago—

SEAN RUADH: You know where he went, don't you?

THE OLD DRUID: —in this very Castle of your father, the King of Ireland—

SEAN RUADH: But what if he gets away? I'll never know what my Fate is.

THE OLD DRUID: *Si sios!*

(Sean drops to the ground as if punched in the stomach. The Old Druid's voice is young and powerful now. The People draw closer, to listen.)

THE OLD DRUID: In this Castle many years ago there lived a beautiful young girl, a Princess, the beloved and only daughter of the King and Queen of Ireland.

SEAN RUADH: My father has no daughters.

THE OLD DRUID: She was as sweet a child as lived in the land, and her voice was like an angel's when she sang.

ONE OF THE PEOPLE: She lit up every room she entered.

ANOTHER: She was like an angel.

ALL THE PEOPLE: An angel!

THE OLD DRUID: But she had her own mind. I warned her not to cross the moat for fear of wild strangers on the road. Her father the very King of Ireland begged her not to walk about by herself. And the Queen her doting mother forbade her to leave the Castle for holy fear. But she was just like you, your sister, she did as she pleased!

SEAN RUADH: My sister! Where is she? Why didn't you ever tell me?

THE OLD DRUID: I'm tellin' you now. You had a sister who listened to no one and walked the roads alone, and she was captured by a Giant.

SEAN RUADH: And died, poor soul.

ONE OF THE PEOPLE: No!

ANOTHER: She lived!

ANOTHER: A curse that she did.

ANOTHER: A curse on us all.

A curse on the Known World!

THE OLD DRUID: Your father and mother offered that Giant everything they had to ransom back their darlin' child but he refused. Now, in those days, there was a beautiful, mysterious land—

ONE OF THE PEOPLE: On the tip
Of the edge
Of the far, far horizon

ANOTHER: Sometimes brighter
Sometimes dimmer

ANOTHER: The land where stories are born

ALL: *Tir-ta-fonn!*

THE OLD DRUID: The Giant put a spell on that misty land and caused it to sink like a stone under the water. He swore your sister would be his prisoner until the day *Tir-ta-fonn* is freed from that undersea enchantment and resides in the Upper World once again. Until that day, no new stories can be born.

ONE OF THE PEOPLE: And since that day

ANOTHER: Famine.

ANOTHER: Want.
And loneliness.

ALL: And famine.

SEAN RUADH: But how would you ever find a land that's under the sea?

THE OLD DRUID: By your mother's request, it appears on the far horizon once every seven years for the length of a single day. If it can be touched with fire on that day it will come again into our World. Then and only then will your sister be free and the story famine ended.

SEAN RUADH: I'll free her! I'll end it! Is that my Fate? Of course it is.

THE OLD DRUID: In the end of all, the Giant left Ireland with your sister, and your mother in her grief walked out in the dead of night and she never returned.

SEAN RUADH: Poor Mam, I never knew. And my Father's been a lonely man ever since.

THE OLD DRUID: He has. But that was his *Diachbha.*

SEAN RUADH: My Bird knows where my sister is, doesn't he? He'll take me to her.

THE OLD DRUID: *(In his human voice.)* Sean. Wait.

SEAN RUADH: I'll cut that Giant open and tear the heart out of his chest!

THE OLD DRUID: Sean Ruadh.

SEAN RUADH: I'll hold fire in the palm of my hand to free my only sister! Is my Bird coming back or should I go find him?
(The King of Ireland enters as if by catapult.)

THE KING OF IRELAND: The most amazing Bird flew past my window just now. Bluer than the sea, great thick wings. It hurt my heart to look at him.

SEAN RUADH: It's my sister's messenger.

THE OLD DRUID: I have told him the story, Sire.

THE PEOPLE: His time is come.

SEAN RUADH: Finally!

THE KING OF IRELAND: No. Please.

SEAN RUADH: I'm going to save her, Father, if I have to shed the blood of a hundred Giants.

THE KING OF IRELAND: Your twelve brothers swore as you swear now, Sean Ruadh, and sure, none of them ever returned.

SEAN RUADH: But I will. What should I take with me, Master? My sword, of course.

THE KING OF IRELAND: He's far too young to be wandering the World alone.

THE OLD DRUID: He's exactly young enough.

THE KING OF IRELAND: He's not going. I forbid it.

SEAN RUADH: You can't do that!

THE KING OF IRELAND: Mind your mouth, you! *(To the Druid.)* I have followed your counsel always, but this is my last son.

THE OLD DRUID: You dare to oppose me?

THE KING OF IRELAND: Yes!

THE PEOPLE: No!

THE KING OF IRELAND: *(After a moment.)* No. But you have to promise me that—

THE OLD DRUID: I promise you that if you keep him here you'll bring down my curse on yourself and him, a curse that will destroy you both.

SEAN RUADH: I'm going, Father.

THE KING OF IRELAND: Would you at least promise to be careful.

SEAN RUADH: Heroes aren't careful. They dare! They dare to do un-careful things.

THE KING OF IRELAND: You're no hero. You know nothing of the World and its ways.

SEAN RUADH: You know nothing of me.

THE OLD DRUID: Your son leaves this night to make his way in the World. Let him leave with the blessing of his father's final gift.

THE KING OF IRELAND: I bless him, how could I not bless him? *(Gives Sean money.)* Here's five quid, my darlin' son. For your journey.

SEAN RUADH: I don't need it.

THE OLD DRUID: Never refuse a gift!

SEAN RUADH: *(Taking it.)* Well. Good-bye so.

THE KING OF IRELAND: Sean.

THE PEOPLE: Wait!

THE KING OF IRELAND: Let the Druid look into the Fire for you.

ONE OF THE PEOPLE: A man of valor knows what he must do, Sean Ruadh.

ANOTHER: And he knows what he must never do!

ANOTHER: You need *geisa* to sharpen your wits.

(The Fire glows more brightly. The Old Druid waves his hawthorn wand over it.)

THE OLD DRUID: Are you ready to take Valor and be a warrior, Sean Ruadh, thirteenth and last son of the King of Ireland?

SEAN RUADH: I am.

(He hands the Druid his sword, which the Druid holds over the fire.)

THE OLD DRUID: *(In the Voice of Prophesy.)* Kneel before the fire and give me your Crown. You are named Sean Ruadh, Sean the Red. Red for—

SEAN RUADH: Blood!

THE OLD DRUID: Red for fiery spirit. In you many hopes live. On the twisty path to your Fate you may take only your father's gift for protection, and your sword, and you must follow the Lonely Crane of *Inish Kea,* who was there at the beginning and will be there at the end of all things. Do you swear before this Fire to find your sister and bring her home?

SEAN RUADH: I swear by this Fire, I will find my sister and bring her home.

THE OLD DRUID: By this smoke are you bound to your Oath

And your Oath to you.

Will you take into your spirit, Sean Ruadh

Your Druid's final gift?

SEAN RUADH: I will.

THE OLD DRUID: I give you three *geisa* to obey without exception until you return.
They are given
As protection, as challenge, as warning.
If you break any one for any reason the pain is:

ALL: Death.

THE OLD DRUID: On pain of death, then, you must:
Never refuse a gift.
Never reveal your royal birth until your sister is free.
And never turn your back on man or beast.

SEAN RUADH: As this wood burns, may I be ignited by my *geisa*.

THE OLD DRUID: Rise now, and meet your Destiny. *(In his human voice.)* Keep your head about you, Sean Ruadh.
(As the last of his words falls upon the Fire, the Lonely Crane of Inish Kea appears once more in the sky above. Sean turns to his Father.)

SEAN RUADH: Don't forget me.
(They embrace. Sean turns and the great Blue Bird turns and they leave together.)

THE KING OF IRELAND: All my family flown away like wild geese. And me alone, and heart-scalded.
(The magical Fire gutters out and with it the light on the land of Ireland. A beat and the lights come up again on a barren place. The Blue Bird swoops on and rides the still air, then flies off again. A second later, Sean rushes on.)

SEAN RUADH: Wait! Waaiittt! Aaugh! He never rests, he never eats, day after day after day. No wonder he's lonely, he's always after flyin' away from yez. I'm run off me feet and still no sister. How long 'til I fight dread beings with my bare hands and rescue her? I wonder now, will I know her when I see her? Will she look like me? Be cripes, I forgot to ask her name. Amn't I a right eejit? But my Bird'll know her, sure, I just have to follow him, that's what my Master said. My head's about me. It's me legs are deserting me. The Great World is so empty—not a breathin' soul anywhere.
(Suddenly there is a most amazing keening sound.)

THE WIDOW WOMAN: *(From off.)* A'chuin, A'chuin!
Why did you die? Why did you die?
Why did you
why did you
why did you
die?
(The Widow Woman has entered by now, dressed in black and crying out in lamentation. She is followed by six people, who travel, and frequently speak, as a group. They carry a coffin; they are The Mourners.)

THE MOURNERS: *(Singing mournfully.)* Aye, tan tinna nah

  Tan tinna nah

  Aye, tan tinna noor anna nandy.

MOURNER: Hard times! Hard times!

MOURNER: He's gone from this World.

MOURNER: Taken in the flush of his years.

MOURNER: Hard, hard times.

THE WIDOW WOMAN: My heart is broken, my heart. Ripped from my body
  and bloody on the ground!

MOURNER: The shame!

MOURNER: Not a cent to her name.

MOURNER: Poor.

MOURNER: Alone in the wide, wide World.

MOURNER: Can't bury her own husband.

MOURNERS: The shame. The terrible, terrible shame!

SEAN RUADH: Excuse me, Ma'am, but would you ever need a handkerchief?

THE WIDOW WOMAN: I would.

  (Suddenly there is a strange, thin otherworldly cry.)

MOURNERS: The Cry of the Banshee!

  Callin' for a soul, a soul to feed her hunger.

  The Banshee, the dread Banshee!

SEAN RUADH: What's happened? Can I help? Please don't cry. I'll fight anybody for you.

THE WIDOW WOMAN: You can't fight the Banshee.

MOURNER: His spirit will never rest.

MOURNER: Stranded at the gates of the Next World.

MOURNER: No rest, no rest ever at all.

SEAN RUADH: Who is this lost soul?

THE WIDOW WOMAN: Aach! It's me darlin' husband in that box, taken be the
  palsy, and I too poor to bury him. If he isn't buried in the cold ground,
  his soul will never leave this earth, never walk through the Gates of Paradise.
  He'll be an eternal prisoner between this World and the Next. *A'chuin!*

MOURNER: All for the want of five quid.

MOURNER: Five quid.

MOURNER: Five quid!

THE WIDOW WOMAN: What'll I do? Where are the *Shanachies* to tell me story?

MOURNERS: They're gone, gone out of this World.

  What can she do?

  She's doomed.

THE WIDOW WOMAN: Where is the hero to save a keening Widow Woman?

SEAN RUADH: Here I am! I'll save you so.

THE WIDOW WOMAN: Where in the World am I going to get a pile of money like five quid? Where? Where?

SEAN RUADH: I have five quid.

THE WIDOW WOMAN: That's a quare handful for a young fella. Is it rich you are?

MOURNERS: A king's son.

He's the son of a king.

SEAN RUADH: Divil a one! I'm poorer than the dirt on the roads.

THE WIDOW WOMAN: You took it then, did you, you thief.

MOURNERS: Thief. Thief!

THE WIDOW WOMAN: Took it from some poor desperate widow woman, I warrant!

SEAN RUADH: Never! It's the due me father gave me.

THE WIDOW WOMAN: I'd give the eye in me head for that sum.

SEAN RUADH: Take it. Free your husband.

THE WIDOW WOMAN: I couldn't take a father's due to his son.

MOURNERS: Never refuse a gift!

SEAN RUADH: An Old Druid said those very words to me not three days ago.

THE WIDOW WOMAN: If the power of the Druids is in it…I'm forgetting all the holy laws. And me manners, too. Thank you, Sir.

SEAN RUADH: May you be comforted.

THE WIDOW WOMAN: He died young, my poor oul' man. But he'll see Paradise this day.

(The Mourners shoulder their burden and the Widow Woman takes up her place behind the coffin. They march off, singing.)

MOURNERS: *(Singing.)* Aye, tan tinna nah

Tan tinna nah

Aye, tan tinna noor anna nandy.

SEAN RUADH: *(To himself.)* The Druid never said "Don't give it away." I had to give it. Didn't I? I have to keep my head about me. Eejit! Where's my Bird anyway? He's meant to advise me and he's nowhere to be found. It's not fair. Has he deserted me maybe because I needed that fiver to ransom my sister? Maybe? Aaugh! I hate all this thinking! Why can't I just fight? *(He starts walking and trips over a small green bush.)*

THE BUSH: *Musha,* there's no call for that.

SEAN RUADH: Who's there?

(The Bush is actually a little green Man who now stands up, affronted.)

THE LITTLE GREEN MAN: You young hooligan! I'm bruised entirely!

SEAN RUADH: A leprechaun!

THE LITTLE GREEN MAN: Where?

SEAN RUADH: You're not a leprechaun?

THE LITTLE GREEN MAN: Me? Are you daft, man?

SEAN RUADH: *(Draws his sword.)* Well what are you then? Who are you? Out with it or I'll carve out your voice box and spear your name on the tip of me sword.

THE LITTLE GREEN MAN: *(Screams wildly.)* Don't kill me, bejeez! Is it money I owe you?

SEAN RUADH: Tell me everything you know about the Giant who captured the King of Ireland's daughter or I'll—

THE LITTLE GREEN MAN: *(Babbling.)* Ireland? What d'ye—I don't—how could I—the King of—

SEAN RUADH: Speak!

THE LITTLE GREEN MAN: Help!

SEAN RUADH: I'll run you through. I'm not afraid of anything at all at all.

THE LITTLE GREEN MAN: I am. I am! Pure terrifried! *(Runs back and forth wildly, squawking with panic.)*

SEAN RUADH: Don't move! Why are you moving? I told you not to move. *(With a groaning cry of battle Sean rushes at The Little Green Man as if to run him through, and somehow in the tussle the sword comes right out of Sean's hand. The Little Green Man snatches it up.)*

THE LITTLE GREEN MAN: Me nerves are in bits. That's as close to death as I— *(He stops himself, and looks around, as though he'd just awakened.)* Be the mortal day!

SEAN RUADH: Go on and kill me. I deserve to die!

THE LITTLE GREEN MAN: Maybe so, but you might want to reconsider. Take it from me, death isn't all it's cracked up to be.

SEAN RUADH: You're not going to kill me?

THE LITTLE GREEN MAN: Too much work, laddie. And besides, that Crane of yours, he wouldn't—

SEAN RUADH: You saw my Bird? Where is he? Show me where he went!

THE LITTLE GREEN MAN: Oh, I couldn't tell you where he was now at all at all. *(He comes upon a bun in his pocket.)* Nourishment! Would you ever share it with me?

SEAN RUADH: No, I have to find my Bird. Oh. Wait! Is that a gift? The bun?

THE LITTLE GREEN MAN: We won't know 'til we taste it. Are you hungry?

SEAN RUADH: I am.

THE LITTLE GREEN MAN: I always think better after I've supped. We'll go looking for your Crane later.

SEAN RUADH: No "we" won't, Sir. I'll be lookin' for my Bird meself, thank you very much.

THE LITTLE GREEN MAN: Really. Why?

SEAN RUADH: Why? Be cripes, I have to. It's my Destiny.

THE LITTLE GREEN MAN: Nobody does anything alone in this World, my son. Except die.

SEAN RUADH: The heroes do. Cuchulainn and Fionn MacCumhaill do, surely.

THE LITTLE GREEN MAN: And you're a hero yourself, are you?

SEAN RUADH: I am.

THE LITTLE GREEN MAN: *(Half to himself.)* Saints preserve us. *(Regarding his bun.)* What's more mairvellocious than a bite of sustenance, I ask you? When you think of it, our stomachs are like heaven for food. My teeth are this bun's pearly gates.

SEAN RUADH: Take a gander at this. *(He executes an extremely awkward jump/leap move.)*

THE LITTLE GREEN MAN: And what was that now?

SEAN RUADH: My salmon leap.

THE LITTLE GREEN MAN: Your salmon leap.

SEAN RUADH: Just like Cuchulainn's when he fought the—what? What's so funny?

THE LITTLE GREEN MAN: "Just like Cuchulainn." It's enough to make a fish laugh.

SEAN RUADH: The *Shanachies* are going to sing ballads about it 'til the end of time. Then you'll be laughing out the other side of your mouth!

THE LITTLE GREEN MAN: Oh, you're goin' to end the story famine all be yourself, is it?

SEAN RUADH: I am. It's my *Diachbha.*

THE LITTLE GREEN MAN: Bejeez, it tires me out just thinkin' about it.

SEAN RUADH: I can't stand here talking all day, I have to find my Bird. Good luck to you so. Thanks for the bite. *(He nearly turns his back, then starts to back away.)*

THE LITTLE GREEN MAN: Here, wait. Ehm. Well. You wouldn't mind a little company, would you?

SEAN RUADH: I would. The Druid never said anything about anybody comin' with me so.

THE LITTLE GREEN MAN: Did he say somebody couldn't come with you?

SEAN RUADH: No.

THE LITTLE GREEN MAN: Then where's the harm in it?

SEAN RUADH: I'm going alone and there's an end.

THE LITTLE GREEN MAN: You'd turn your back on a poor wee brussels sprout of a fella like me?

SEAN RUADH: I didn't turn my back!

THE LITTLE GREEN MAN: That was the feeling of it. You wounded me, sure, and me after savin' your sorry life not five minutes ago.

SEAN RUADH: I didn't mean to—it's just that I—

THE LITTLE GREEN MAN: No harm done. I'll come with you and not another word spoken.

SEAN RUADH: No! It's my Bird and my Destiny.

THE LITTLE GREEN MAN: I offer the lad the pleasure, the pure *gift* of my company, a thing most men would weep to get even the smell of and it's no, he says. Picture it!

SEAN RUADH: Wait, don't go. I—however did you know? It's not fair! *(After a moment.)* I have to fight all the battles.

THE LITTLE GREEN MAN: I take a dread Oath to leave all the bloodshed to you. *(He starts off, Sean doesn't move.)* Ah, don't get a puss on it's not worth it. I'm Shaking-Head.

SEAN RUADH: Sean Ruadh.

SHAKING-HEAD: Sean the Red. Aren't you the fiery fella with your salmon leap and all. And remind me now, whose son are you when you're at home?

SEAN RUADH: The wide roads are my home.

SHAKING-HEAD: Good lad, that's a good lad. All that walkin' ahead. Makes you wish you could travel by catapult. *(Takes out a penny whistle.)* How about a bit of a sing? I'm a great wee man for a song. *(Plays "Since I Left Skibbereen.")*

SEAN RUADH: That one has fourteen verses.

SHAKING-HEAD: I've got the wind.

(They walk off and instantly, as if by catapult, two men enter: The King of the Western World who drags a poor, ragged Old Shanachie, who has a harp on his back.)

THE OLD SHANACHIE: Not so fast, Sire, I can hardly breathe.

THE KING OF THE WESTERN WORLD: *(Scanning the far horizon.)* Well? Where is it? Show me your almighty *Tir-ta-fonn!* You said it was coming.

THE OLD SHANACHIE: I didn't. I said there were signs it was coming. I said seven years are—

THE KING OF THE WESTERN WORLD: Liar! All you *Shanachies* are the same, all lies and liars. I should know better than to believe yez, but what's a poor desperate father to do?

THE OLD SHANACHIE: Wait and hope, Sire, like the rest of us.

THE KING OF THE WESTERN WORLD: I won't. I can't. Play your harp and summon *Tir-ta-fonn!* Without it we've no hope of a hero, sure.

THE OLD SHANACHIE: It won't work, Sire. Stories unfold in their own way. Even I can't compel them.

THE KING OF THE WESTERN WORLD: My daughter is not "a story"! Do as I say or I'll tear the liver out of ye.
(The Old Shanachie plays a run of notes. Sean catapults on and Shaking-Head limps tiredly into view behind him.)

THE KING OF THE WESTERN WORLD: Glory be to God it's a sign! It must be.

THE OLD SHANACHIE: Wait and see, Sire.

SEAN RUADH: *(To Shaking-Head.)* I'm sure I saw him over yonder.

SHAKING-HEAD: You keep saying that and we never find him. Bejeez, me legs are two old men.

THE KING OF THE WESTERN WORLD: All the bounty of my kingdom is at your feet, Sir!

SEAN RUADH: Thanks, I'm sure. I'm looking for a notorious great blue bird. Have you seen him, be any chance?

SHAKING-HEAD: It's the Lonely Crane of *Inish Kea* he's talkin' about, if you don't mind.

SEAN RUADH: *(To Shaking-Head.)* Will you *whisht!*

THE OLD SHANACHIE: Oh, Old Spirit! The Lonely Crane.

THE KING OF THE WESTERN WORLD: Help me, Sir! Help a poor misfortunate father. Save my darlin' daughter from the *Urfeist,* you're her only hope!

SEAN RUADH: *(Drawing his sword.)* I'll save her, sure! Where is she? What's an *Urfeist?*

THE OLD SHANACHIE: A bloodthirsty sea serpent. Every seven years the *Urfeist* comes on to the land to destroy the most beautiful and good thing it can find.

THE KING OF THE WESTERN WORLD: Seven years ago that hideous creature ate the daughter of the King of the Eastern World. I've lived in terror all this time that my daughter would be next, and none to save her.

SEAN RUADH: I'll slice him up into stewing meat! *(He starts off.)*

THE OLD SHANACHIE: Mind now, you have to be a king's son to fight the *Urfeist.*
(Sean stops.)

THE KING OF THE WESTERN WORLD: No you don't. Go Sir, fight!
(Sean starts to go again.)

THE OLD SHANACHIE: Yes you do. Stay, young man.
(Sean stops again.)

SHAKING-HEAD: *(To Sean.)* Mind where you swing that sword, you'll decas-
   tricate me.

THE OLD SHANACHIE: Your Majesty, your Druid said only a king's son can kill
   the *Urfeist*. *(To Sean.)* Now, sir, are you a king's son or no?

SEAN RUADH: Well…no. I'm not. No. But I'd fight him anyway.

THE OLD SHANACHIE: The Lonely Crane is with you but you're not a king's
   son?

(The air is rent into smithereens by a great cacaphonous mooing.)

SEAN RUADH: Come here to me, I'll fight y', whatever y' are!

THE OLD SHANACHIE: Put up your weapon, it's only the poor cows. Starvin'
   like the rest of us.

SEAN RUADH: Cows?

THE OLD SHANACHIE: A pure tragedy, Sir. They used to give the best milk in
   the Known World.

THE KING OF THE WESTERN WORLD: 'Til this *Urfeist* terror dried them clean
   up. The Royal Cowboy felt so helpless he quit. I haven't had a glass of
   milk in weeks. I don't even want to think about how lonely the world is
   without cheese in it.

THE OLD SHANACHIE: *(To the audience.)* No wonder I'm wastin' away to a nub.
   No man can write a stirring ballad called "I'm Lonely for Cheese," now
   can he.

(Another, louder chorus of moos strafes the air.)

SHAKING-HEAD: I can't keep silent a minute longer. Sean Ruadh here is the
   greatest cowboy in all of the land of Ireland!

SEAN RUADH: What're y' talkin' about? I am not.

SHAKING-HEAD: If anybody can bring your cows back to their milkiness, Your
   Majesteriality, it's this fella here.

THE KING OF THE WESTERN WORLD: What do I care if he's the greatest cowboy the world has ever seen. I need an *Urfeist* killer.

SEAN RUADH: *(Taking Shaking-Head aside.)* Will you *whisht!* What're you thinkin'
   of?

SHAKING-HEAD: *Whisht* yourself. Your Bird is gone. You can't find your Destiny
   without him. Stay put and I wager he'll come back to find you.

SEAN RUADH: But my Destiny's got nothin' to do with cows.

SHAKING-HEAD: So you're just going to turn your back on them?

SEAN RUADH: Of course I'm not going to—will you just stay out of it please?

THE KING OF THE WESTERN WORLD: Stop all this demented whispering! I won't
   have whispering in the Western World. The King has spoken. *(To the
   Shanachie.)* Now the man himself is here, I've no further need of ye. Leave

my kingdom at once. If I ever see you here again I'll chop up your harp for kindling and burn you on the fire.

THE SHANACHIE: But Sire—

THE KING OF THE WESTERN WORLD: Get out before I tear the eyebrows off you! Go!

(The Old Shanachie exits swiftly.)

THE KING OF THE WESTERN WORLD: *(He turns to Sean.)* You're going to fight that serpent and save my daughter, be you king's son or tinker's son. Or I'll have you fed to wild dogs. In the between while, you'll tend to my poor bastes. The cow pasture's that way.

(Light change. A pained, backed-up mooing begins. Sean and Shaking-Head, are in the cow pasture, both greatly the worse for wear. It is near dark, a moon is rising.)

SEAN RUADH: Don't you dare complain! It's your fault we're up to our hunkers in mud, pure famished for food, congregating with cows.

SHAKING-HEAD: Aach, put a cork in it.

SEAN RUADH: My Bird's deserted me, sure.

SHAKING-HEAD: He hasn't.

SEAN RUADH: Where is he then? What do you know about it, anyway? *(To himself.)* It all started with the five quid. *(To Shaking-Head.)* I never should've let you come with me. You've wrecked everything!

SHAKING-HEAD: Haven't you got a puss on!

SEAN RUADH: You're the biggest coward I ever met.

SHAKING-HEAD: Is that so? And what's the difference between a coward and a brave man, accordin' t' you?

SEAN RUADH: It's Fate.

SHAKING-HEAD: No it isn't. It's Faith.

SEAN RUADH: It's not! You have to be born fearless.

SHAKING-HEAD: What if you weren't? There's more to it than that.

SEAN RUADH: There isn't. Look at my twelve brothers. Not one of them was a brave man born. So they all died.

SHAKING-HEAD: How do you know they're dead? They might not be.

SEAN RUADH: They are. I know they are.

SHAKING-HEAD: A brave man has Faith and pursues the unknown end. That's what I think.

SEAN RUADH: Listen to him! Never did a brave thing in your life, I bet. Faith in what?

SHAKING-HEAD: I don't know. Just Faith.

(The sweetest music imaginable drifts over them. It quiets even the agony of

the cows. In a delicate stillness, the music plays, the moon rises and an other-worldly light shines behind the two of them.)

SHAKING-HEAD: Bedad, it must be the Feast of *Lugh*. It's the only night in the whole year the Door to the Other World is open.

(Sean goes toward the light.)

SHAKING-HEAD: Are you daft? Sean, wait! It's perilocious in there! *(Shaking-Head catches up to Sean just in time to slip a knife into his hand.)* Keep this the whole time! Be polite to 'em and whatever you do, don't eat or drink anything.

(Joyous, celebratory music blasts from the open door. Sean Ruadh and Shaking-Head enter Faery Land. There is a golden goblet on a crystal pedestal that Sean goes toward. Before he can touch the cup, a beautiful Faery Girl appears. She turns Shaking-Head to show him something offstage and he goes off as though enchanted.)

THE FAERY GIRL: Welcome to the Isles of the Blessed, Sean Ruadh.

SEAN RUADH: However did you know my name?

THE FAERY GIRL: I've been waiting for you. I'm Caer.

SEAN RUADH: *(Pointing to the goblet.)* Could I ever ask you, Caer, what is that?

CAER: Dagda's Cup of Truth from the heavenly city of Murias. He gave it into the keeping of the Good People so it would never be broken by human Untruth.

SEAN RUADH: Your folk are the Good People?

CAER: They are. Whatever you truly love to eat and drink, you will taste in that Cup. It never runs out of nourishment. Come away now, and don't be asking to drink from it. Only a brave man born, a pure hero, can drink from Dagda's Cup.

SEAN RUADH: I'm a hero.

CAER: It's trying to fool me you are! Don't I know there's a story famine these many years and no more heroes in the Human World because of it.

SEAN RUADH: I'm a brave man born, I know I am. *(He goes to take the cup.)*

CAER: *(Preventing him.)* Dagda's Cup will burn a coward if he touches it.

SEAN RUADH: Then I have nothin' to fear. *(He takes up the cup.)* See there! I'm not burned at all at all.

CAER: You're the bravest man that ever was!

SEAN RUADH: I am. Seeking my Destiny in the Great World and—you're laughing.

CAER: You human lads all talk of your Destiny like a lost button you're trying to find.

SEAN RUADH: Your hair smells like mist.

CAER: Three of your brothers are here, Sean Ruadh.

SEAN RUADH: Where? Take me to them! Is Eamon here? I loved Eamon the best.

CAER: Drink from Dagda's Cup and you'll see all three of your brothers again, and I'll never leave your side, my Sean.

SEAN RUADH: My Caer. I love your name. *(He raises the cup to his lips, stops.)* Wait now. I should rescue my sister first. The Druid said that's my *Diachbha.*

CAER: What are you talkin' about? You never had a sister!

SEAN RUADH: I did. Everybody said I did. How would you know anyway?

CAER: Did you ever actually see her? We know all about the Human World here and you have no sister, you never did.

SEAN RUADH: But the Druid—I took Valor. An old *Shanachie* said I'd be a hero.

CAER: My hero. There's Destiny between us, my Sean, can't you feel it?

SEAN RUADH: Could I ever kiss you, Caer?

CAER: As many times as you may wish. After you drink.
(Shaking-Head enters, reeling, as though he's trying to escape something. He sees Sean about to drink.)

SHAKING-HEAD: Sean Ruadh! Sean, stop now! She's tryin' to trick you.

CAER: You're not goin' to believe a notorious oul' coward like him are you? Drink.

SHAKING-HEAD: We're leaving. *(He starts to drag Sean away.)*

SEAN RUADH: Let me go, I want to stay with her.

SHAKING-HEAD: Where's your head? One drink and you're trapped for all eternity.

CAER: One drink and I'm yours. One drink and you'll never die.

SEAN RUADH: She's my Destiny.

SHAKING-HEAD: Is that what your Druid said? Look at me! Is it?
(Sound of a large, creaky door moving to close. The sound builds and builds to the end of this scene.)

SHAKING-HEAD: The Door's closing, Sean!

SEAN RUADH: *(To Caer.)* My sister needs me.

CAER: I need you.

SEAN RUADH: *(To Shaking-Head.)* I don't know what to do.

CAER: Don't turn your back on me, my Sean. Drink!

SHAKING-HEAD: *(As Sean is about to drink.)* Keep your head about you! Think!

SEAN RUADH: *(To Shaking-Head.)* I have to drink it! I can't turn my back on— wait. Wait. No. *(To Caer.)* You're neither man nor beast! It's my sister needs me, not you. *(He tries to throw the cup to Caer several times but it won't leave his hand.)*

SHAKING-HEAD: The Door! Sean, hurry!

(They race and manage to get out just before it slams shut like a clap of thunder.)

SHAKING-HEAD: They almost had us in the right oul' style.

SEAN RUADH: I'm a failure! I'm destroyed entirely!

SHAKING-HEAD: What're you talkin' about, you won your first fight.

SEAN RUADH: That wasn't a fight. I didn't keep my head about me, eejit! I forgot my Druid and I believed her totally. I believed everything she said.

SHAKING-HEAD: Don't be disforkulant, many a fine fella's been bested by a faery girl. But you weren't.

SEAN RUADH: Only because you saved me.

SHAKING-HEAD: *(Dismissing it.)* A bag of shells. You fought your own bad angel and won the Cup of Truth. I could never have done the like of that. You can take a sip of it now.
(Sean sips.)

SHAKING-HEAD: How does it taste?

SEAN RUADH: Like water from the angels' own spring. *(Offers it to Shaking-Head.)*

SHAKING-HEAD: Oh no thanks, thank you no. It'd burn me to cinders.

SEAN RUADH: I didn't mean to—before, I mean, when I—drink! You're a brave man too.

SHAKING-HEAD: I'm not. I'm a right trepidoshious coward and you know it.
(They are firmly back in the Western World, the moon now high in the night sky, the cows lowing in the darkness.)

SEAN RUADH: Never thought I'd be glad to hear those poor bastes complain.

THE OLD SHANACHIE: *(Whispering.)* Oh my sweet soul, it's Dagda's Cup of Truth!

SEAN RUADH AND SHAKING-HEAD: Aaugh! Who's there?

SEAN RUADH: The King said he'd roast you alive if he ever caught you here again.

THE OLD SHANACHIE: I knew you were the man! The Lonely Crane, and now the Cup of Truth. I mind the signs.

SHAKING-HEAD: He fought like a *Fomorian* for it he was near shredded to fragmenteens!

SEAN RUADH: Shaking-Head.

THE OLD SHANACHIE: The Powers beyond are with him, that's sure.

SEAN RUADH: Because I'm a brave man born.

SHAKING-HEAD: No. Because you had faith.

THE OLD SHANACHIE: Dagda's Cup is a potent weapon. One sip can revive a man on the lip of death to full fighting strength again. But its Power cuts both ways. Take care you never speak a lie over the Cup.

SHAKING-HEAD: That's right. I remember that.

THE OLD SHANACHIE: If three Untruths are told over it, it smashes to bits, and the great Powers will turn on you and nothin' in the Wide World can save you then. Mind what I'm tellin' you.

SHAKING-HEAD: You'll be the champion fighter now. Walkin' away! Never mind that desperate salmon leap.

THE OLD SHANACHIE: He's got a salmon leap? *(He looks to Sean, hoping to see it.)*

SHAKING-HEAD: He has to save it for battle so.

THE OLD SHANACHIE: Fair play to you. *(He starts to tune his harp.)* Here I thought I'd lived too long and it turns out I've lived exactly long enough.

SEAN RUADH: *(To Shaking-Head, who has found nourishment in his pocket and is eating.)* You're forever eating! You'll explode, sure.

SHAKING-HEAD: I'm only fortifryin' meself, so. We fight the *Urfeist* today.

SEAN RUADH: Oh, it's "we" now, is it?

SHAKING-HEAD: Amn't I meant to cheer you on? You don't want me to faint with hunger at the critical moment.

(The Shanachie strums his harp: It's in tune. The music seems to make the light change all of a sudden, revealing a Tower. At a window is a Beautiful Young Girl.)

SEAN RUADH: Who's she?

THE OLD SHANACHIE: I can't tell rightly. Me eyes aren't what they were.

SHAKING-HEAD: Only your eyes?

THE BEAUTIFUL YOUNG GIRL: *(Singing.)* For you took what's before me and what's behind me
took East and West from all around me
the sun, moon and stars from me you've taken
and God himself if I'm not mistaken.

SEAN RUADH: You sing like an angel!

THE BEAUTIFUL YOUNG GIRL: Leave me alone.

SEAN RUADH: Where did you come from? I never saw this Tower before.

THE BEAUTIFUL YOUNG GIRL: Of course you didn't, you fool! It wasn't here.

SEAN RUADH: Where was it then? Oh! Would you be Princess Finola?

THE BEAUTIFUL YOUNG GIRL: I wouldn't. Go 'way.

SEAN RUADH: Are you watching for the *Urfeist?* I'm going to kill him.

THE BEAUTIFUL YOUNG GIRL: You're goin' to die like all the rest. Every seven years it's the same shtupid thing!

SEAN RUADH: It's not! I'm going to save Princess Finola.

(The Young Girl hurls a stone with rather amazing force. She very nearly hits Sean with it.)

SEAN RUADH: Whyever did she do that!

SHAKING-HEAD: Some folk aren't sociable.

THE BEAUTIFUL YOUNG GIRL: Next you'll be tellin' me you're bringin' back the land of *Tir-ta-fonn*.

SEAN RUADH: I am. I will.

THE BEAUTIFUL YOUNG GIRL: Loud promises are easy made and hard kept.

SHAKING-HEAD: Let's leave her be before she pelts us with arrows.

SEAN RUADH: I'm not running away from her. *(Holding up The Cup of Truth.)* Take a gander at this. I won it from the Powers Beyond.

THE BEAUTIFUL YOUNG GIRL: You won Dagda's Cup? I don't believe it.

SEAN RUADH: I'm the man himself. The Lonely Crane of *Inish Kea* is traveling with me.

THE BEAUTIFUL YOUNG GIRL: Traveling with you, is it? I don't see him anywhere. Looks to me like he's given up on you, Mr. Man Himself.

SEAN RUADH: He hasn't! You'll see, I'll do everything I said I'd do, and free my darlin' sister into the bargain. She's everything you're not! Sweet and gentle and grateful—she'll put the likes of you to shame.

THE BEAUTIFUL YOUNG GIRL: Aach, what do I care for your shtupid sister?

SEAN RUADH: How dare you insult her? *(He starts toward the Tower, a sound stops him.)*

THE BEAUTIFUL YOUNG GIRL: Now you've wakened the Giant, and worse than stones will smite you.

(A Giant appears.)

SHAKING-HEAD: *(Taking cover and cowering.)* Help!

THE GIANT: WHO'S THERE?

SEAN RUADH: Me, you great *omadhaun*.

THE GIANT: Who DARES, who has the NECK to call me an OMADHAUN?

SEAN RUADH: Me again, you pig-faced oul' sack of pus!

THE GIANT: ONE MORE WORD AND YOU'LL BE IMPALED ON MY SLUMBER PIN!

(A long slender needle appears above Sean's head. It is very spiky and unfriendly looking.)

SHAKING-HEAD: We'll be annunciated!

SEAN RUADH: Leave now or I'll gut you like a chicken and roast you over a spit 'til you cough up your organs!

(The slumber pin swipes at Sean.)

SEAN RUADH: You'll pay dear for tryin' to stab me.

THE GIANT: *(Chuckling.)* HOW? HOW WILL YOU MAKE ME PAY?

SEAN RUADH: *(Drawing his sword.)* With this!

(The slumber pin descends and a duel ensues. Sean seems to get the upper hand but then he makes one desperate and desperately pathetic salmon leap. It misses spectacularly, but the Pin stops in midair.)

THE GIANT: WHAT was THAT?

SEAN RUADH: My salmon leap.

SHAKING-HEAD: The terror of the Known World! Run away while you still can!
(The Giant starts to laugh. In the midst of his hilarity, he stabs himself with the Slumber Pin and promptly falls into a deep sleep, snoring magnificently.)

THE OLD SHANACHIE: *(To the audience.)* Would you believe he stabbed himself with his own Slumber Pin?

TREMBLING: He'll sleep for a thousand years now!

THE OLD SHANACHIE: *(Singing.)* What's your tour-rye-ah

Faddle diddle dah

Tour-rye-oor-rye-oor-rye-ahh.

SEAN RUADH: *(To the Beautiful Young Girl.)* He was bigger than a stone and I bested him.

THE BEAUTIFUL YOUNG GIRL: You did. I never saw the like in all me life. You were fierce!

SEAN RUADH: Maybe you'd like to eat your words now and admit that I'm the man.

THE BEAUTIFUL YOUNG GIRL: You've come to rescue me, then? That's why you're here?

SEAN RUADH: *(Aside to Shaking-Head.)* Another one!

SHAKING-HEAD: *(Same.)* It's a hard country.

SEAN RUADH: Well…what do you need to be rescued from?

THE BEAUTIFUL YOUNG GIRL: I can't tell you that.

SEAN RUADH: Why not?

THE BEAUTIFUL YOUNG GIRL: I can't tell you!

SEAN RUADH: You mean, you're under a spell, like?

THE BEAUTIFUL YOUNG GIRL: My name is Trembling. That's all I can tell yez.
(She turns and picks something up.) But there's something I can do for you, sure. I never thought this day would come but—

SEAN RUADH: Fair play to you, Trembling, but first things first. You owe me a gift.

TREMBLING: What?

SHAKING-HEAD: You can't *ask* for your due, it has to be given to you.

SEAN RUADH: Well, what's she waiting for? How many more Giants do I have to kill?
(There is a loud crack.)

TREMBLING: You didn't kill him he fell on his own Slumber Pin.

SEAN RUADH: Because I tricked him into it.

TREMBLING: Oh, be cripes, how hard was that? He was as shtupid as a basswood stump!

SEAN RUADH: Give me a gift.

TREMBLING: I won't!

SEAN RUADH: Then I won't help you.

TREMBLING: I don't need your help. I don't need anybody!

(There is another audible crack.)

THE OLD SHANACHIE: *Whisht* now! Did you hear that?

SEAN RUADH: Fine then, I don't care two pins. I've got me own *Diachbha* to attend to.

TREMBLING: So do I.

SEAN RUADH: Girls don't have *Diachbhas!*

TREMBLING: We do. And *geisa* too. You know nothin' about girls.

SEAN RUADH: I know everything about everything!

(There is a third, definitive, and very loud crack!)

THE OLD SHANACHIE: *(Falling to his knees.)* Evil and despair! You've smashed the Cup of Truth.

(Indeed it lies in fragmenteens on the ground.)

SEAN RUADH: Now look what you've done!

TREMBLING: You did it.

SHAKING-HEAD: This is catastrophious.

THE OLD SHANACHIE: You'll pay with your life for breaking that Cup and no escape for it. *(He lays down his harp and starts to leave, slowly.)*

SEAN RUADH: But I didn't mean to! I—where are you going?

THE OLD SHANACHIE: Between the jaws of Death and out of this World altogether.

SEAN RUADH: No, wait. Don't go. I'll fix it. I'll—

THE OLD SHANACHIE: There's no fixing anything now. You'll die tomorrow at the hands of Fate and any hope for new stories will die with you. *(He exits.)*

SEAN RUADH: There must be something I can do. Wait, please!

SHAKING-HEAD: You didn't keep your head about you.

SEAN RUADH: I know that, sure! I don't need you to tell me that!

TREMBLING: No, of course not. You're the man himself.

SEAN RUADH: I'm sorry.

TREMBLING: It's mad late for "sorry" now, dog-late for it.

SHAKING-HEAD: We're doomed.

SEAN RUADH: I'm sorry, Father! I'm so sorry.

END OF ACT I

ACT II

Light comes up on Sean Ruadh, alone, as he was when we last saw him, looking up, searching for the Lonely Crane. The light expands and as before Shaking-Head and Trembling are there.

SEAN RUADH: I'm sorry, Father! I'm so sorry.

SHAKING-HEAD: Let's go for ourselves, Sean Ruadh, away from here, while we've still got our skins on us.

SEAN RUADH: What happened to "have faith and pursue the unknown end"?

SHAKING-HEAD: What good can come of stayin' now?

SEAN RUADH: *(Almost giving in.)* We could go lookin' for my Bird, maybe…

TREMBLING: *(Looking off to the horizon.)* Bless us and save us!

SEAN RUADH: What? What is it?

TREMBLING: Never you mind it's no concern of yours. Be on your way now.

SEAN RUADH: The *Urfeist*. It's coming for Princess Finola.

SHAKING-HEAD: Sean, I'm beggin' yez, let's go! Before we're masticulated to a powder!

TREMBLING: "I'm the Man Himself," he says and then he turns his back on us all at the first sign of trouble.

SEAN RUADH: I never turned my back.

TREMBLING: You're about to!

SEAN RUADH: I'm not!

TREMBLING: What're you goin' to do then? Well? What?

SEAN RUADH: Well, I reckon I'll…fight the *Urfeist*.

SHAKING-HEAD: You can't do that! The Great Powers are against you.

SEAN RUADH: I'll do no running and there's an end. *(A beat.)* Go to the water's edge.

SHAKING-HEAD: I? Me? Be meself? No, Sean, please, I'm scared liquid of monsters.

SEAN RUADH: Tell 'em I'm comin' right after you. Go now, go!
(With palpable reluctance Shaking-Head goes.)

SEAN RUADH: *(Half to himself.)* Now where am I going to get clothes fit for a prince?

TREMBLING: What do you need them for?

SEAN RUADH: You have to be a king's son to fight the *Urfeist*.

TREMBLING: *(Beat.)* That Giant killed many a prince in his time, the manky oul' beggar.

SEAN RUADH: Would you—do you think you might have—I'd only borrow the clothes, like.

TREMBLING: They won't help you, sure. You'll die anyway.

SEAN RUADH: Fighting. I'll die fighting.

(Lights to the water's edge. There we see: Princess Finola, her father, the King of the Western World, and a Man with a bodhran. Princess Finola has a sword drawn and she's practicing her fancy moves with it, slicing up the air with great ferocity.)

THE KING OF THE WESTERN WORLD: *(To the Man.)* Tell me straight or I'll tear the ears off you!

THE SECOND SHANACHIE: *(Singing.)* I am a rambling Irish man...

THE KING OF THE WESTERN WORLD: You're a *Shanachie,* don't lie to me, you liar! One more note out of you—

THE SECOND SHANACHIE: Sorry about the song. I'm just startin' out, you see. I only finished making the *bodhran* a week ago Sunday and I'm going to make my first-ever ballad on the *gallous* hero who rescues Princess Finola!

PRINCESS FINOLA: I'm goin' to rescue myself, thank you.

THE SECOND SHANACHIE: That can't be right, now.

THE KING OF THE WESTERN WORLD: Amn't I just after tellin' you, Finola, you can't rescue yourself! I'm sure the Druid said that.

PRINCESS FINOLA: He didn't, Father. He said be sure to look my tormentors square in the eye. Be sure to question a gift, he said, and be sure to take my shoes off to the man I love. No word did he say about not rescuing meself from harm.

THE KING OF THE WESTERN WORLD: That blasted Druid swore a king's son would save you and marry you, too. And I believed it! I had to believe it, sure. Now the *Urfeist* is nearly upon us and not even that cowboy is anywhere to be found. Will you stand back from the water, Finola! You'll tear the heart from me chest.

PRINCESS FINOLA: I'll not be dyin' this day, Father, I promise you.

(Shaking-Head enters, trepidoshiously.)

SHAKING-HEAD: Is the *Urfeist* here yet?

ALL: No. Not yet. He's a ways out yet.

SHAKING-HEAD: Princess Finola will be saved this day! There I've told yez. *Tirrah!*
(He turns to go.)

THE SECOND SHANACHIE: You see, Sire? Even the leprechaun says so.

SHAKING-HEAD: I am not a leprechaun! Bejeez, are y' blind or what?

PRINCESS FINOLA: I'm not goin' to saved by you, sure.

SHAKING-HEAD: Me? I? Oh no, gracious me no. I couldn't save me own toe from a stubbing. *(To the Shanachie.)* Quite a *bodhran* you've got there.

THE SECOND SHANACHIE: Made it meself, I did. Finished it a week ago Sunday.

SHAKING-HEAD: Could I ever play with yez, maybe? I've a penny whistle.

THE KING OF THE WESTERN WORLD: No music, I'll have no music in the Western World.

THE SECOND SHANACHIE: Sure, it's only the words, now, Sire. *(To Shaking-Head.)* I'm new at this but I thought something like: *(Sings.)*
There it began, at the edge of the sea
But no man came forward to be saving she.

SHAKING-HEAD: Aye. And then what?

THE SECOND SHANACHIE: Well I don't know, nothin's happened yet has it? *(Sean Ruadh catapults into the scene. He is dressed entirely in black from head to foot: disguised as the Black Prince. He carries his sword. When he and Princess Finola see each other there is a long moment. They are stopped cold by each other. They stare.)*

THE BLACK PRINCE: I'm here to save you, Princess Finola!

PRINCESS FINOLA: I'm not in danger.

THE KING OF THE WESTERN WORLD: One man of Valor in the whole of the Known World! Where've you been, man, we've had our eyes out on pot sticks for you.

THE SECOND SHANACHIE: What did I tell you, Sire. He's here and time to spare.

PRINCESS FINOLA: Who are you when you're at home?

THE BLACK PRINCE: I'm…the Black Prince, world famous *Urfeist* Killer! Nothing and no one will touch a hair of your head while I'm here!

SHAKING-HEAD: *(Aside.)* Sean? Sean Ruadh, is that you under all that darkness?

THE BLACK PRINCE: *(Sean Ruadh. Aside.)* Whisht now. I know what I'm doin'.

PRINCESS FINOLA: Would you ever sit down, Black Prince, while we're waiting?

THE BLACK PRINCE: I would. *(He sits, then gets up again.)* No. No! I have to be ready for him.

PRINCESS FINOLA: What's the best way to fight an *Urfeist,* do you think?

THE BLACK PRINCE: I wouldn't know. I've never seen one before.

PRINCESS FINOLA: But I thought you said—

THE BLACK PRINCE: I like your hair.

PRINCESS FINOLA: Sure, it's just hair. I like your sword.

THE BLACK PRINCE: I'm a fearsome swordsman, me. You've nothin' to be afraid of.

PRINCESS FINOLA: My father's afraid. I'm not.

THE BLACK PRINCE: That's grand. But you want to take care, now. You're going to be—

PRINCESS FINOLA: *(Jumps up, swings her sword.)* Killing the *Urfeist* before the morning is done!

THE BLACK PRINCE: Here, now just a minute, you can't save yourself.

PRINCESS FINOLA: I can. I will! There was a Druid saw Valor in me when I was in me cradle.

THE BLACK PRINCE: But…what would I be doing here if you could save yourself?

PRINCESS FINOLA: Entertainin' me. You wouldn't be thinkin' you're a better fighter than me?

THE BLACK PRINCE: I would so.

PRINCESS FINOLA: *(Assuming an "en garde" position, looking him dead in the eye.)* Prove it!

(The Black Prince responds to her challenge. They joust with great spirit and skill, and are very evenly matched. The Second Shanachie continues his composing.)

THE SECOND SHANACHIE: *(Singing.)* The Black Prince came at the lip of day
To snatch Princess Finola from the teeth of the grave.

PRINCESS FINOLA: *(To the Shanachie, as she's fighting.)* He'll have to get past me first!

THE BLACK PRINCE: How hard can that be?

PRINCESS FINOLA: You couldn't do it if you had the Magical Egg of Fire itself on your side!

(She comes at him ferociously. They thrust and parry and provoke each other to great flourishes of swordsman/womanship.)

SHAKING-HEAD: *(To the Second Shanachie after a particularly sizzling exchange in the duel.)* Could we stand a wee bit further back, do you think?

(Suddenly the waters roll and roil and there is a fearsome smack on the water. We see the long, very spiky tail of the Urfeist *parting the mists on the sea. The duel ends: no clear winner. The tail slaps the water again, making a bone-chilling sound.)*

SHAKING-HEAD: *(Screaming.)* Save me in the name of the angels! I'm liquifying with fear.

THE KING OF THE WESTERN WORLD: Fight it, young man! You're her only hope!

PRINCESS FINOLA: Ahh, quit your wailin', Father.

SEAN RUADH: *(Aside to Shaking-Head.)* Should I do my salmon leap?

SHAKING-HEAD: *(Aside.)* You shouldn't.

THE SECOND SHANACHIE: He's got a salmon leap?

THE BLACK PRINCE: Stand back now, Finola.

PRINCESS FINOLA: Stand back yourself! I'll fight alone or I'll fight alongside but I'm fightin'.

(A third, soul-piercing smack on the water and The Black Prince turns, raising his sword and swinging it impressively over his head. Finola joins him, her own sword in action. But suddenly, the tail sinks back into the sea and out of sight.)

THE KING OF THE WESTERN WORLD: That was *gallous!* Well done, Prince of Fighters!

THE BLACK FIGHTER: But—nothing happened. Nobody died. There wasn't even any blood.

THE KING OF THE WESTERN WORLD: It's a miracle!

PRINCESS FINOLA AND THE BLACK PRINCE: It's not!

THE BLACK PRINCE: *(To Shaking-Head.)* The Powers Beyond won't even let me fight? It's not fair!

THE SECOND SHANACHIE: *(Who's been composing.)* I've got it! Try this one on: *(Singing.)* He sank back to the deepy, deepy sea

The Black Prince never even wounded he.

There wasn't any blood, and there wasn't any death—

THE BLACK FIGHTER: Stop! Why are you singing? There's nothin' to sing about. *(Our Shanachie, the old man, comes rushing in, dragging his harp with him.)*

OUR SHANACHIE: What kind of a heroic ballad is that? Here I am, snatched from the lips of Death by the most demented warbling that ever cracked me eardrums. In the name of *Tir-ta-fonn,* I ought to break that *bodhran* over your head, man.

THE SECOND SHANACHIE: You'd take the *bodhran* of a *Shanachie?* And I only made it last Sunday, now!

OUR SHANACHIE: A *Shanachie,* he says! *(To Shaking-Head.)* What is it with the young?

SHAKING-HEAD: They know everythin'. They just don't know what order it goes in.

OUR SHANACHIE: *(To the other Shanachie.)* You start with the chorus, man, the chorus! *(Singing.)* Come a tour-rye-ah

Faddle diddle dah—

THE SECOND SHANACHIE: You don't! You start with whatever moves you!

THE BLACK PRINCE: I'm goin' to fight him. That's what I came for and that's what I'm goin' to do. Make him come back.

PRINCESS FINOLA: He'll only come back tomorrow, Black Prince.

THE BLACK PRINCE: Then so will I, Finola!

(He catapults off. Shaking-Head hustles after him. Finola reaches out her hand to stop him, but she comes up with only…)

PRINCESS FINOLA: A single strand of his hair!

THE KING OF THE WESTERN WORLD: *(Recognizing Our Shanachie.)* You!

OUR SHANACHIE: Didn't I tell you your daughter would be saved? *(Referring to The Black Prince.)* Who's that fella now? Where did he come from? *(The lights change. Sean and Shaking-Head stand below Trembling's window. It is nearly night, late dusk. Trembling is at the window.)*

SEAN RUADH: Admit it, you were wrong! You thought I'd be serpent meat be now.

TREMBLING: Maybe the *Urfeist* didn't think you were worth fightin'.

SEAN RUADH: He's comin' back tomorrow! Herself said so. I'll finish him off then, in notorious bloody style! You'll see.

TREMBLING: Without the help of the Greater Powers, you'll be the one finished, Mr. Man Himself.

SEAN RUADH: There's a Magical Egg. Well. Princess Finola mentioned it. Do you know it? I was thinkin' if I could get that—

TREMBLING: The World and its wife knows about the Magical Egg of Fire in the Rattlin' Bog! But you're as likely to live in *Tir-ta-fonn* as find it.

SEAN RUADH: Why? Where is it?

TREMBLING: It lives in a riddle, wrapped in a tale, under a pile of twisty words. The old people say it can only be found inside the Wild Duck.

SHAKING-HEAD: Bejeez, how would you ever find it if it was inside a duck?

TREMBLING: Indeed, you'd have to seek her nest, and it nestled at the top of a tall, tall tree and that tree in a particular hole and that hole in the very ground of a great Rattlin' Bog to the West of a Western place.

SEAN RUADH: Could we get to the Bog and back tonight, do you think?

TREMBLING: Sure, how would I know? I'm an eternal prisoner in this Tower! But you don't care about me, sure. What does anybody care about me?

SEAN RUADH: I'll rescue you, too. I promise.

TREMBLING: Ah, don't make promises. I hate promises. They're all as broken as your Cup of Truth in the end.

SEAN RUADH: They're not. You have to have faith, Trembling. *(To Shaking-Head.)* We need to go to the Bog.

SHAKING-HEAD: Not tonight, please.

SEAN RUADH: Herself said the *Urfeist's* comin' back tomorrow. We have to go now.

SHAKING-HEAD: *Musha*, walkin' all night, I'll be brittle as an old stick.

SEAN RUADH: Herself wouldn't have—

TREMBLING: "Herself this, herself that"—why is she so smart all of a sudden?

SEAN RUADH: She's a holy livin' terror, she is. Fights with a sword! Stood right next to me and faced the *Urfeist* and not afraid at all at all.

TREMBLING: She tried to rescue herself, like? She can't do that.

SEAN RUADH: I know. But she did it anyway! She knows her own mind, sure.

TREMBLING: You like her.

SEAN RUADH: I do. Well. I mean. She's—never mind. *(To Shaking-Head.)* Let's be on our way.

SHAKING-HEAD: It'll be all dark and squooshy, spirits abroad everywhere…I don't want to.

SEAN RUADH: I'm off for meself, then.

TREMBLING: You'd go alone in the dark and no promise of getting the Egg?

SEAN RUADH: No promise I won't get it either. I'm more than a match for a manky oul' duck!

TREMBLING: Wait. You're owed a gift, Sean Ruadh, for besting the Giant. *(She takes up a great Sword.)*

SHAKING-HEAD: Dear me Duchess! It's the Sword of Light, the greatest gift of them all.

TREMBLING: The Giant stole it, but its true owner was the old heroes, the men of the *Fianna*. It never fails to kill at one blow.

SEAN RUADH: Thanks, Trembling.

TREMBLING: You were owed it.

SEAN RUADH: The hilt's all marked up.

TREMBLING: A message the ancients wrote in their own hand for the man who carries the Sword.

SHAKING-HEAD: That'd be the *ogham* alphabet.

SEAN RUADH: What does it say?

SHAKING-HEAD: I can't read *ogham*. Never learned.

SEAN RUADH: Eamon tried to teach me once…I told him I'd never need it. Eejit!…something about blue…man in blue, maybe?

TREMBLING: You have to wear blue the first time you carry it, or the Sword won't lend you its power.

SHAKING-HEAD: We'll kill the *Urfeist* with this, now! No need to go traipsin' all over Creation lookin' for an Egg.

SEAN RUADH: Are you sure? Maybe we should go to the Bog anyway.

SHAKING-HEAD: Isn't he the worrier? We should eat a notorious great supper and have a cuppa tay before we sleep. That'll do us up right for tomorrow. *(Light changes to Finola who is brushing her long hair by the water's edge, long slow strokes. Her father is with her, and the two familiar Shanachies.)*

THE KING OF THE WESTERN WORLD: Where is he? He said he'd be back tomorrow! Dear God!

PRINCESS FINOLA: He'll be here, Father. Not that I care two pins.

OUR SHANACHIE: *(To The Second Shanachie.)* Tell Me Ma.

THE SECOND SHANACHIE: That's so old! Can't we keep working on the new one we've got going?

OUR SHANACHIE: The old ones help us write the new ones, you eejit! Play!

THE SECOND SHANACHIE: I won't. Why do you get to choose the songs? I was here first.

OUR SHANACHIE: *(To the audience.)* Here first, he says! *(Singing.)* Tell me Ma when I go home

The boys won't leave the girls alone.

They pull me hair, they stole me comb

Well that's all right 'til I go home.

BOTH SHANACHIE: *(Chorus.)* She is handsome, she is pretty

She is the queen of my heart's City.

She's come a-courtin' one, two, three

Please won't you tell me, who is she?

Let the wind and the rain and the hail blow high,

And the snow come tumbling from the sky

She's as nice as apple pie,

She'll get her own lad by and by.

(Sean Ruadh leaps into the picture, with Shaking-Head loping furiously along behind him. Sean, disguised, this time as The Blue Prince, in blue down to a pair of fancy blue glass boots.)

SEAN RUADH: Here I am, you soul-sucking sea serpent! Fight me to the bloody end!

PRINCESS FINOLA: Who are you?

SEAN RUADH: *(The Prince of the Blue Waves.)* I'm the Prince of the Blue Waves, the greatest *Urfeist* Killer on land or sea!

THE KING OF THE WESTERN WORLD: Dog-late, young man. But in the nick. Where's the other fella?

PRINCESS FINOLA: Yes. Did you see a fella all in black on his way to us, be any chance?

THE PRINCE OF THE BLUE WAVES: That I did. Dead be the side of the road he was.

PRINCESS FINOLA: He wasn't!

THE PRINCE OF THE BLUE WAVES: He'll never be seen in this World again.

PRINCESS FINOLA: Away with ye, now, we don't need the likes of you. I'll be fighting the *Urfeist* all on my own.

THE PRINCE OF THE BLUE WAVES: I'd go, sure, I would. But I can't ever leave you, Princess Finola.

PRINCESS FINOLA: Aach, what're ye talkin' about you shtupid—

(Our Shanachie plays a chord on his harp just as Princess Finola turns to look The Blue Prince dead in the eye. Maybe it's the music and maybe not but she sees something familiar in the Blue Prince's eyes.)

PRINCESS FINOLA: Are you—do I know you, now? I'm thinkin' I do but…could I see your Sword, maybe?

THE PRINCE OF THE BLUE WAVES: No you couldn't, no. I only unsheath it for battle, me.

PRINCESS FINOLA: Aye so. I see.

THE SECOND SHANACHIE: *(To Our Shanachie, referring to the harp and its effect.)* That was—how did you ever do that? Could I do the like with me *bodhran?*

OUR SHANACHIE: And more. If you'd a mind to listen to your elders the odd time.

THE PRINCE OF THE BLUE WAVES: Could I ever brush your hair, Finola?

PRINCESS FINOLA: You could. If you'd a mind to.

(He takes the brush and copies her long, slow strokes. The Shanachies are delighted at this and sing under, softly.)

THE SHANACHIES: She is handsome, she is pretty.

She is the queen of my heart's City.

She's come a-courtin' one, two, three

Please won't you tell me who is she?

(Without warning the waters part and the Urfeist rises out of the water and strikes Sean hard! He falls to the ground and the great serpent is just about to grip Sean between his horrifying teeth when…)

PRINCESS FINOLA: My Blue Prince! He's killed my Blue Prince! *(She draws her sword.)*

THE KING OF THE WESTERN WORLD: Finola! Noooo!

(Finola lets out a piercing cry that startles the beast briefly and Sean gets to his feet. He is very badly injured and even a little disoriented. Finola keeps the serpent distracted but she's over-matched.)

SHAKING-HEAD: *(To Sean.)* The Sword! Get out the Sword!

(Sean pulls it from its sheath but it's his own, un-magical weapon, and not the Sword of Light.)

SHAKING-HEAD: Don't tell me you forgot it! Where's your head?

SEAN RUADH: I don't need it anyway! I'll fight him with me bare hands!

(The Urfeist charges and they engage in, fierce, bitter combat, with Finola adding her own strokes when and where she can. But it is mostly Sean and

the serpent. Sean takes many blows but manages one last effort and gashes the Urfeist. *It cries out and turns back toward the outer waters. The Blue Prince, seemingly badly wounded, staggers off.)*

THE KING OF THE WESTERN WORLD: Would you believe it? She's saved again!

PRINCESS FINOLA: I'm not ever saved yet, Father. The *Urfeist* will be back tomorrow.

(Shaking-Head races off after Sean and Finola comes upon a single blue glass boot.)

PRINCESS FINOLA: He's the same! I know he's the same man!

THE KING OF THE WESTERN WORLD: Who's the same man?

PRINCESS FINOLA: Whichever man's foot fits in this fine glass boot, that man is my Black Prince and my Blue Champion and the man I must have for my own.

(Lights out on them and up on Trembling's Tower. Sean is on the ground, badly injured and Shaking-Head tends to him.)

TREMBLING: We need the Magical Egg of Fire to win.

SHAKING-HEAD: We can't get it now, sure, look at him, he's a wreck entirely.

SEAN RUADH: I'm not! *(He tries to get up, fails.)*

TREMBLING: You have to go.

SHAKING-HEAD: Me? I? Alone? Oh no. No no no no no.

SEAN RUADH: A notorious oul' coward like him? Never!

TREMBLING: *Whisht,* now, you fought a hard fight.

SEAN RUADH: I didn't! That wasn't a real battle, sure. A real battle is a fight to the death.

SHAKING-HEAD: Lucky for you it wasn't.

TREMBLING: Shaking-Head, you have to go. We need that Egg.

SEAN RUADH: Oh it's "we" now, is it?

SHAKING-HEAD: I'm not your servant. Why don't you get it yourself?

TREMBLING: I can't, you know I can't! I'm a prisoner.

SEAN RUADH: Whose prisoner? I don't see anybody keepin' you up there but yourself. You know what has to be done, why don't you come down and do it?

SHAKING-HEAD: *(After a pause.)* Well? What would happen if you did, now?

TREMBLING: I'd be struck dead.

SHAKING-HEAD: Be what? The Giant? He's a long gone *omadhaun.*

SEAN RUADH: The only reason you won't come down is you're afraid. Plain afraid.

TREMBLING: I'm not.

SEAN RUADH: You are! You're afraid of everything. You just sit up there thinkin' the worst of us all, criticizin' everything night, noon, and mornin' I'd like to know what you ever did that gives you the right to judge me.

TREMBLING: Nothing.

SEAN RUADH: That's right, so. Nothing at all at all. So leave off torturin' me now in the name of the angels! You can go on and save yourself for all I care.

TREMBLING: Do you need me to help you, Sean Ruadh?

SEAN RUADH: Aach, never mind.

TREMBLING: I'm askin' you, now, just answer me yes or no. Do you need me to help you?

SEAN RUADH: How could you ever help me?

TREMBLING: Yes or no.

SEAN RUADH: It's too late now anyway.

TREMBLING: Yes or no.

SEAN RUADH: Yes, be cripes, yes! Are you happy now? Yes, I need you to help me!
(A distinct, but unrecognizable sound is heard. Trembling comes down from the Tower.)

SHAKING-HEAD: Aren't you the brave one!

TREMBLING: I'm not. The skin's shakin' off me bones I'm so terrified.
(That sound again.)

SEAN RUADH: So am I. So am I, too.
(A third, very definitive sound.)

SHAKING-HEAD: Oh, my sweet Soul. Trembling, Sean.

TREMBLING AND SEAN RUADH: What? What is it?

SHAKING-HEAD: Dagda's Cup.
(There on the ground, pristine and whole once more, is the reconstituted Cup of Truth.)

SHAKING-HEAD: I remember now! Speak three lies over the Cup and break it, speak three truths over it and un-break it. The Powers Beyond are with us again!

SEAN RUADH: You see? You didn't need me, Trembling. You've saved yourself.

TREMBLING: No. Not yet! I have to—

SEAN RUADH: *Whisht* now! You can't say!

TREMBLING: You're right. Ta.

SHAKING-HEAD: Sean. Drink!

SEAN RUADH: I can't. Only a brave man born can drink from Dagda's Cup. It'd burn me.

TREMBLING: Maybe sometimes the bravest thing you can do is admit you're afraid. *(She dares to touch the cup: She is unburned.)* You're no coward, Sean Ruadh. Drink, now, drink.

(Sean is cured.)

TREMBLING: Be off with yez now, it's a long way to the Bog and back in one night.

SEAN RUADH: You're coming with us.

TREMBLING: No. I've me own *Diachbha* to attend to, Mr. Man Himself.

SHAKING-HEAD: Where are you going?

TREMBLING AND SEAN RUADH: Are you shtupid or what are you?! I can't say! She can't say!

(They take their leave of each other as the lights change. A keening scream starts faintly and it rides right through the change of scene. It is deep night, there is a sky full of stars. Sean Ruadh and a bone-exhausted Shaking-Head have arrived at the famous Rattlin' Bog of song and story. They stare in wonderment at the quaking pudding before them.)

SHAKING-HEAD: It's enough to cut the socks off you!

SEAN RUADH: *(Finds food in his pocket, offers it.)* Nourishment!

SHAKING-HEAD: Eat it for yourself now, I'm not hungry.

SEAN RUADH: What? Are you sick? *(He eats, after a moment he turns and Shaking-Head is crying.)* Here, what's this?

SHAKING-HEAD: Ah, Sean. I did everything wrong me whole life. A hard-headed cuss, I was, nobody could ever tell me anything. And here I am after all that, sittin' on me hunkers, letting you down.

SEAN RUADH: You're not! Don't cry. What're you crying for?

SHAKING-HEAD: Ahhh…to be a human being, a livin', breathin', heart-shaked, blood and bones human being.

(A woman catapults into view: red hair, flaming red cheeks, ablaze with life! She is Auburn Mary, the Hag of the Rattlin' Bog. She carries a lantern.)

AUBURN MARY: Aach, quit your blubberin'! I hate pointless blubberin'.

SEAN RUADH: Who're you?

AUBURN MARY: Who're you yourself? And what're you doin' clutterin' up me Bog? Speak quick or I'll blow you out me nose!

SEAN RUADH: I'm Sean Ruadh and this is my friend Shaking-Head and—

AUBURN MARY: You smell like a cow pasture, the pair of yez.

SEAN RUADH: You're smellin' the perfume of great *Urfeist* fighters.

AUBURN MARY: It's a vicious assault on a poor woman's nose.

SEAN RUADH: We're looking for the Magical Egg of Fire. Ma'am.

AUBURN MARY: Stick a cork in that "ma'am"! Amn't I Auburn Mary, Hag of the Rattlin' Bog? And didn't I get to be a ravin' old Hag from listenin' to—you say one word of that desperate riddle and I'll cut out your tongue with a blunt knife! D'ye hear? Now. What do you want the Egg for? And no word of the riddle, mind.

SHAKING-HEAD: It's a bit of a long story.

AUBURN MARY: A long story is a teejous story! I flay the skins off lads that tell me teejous stories. Right?

SEAN RUADH: Right. Well, in short—you're fierce!—it started in Ireland with the Druid.

AUBURN MARY: Ireland, you say? In Ireland?

SHAKING-HEAD: The thing of it is, he's tryin' to save a Princess from the jaws of a whacking great *Urfeist* and—

SEAN RUADH: But saving Finola isn't my *Diachbha*. I'm really supposed to save my sister from a Giant, and to do that I have to—

AUBURN MARY: *(Her hand on her heart.)* A Giant…?

SEAN RUADH: —free the underwater land of *Tir-ta-fonn* and get it to stay above water—

AUBURN MARY: Stop. Now, stop! *Tir-ta-fonn,* did you say?

SEAN RUADH: I did. And—

SHAKING-HEAD: *Whisht!* Or she'll be cuttin' up your carcass for bog feed!

AUBURN MARY: My heart is in that land! There's only one way into the Bog that doesn't rattle at all at all. Stay close to me now and I'll take yez through. Ah, *Tir-ta-fonn!*

SHAKING-HEAD: Thank you kindly, that's dacent of you.

AUBURN MARY: Suck back your jabber, I'm talkin' to the lad now!
(She starts off and they follow as best they can.)

AUBURN MARY: Take ten steps right and ten steps left, then fifteen steps forward and thirteen steps sideways and four quick little leaps and here's your Tree in the Hole, and you're safe inside your skin. Just climb straight up over seven branches and at the top, only a wee ways out on the limb you'll find the nest and inside it the Wild Duck. Do you but lift her up—carefully, mind! She's an old duck—and there will be your wretched Egg of Fire.

SHAKING-HEAD: Thank you! Good-bye now! Come on.

SEAN RUADH: Just a minute. Wouldn't it be hard to hold in my hand, the Egg I mean, being as how it's made of fire.

AUBURN MARY: There's a thinking lad! It wouldn't! Not if you carried it in this Bag. Take care to wear only red to protect yez if you're goin' to be usin' the Egg.

SEAN RUADH: Red is my color.

AUBURN MARY: Is it now? Well climb if you're climbing. Take care you don't get bit by the Duck, now, she's a vicious temper on her. Go!

(The lights go to Finola and her Father by the water with the Shanachies. Trembling sits off by herself. She is gathering stones into a pile and staring intently out to sea.)

THE KING OF THE WESTERN WORLD: It's the waitin' tears the liver out of ye.

OUR SHANACHIE: Aye. It's like tryin' to sit down on the point of a knife.

PRINCESS FINOLA: He'll come back. Didn't he say he would?

THE KING OF THE WESTERN WORLD: He did. He's leavin' it to the last minute, sure.

(Lights change and Sean Ruadh and Shaking-Head are walking in the dark. A ragged white moon lights their way and a shadowy cemetery is faintly visible beyond them. A long, low, thin cry is heard: The Cry of the Banshee. Shaking-Head stops cold. He shivers.)

SEAN RUADH: It's only a poor sad creature cryin' in the night. Stay close to me, I'll protect yez.

SHAKING-HEAD: Now we've got the Egg and everything's—tell me how you came to meet me, Sean Ruadh. Tell me the story of it.

SEAN RUADH: Now? Why?

SHAKING-HEAD: To cam me down. Tell me and then you can go on.

SEAN RUADH: It's not a very long story.

SHAKING-HEAD: Sure, haven't we been told a long story is a teejous story.

SEAN RUADH: The Old Druid says what's the point of a short story. But all right, in short. I was sitting with The Old Druid himself one night, and he told me about my sister and the Giant and *Tir-ta-fonn* and my Destiny. Now, my father was sad to see me go but he knew it was time and he gave me five quid for my journey.

SHAKING-HEAD: Why five quid?

SEAN RUADH: That's what he gave all my brothers. So I set out and the first thing that happened was I met a Widow Woman crying on the road. She was a wreck entirely because she couldn't bury her husband, for the want of five quid. I gave her the fiver to bury her poor husband and—that's all. I met you right after that.

SHAKING-HEAD: It's a good story.

SEAN RUADH: I remember she said if they buried her husband he'd go to Paradise that very day.

SHAKING-HEAD: He didn't go.

SEAN RUADH: What're you talking about? How do you know?

SHAKING-HEAD: I'm the husband of that weeping woman. It was my dead body you did a service for, and my darlin' wife you saved from shame. So I came with you, to do you a good turn in my turn before I left this delicious World for good and all.

SEAN RUADH: You mean, you're—a ghost, like?

SHAKING-HEAD: I am what I am.

SEAN RUADH: Wait a minute, what's—why are you telling me now all of a sudden?

SHAKING-HEAD: Well, because here's where we have to part ways.

SEAN RUADH: No! Why? You can't go! What'll I do without you?

SHAKING-HEAD: You have your *Diachbha* and I have mine.

SEAN RUADH: I'll do anything to save you!

SHAKING-HEAD: You did save me, Sean Ruadh. And I saved you. So we're even.

SEAN RUADH: You were right about having Faith. You never let me down...I don't want to say good-bye to you.

SHAKING-HEAD: Ah, Sean. What human beings want is a matter of total indiffer in the Great World. You know that.

SEAN RUADH: I do. And it breaks my heart.

SHAKING-HEAD: Mine too.

(Sean Ruadh is overcome.)

SHAKING-HEAD: Here now, what's this?

SEAN RUADH: Me bladder's near me eye.

SHAKING-HEAD: Well. *Slaun latt, cara mo chroi.*

SEAN RUADH: What does that mean?

SHAKING-HEAD: It means: Good-bye, friend of my heart. *(Beat.)* Keep your head about you.

(They embrace and Shaking-Head walks into the graveyard. Above his head the Lonely Crane of Inish Kea flies over the face of the moon. Sean Ruadh watches his friend go and looks up to see his Spirit's guide. He stretches out his arm to the Bird.)

SEAN RUADH: Oh, Old Spirit! Now I'm lonely too.

(Lights go to the water's edge again. Suddenly on the far, far horizon is a shimmering vision.)

TREMBLING: Look!
   On the tip
   Of the edge
   Of the far, far horizon!

OUR SHANACHIE: Is it?
   Can it be?

TREMBLING: Seven long years since we saw you last!

THE KING OF IRELAND'S SON 239

ALL: *Tir-ta-fonn!*

TREMBLING: Visible for one short day.

OUR SHANACHIE: Unless it can be touched with fire before nightfall.

(Trembling has sticks that she's lit and she tries to throw them toward the misty Isle but they fall short. Everyone else is watching her and they don't see the Urfeist rising silently from the depths of the sea. Its filthy, scabrous tongue is about to wrap itself around Finola when Sean Ruadh dashes in, as if by catapult, dressed in his own color, red, and accompanied by the Bird.)

SEAN RUADH: Finola! Watch your back!

(She turns and just when it seems she will be consumed, a perfectly aimed stone thrown by Trembling hits the Urfeist. Finola draws her sword, and Sean joins her, carrying the blazing Sword of Light.)

SEAN RUADH AND PRINCESS FINOLA: Come to me, now

You murthering evildoer!

SEAN RUADH: I'll make ragged bloody shreds of you!

PRINCESS FINOLA: Snap your spine

SEAN RUADH: Slice your neck through

PRINCESS FINOLA: Carve out your teeth

SEAN RUADH: Spear your eyeballs

And let your eye juice gush into your mouth!

SEAN RUADH AND PRINCESS FINOLA: Come to me and

Taste my Sword!

(With a warrior cry, Sean puts all of his strength into a run at the Urfeist, slicing it down the middle. A huge cheer goes up. Quickly, Sean takes out the Egg of Fire.)

PRINCESS FINOLA: The Magical Egg of Fire!

(Sean Ruadh then performs one amazing arcing salmon leap to be spoken of for years to come. He flings the Egg into the fallen serpent and it bursts into flames, flames that consume every serpentine inch of the monster to the end of its spiky tail that just barely touches the shimmering land of Tir-ta-fonn on the far horizon. It swims brilliantly and solidly into focus: an above-ground place once more. The Lonely Crane flaps its mighty wings and flies off.)

THE KING OF THE WESTERN WORLD: Be glory, me darlin' daughter is saved from slaughter! You earned the name of Valor this day, young man. Who are you? Where do you come from?

TREMBLING: He's my brother, he must be, for he's set me free at last!

SEAN RUADH: You're my sister? You?

TREMBLING: I am.

SEAN RUADH: Wait, now. I did it? This was my Fate?

OUR SHANACHIE: That salmon leap would put Cuchulainn himself to shame!

SEAN RUADH: But I thought…I thought I was only helping Finola. Does it count? Can you fulfill your *Diachbha* even if you don't know you're doing it?

PRINCESS FINOLA: Everything counts!

(The air is rent into smithereens by a huge majesterially milky moo from the offstage cows. This is followed by the oceanic sound of their milk, flowing free into the Western World, the promise of cheese to come.)

OUR SHANACHIE: The cows are giving milk again! Cheese has returned to the Western World!

(Auburn Mary arrives with her usual definitiveness. She is no longer a hag. She wears a rich mantle and carries a small basket. She seems almost serene, as though a cloud has been lifted from her.)

AUBURN MARY: Lucky I am to have seen what I have seen here today! The like of that lad.

SEAN RUADH: Auburn Mary?

(She agrees with this assessment.)

SEAN RUADH: The Egg worked!

AUBURN MARY: Didn't I say it would, sure.

OUR SHANACHIE: Tell us the truth now at the end of all. Whose son are you, Sir?

PRINCESS FINOLA: *(With the blue boot in hand.)* Surely you, Red Warrior, are also my Black Prince and my Blue Champion and the man I must have for my own. Say you are.

SEAN RUADH: Well, I'm Sean Ruadh, and I'm the King of Ireland's son and I'll fight beside you any day in any color you like.

(With that the blue boot leaps out of Finola's hand and runs to Sean, and she after it.)

AUBURN MARY: Stop! Now, stop. You're the King of Ireland's son. You swear it?

SEAN RUADH: I am. I do.

AUBURN MARY: *(To Trembling.)* Then sure you must be the King of Ireland's divil of a daughter.

TREMBLING: I am.

AUBURN MARY: *(From her basket she takes a gold circlet and places it on Trembling's head.)* I walked all the wild roads of this World looking for you, my darling child!

SEAN RUADH AND TREMBLING: Mam! Mam!

(All three throw themselves into a huge embrace. The lights change and the two Shanachies step forward, alone.)

OUR SHANACHIE: And a great age of heroes came after that, with stories to nourish a whole nation of storytellers.

THE SECOND SHANACHIE: But there was none greater than the first, Sean Ruadh, the King of Ireland's Son.

OUR SHANACHIE: Indeed. And many ballads and songs carried his name far from the land of his birth, to mountainous places, and darkened rooms like this one.

THE SECOND SHANACHIE: The *Shanachies* say that the King of Ireland wept when he saw them coming: his lost wife and his headstrong daughter…

OUR SHANACHIE: …and his reckless youngest son. And the next day the Old Druid blessed the marriage of Sean Ruadh and Princess Finola.

THE SECOND SHANACHIE: Wasn't I there meself? But all I got for it was a bag of porridge and a pair of paper shoes!

OUR SHANACHIE: Weren't you the lucky one? All I got was a grain of rice and a cup of sour milk!

THE SECOND SHANACHIE: They say the wedding lasted nine days and…

OUR SHANACHIE: The last day was better than the first. And that's all I'm goin' to tell yez.

(They play and sing very, very softly.)

THE SHANACHIES: *(Singing.)* If it should fall unto my lot
That I should rise and you should not
Then I'll gently rise and softly call:
Good night, and joy be with you all…

THE END

THE TASTE OF SUNRISE: TUC'S STORY

by Suzan L. Zeder

Dedicated to
Billy Seago and the host of Deaf artists
who have graced this play
with their insight and support

ORIGINAL PRODUCTION

The Taste of Sunrise: Tuc's Story was originally produced by Seattle Children's Theatre on September 20, 1996. The American Sign Language translation was by Billy Seago. It was directed by Linda Hartzell. Deborah Lynn Frockt was the dramaturg. Renée Roub* and Anna Jo Gender* were the stage managers. The cast was:

Voice of Tuc/Ensemble . . . . John Abramson
Young Tuc . . . . Jay Bunnag
Ensemble . . . . Alissa Bural*
Ensemble . . . . Kymberli Colbourne
Youngest Tuc . . . . Nathan Elliott/Ashton Sanderson
Maizie . . . . Patricia Ferguson*
Nell . . . . Mary Kae Irvin
Emma . . . . Jane Ryan*
Adult Tuc . . . . Billy Seago*
Dr. Mann/Ensemble . . . . David Scully*
Jonas . . . . Paul Morgan Stetler*
Dr. Graham/Nurse . . . . Amy Thone*
Roscoe . . . . Brent Wiggins

Understudy . . . . Robert Barnett

* Members of Actors' Equity Association, the union for stage professionals

AUTHOR'S NOTE

There is a scene in my play, *Mother Hicks* in which Tuc, a Deaf Man, turns to Girl and signs:

> You look at me and only see the things I cannot do, things I cannot be; but I can taste the cool spring water and know what month it is. I can smell the difference between the smoke of hickory and apple wood. I can see the sharp sting of honey, and I can taste the sunrise.

The moment those words flew out of my fingertips onto the keyboard of my typewriter, I knew that someday Tuc would need a play of his own to tell us who he is and how he came to be. This is that play. It took me thirteen years to write it.

This is a play of two worlds, Deafness and Hearing. I inhabit only one of those worlds. This is a play of two languages: English and American Sign Language. I speak only one of those languages. It is therefore with profound gratitude that I thank all of the Deaf artists who have touched this play with their wisdom and their grace. They have let me borrow pieces of their lives, they have shared the depth of their thoughts, feelings, and memories. They have done me the inestimable honor of trusting me with both their anger and their hope. I have provided a time and place for this play and a host of characters drawn from careful research, but it is the Deaf actors, and teachers, and historians, and students from Seattle to Washington D.C., who have given Tuc his voice and his soul. This is your play, not mine!

If you decide to produce this play, it will not be because it is easy, inexpensive, or because it fits comfortably into a usual production structure. I encourage you to seek partnerships, co-productions, and relationships between Deaf and hearing artists to create something together that neither could do as well alone. If you decide to produce this play, it will be because it touches something within you that demands that you stretch yourself and your community beyond your usual resources, because these words need to be spoken, these signs need to be seen, because Tuc's life needs to be shared with others who only see what people cannot do and cannot be. My life has been profoundly changed by every production of this play that I have seen. I hope yours will be too.

CHARACTERS**

TUC: A Deaf man in his late teens or twenties***

JONAS TUCKER: Tuc's father, thirties.

EMMA FLYNN: Housekeeper for Jonas Tucker

NELL HICKS: Midwife, thirties

TOWNSPEOPLE:

>   CLOVIS P. EUDY
>
>   IZZY SUE RICKS
>
>   PATRONS OF THE SODA FOUNTAIN ONE AND TWO

DR. ALEXIS GRAHAM: Teacher at the Central Institute for the Deaf

DR. GRINDLY MANN: Superintendent, Central Institute for the Deaf

ROSCOE: Deaf boy at the School for the Deaf.

AUDIOLOGISTS ONE AND TWO

MAIZIE: A wild child of the '20s, sixteen years old.

STUDENTS AT THE DEAF SCHOOL

HUNTERS ONE AND TWO

NURSE AND DOCTOR: Illinois State Home

VOICES OF TUC, MAIZIE, AND ROSCOE****

** Cast size may be as small as eight, but must include actors who can sign for all speaking characters, and voice for all signing characters. Optimum cast size is nine to assist with interpreting.

*** Tuc will play himself at a variety of ages. In some productions one or more young actors have been used for Tuc as a child. In others, the adult Tuc has played himself at all ages.

**** Maizie and Roscoe's signed lines should be voiced by the same ensemble member consistently.

SETTING

Tuc's Farm, Township of Ware, Central Institute for the Deaf, Dug Hill, Illinois State Home

TIME

1917–1928

NOTE

The play takes place in the mind and memory of Tuc, a young Deaf man. The set consists of a large open raked space, surrounded by higher platforms to accommodate the various locations of the play and to allow the signers—who interpret the spoken words of hearing characters in sign language—the closest proximity to the action. It is my intention that all spoken words of all characters are also signed by other Ensemble Members and that all signed speeches are voiced.

On top of the highest platform is an abstract wooden structure that will indicate a tree in the subsequent action.

There is a cyclorama upon which to paint the colors of the sky.

The many locations of the play are suggested by minimal set pieces and a few props. These seem to appear out of the air with the same grace and ease Tuc displays as he tells his story in the visual, spatial language of sign. Time is memory, without literal boundaries as day folds into night and years pass in a single gesture.

ACT I

At rise: Pre-show music fades. Lights dim to black. A moment of silence. Lights up on Tuc. His hands and face are clearly visible. Nearby is Jonas in partial shadow. Tuc signs "Wind." The sound of wind is heard. Jonas looks at his own hands. Tuc signs "Water." The sound of flowing water is heard. Jonas moves his fingers tentatively. Tuc signs "Bird." The sound of birds are heard. Tuc moves his hands in a sweeping gesture like a bird soaring. Jonas copies the gesture, their hands almost touch...almost. Jonas follows his hands off-stage as Tuc reaches toward him. Tuc claps his hands together and there is the sound of thunder. Tuc signs out front as Ensemble Member voices.

TUC: **Long ago, I remember sound.***

(Tuc claps his hands again and there is another peal of thunder. Lights and sound create a fever dream. There is the echoing sound of a small child crying. Jonas rises and crosses upstage. Lights up on two chairs that indicate a small bed. Emma enters with a sheet. Jonas paces, holding a muslin bundle. This bundle will be treated as if it is a very small, very sick, child.)

TUC: **Fever burning in the night**
Lightning shatter
Thunder crack
Voices echo,
Echo
Echo
Deep inside my mind...

JONAS: He just keeps screaming and screaming!

EMMA: I've stoked the fire! Wrap him in another quilt.

(Jonas places the bundle, "Baby Tuc," in the bed as Emma covers him up.)

JONAS: It's hot as Hades in here!

EMMA: Doc Gunner said to burn the fever out.

(Nell Hicks enters and knocks.)

EMMA: That will be the doctor!

JONAS: Finally!

(Emma crosses to Nell and mimes opening a door. Nell enters the playing space.)

EMMA: Don't you see the red flag on the door? That means we got Scarlet Fever here.

---

*All lines written in this style should be signed by the character and spoken by an Ensemble member.

NELL: That's why I came.

EMMA: We've been waiting for Doc Gunner.

JONAS: Who is it, Emma?

EMMA: Are you a nurse?

NELL: Midwife, but I've seen my share of fever.

JONAS: Please, hurry!

EMMA: Mr. Tucker, I've never seen her before in my life.

JONAS: Emma, my boy is burning up. I ain't about to sit around and watch him die.

(Nell crosses to the bed.)

NELL: Bring me a basin of cool vinegar water.

(Jonas turns upstage slightly and fetches a basin.)

NELL: Put out the fire!

EMMA: What?

NELL: Get rid of these blankets and quilts… *(Nell pulls a small bottle out of her pocket.)* Dose him strong with Belladonna.

EMMA: Deadly nightshade?

NELL: It's for the fever!

JONAS: Here's the water!

EMMA: Doc Gunner said to starve a fever…

JONAS: He's going to be all right, isn't he?

(Nell looks at him with worry and throws the sheet to Emma.)

NELL: Dip this sheet in well water, and bring it back here wringing wet.

EMMA: But Doc Gunner said…

NELL: The boy's dying! Do as I say!

JONAS: Do as she says!

NELL: Hold on, hold on little one; we'll get you cooled down. *(Nell holds the baby, sits on the bed and sings.)*

TUC: **Fever burning.**
Lightning flash.
Thunder crack.
Inside body, smoke,
Voices echo into smoke.

EMMA: She's singing! Why in God's name is she singing?

(The song is a haunting, pure tone. Tuc's signing mirrors the cresting and gradual abatement of the fever. Fever lights change to cool tones.)

TUC: **Singing spell**
Children ride her voice away
Past the burning

Past the pain
Sound, cool as water
Sound of final grace
Sound beyond sound
Into silence, into...

NELL: Fever's broke.

JONAS: What do we do now?

NELL: Wait. Wait and pray.

(Nell exits as Jonas keeps vigil.)

TUC: **Jonas Tucker, father, mine.**
Mother died when I was born
Father always carry me
To the fields. To the town
People see and say
"There goes Jonas Tucker and his little Tuc."
Now, Father sits by my bed waiting
Watching
Waiting.

(Emma enters.)

EMMA: Mr. Tucker, is there anything you need before I go home?

JONAS: You go ahead, Emma. He's sleeping again.

EMMA: Your supper's keeping warm on the stove. *(Looking at the shape on the bed.)* Still hasn't made a sound?

JONAS: No.

(There is a low rumble of thunder.)

JONAS: I heard voices just now.

EMMA: *(Archly.)* That...woman was by to see about the boy. She left some bitterroot tea and ox blood soup to build his strength. I told her he was sleeping.

JONAS: I never got a chance to thank her properly. I didn't even get her name.

EMMA: The whole town's talking about her. Her name is Hicks, Nell Hicks. Some say she's from Jonesboro, others from Mound City. Some say she's got a husband on the riverboats, others say he's a snake oil salesman on the run.

JONAS: What does she say?

EMMA: Nothing. She don't say nothin' about nothin'. All anyone knows is she has rented a room above the pharmacy. She's looking for work, midwifing or nursing or whatever.

JONAS: All I know is she saved Tuc's life and I'm grateful.

EMMA: She nursed the Collins boy, sang to him, and he woke up blind. She also left this bundle of Devil's wort and purple sage for you to burn; she says it's to ease his breathing.

(There is another rumble.)

JONAS: You'd best get home to your family before the storm breaks.

EMMA: Mr. Tucker, I'd think twice before I'd burn that stuff near the boy.

JONAS: Thank you, Emma. I'll see to Tuc, before he wakes up frightened by the thunder.

(There is another rumble. Jonas crosses to the bed. Emma exits.)

JONAS: It's all right, son. I'm here. You're all right. You're...

(As the thunder rolls again, Jonas stops short and looks at the bed.)

JONAS: ...sleeping. *(Jonas claps over the bed. He leans down and claps.)* Tuc? Can you hear that, son? Tuc! Come on Tuc! TUC!!!!!

TUC: **Father shouting long ago**
I hear his voice in memory.

(Tuc snaps the sheet on the bed open and tosses it high in the air.)

TUC: **Years pass since the fever night.**

(During the following speech, Tuc becomes himself as a young boy.)

TUC: **Ten years pass.**
I am a boy with legs to run and arms to hold
and eyes to see
and ears...to keep my hat from falling down!

(Jonas and Tuc wrestle and play. Emma enters.)

EMMA: Jonas Tucker, that boy is getting too big for you to tote him around on your back like a baby possum!

JONAS: Emma, the menfolk are going on a honey hunt!

(Jonas picks up a pail as he and Tuc stalk across the stage in search of bees. The sound of buzzing is heard. Tuc points.)

JONAS: You got the eyes of an eagle, son. Now follow the bee line straight to the...

(The wooden structure on the upper platform becomes the "honey tree." Jonas and Tuc cross to it carefully. Jonas teaches Tuc how to harvest the honey. Tuc reaches into the hive and brings his hands slowly up in the air holding an imaginary honey comb.)

JONAS: Feel 'em on your hands. They'll tell you if they're angry. *(With a bit of awe.)* Can't hear that buzzin' to scare you none. You're a natural born bee man, son.

(Tuc makes a gesture of thanks to the bees.)

JONAS: That's right, thank the bees! Let's go home.

(Jonas and Tuc cross to a chair.)

TUC: **In father's chair, we sit together.**

Many jokes and stories he tells to me.

His body talks to my body.

(*Jonas mimes telling a story to the child in his lap.*)

TUC: **Father talk has no need for words.**

Talk how? Breath.

Talk how? Heartbeats.

Talk how? Mind thoughts.

Words too small for everything we say.

(*Lights change, as Nell enters carrying a muslin bundle and a basket of yellow flowers.*)

NELL: That's Arnica Montana for sprains and bruises, and Chamomile blossoms for sleep.

(*Jonas and Tuc cross down to Nell.*)

JONAS: Good day to you, Nell Hicks.

(*Two sharp shafts of light come up on Izzy and Emma on the platforms directly above.*)

IZZY: I saw her in town, big as life, and I said, "Why Nell Hicks, you've been away…

JONAS: (*To Nell, overlapping.*) You've been away.

IZZY: And she said…

NELL: (*To Jonas.*) I have.

JONAS: What brings you out our way today?

NELL: We're gathering a basket full of sunshine.

JONAS: We?

IZZY: And I swear she had a baby with her.

EMMA: A baby?

NELL: (*Indicating the bundle.*) This is May -ry.

JONAS: Mary?

NELL: It's not Mary and it's not Marie, it's May -ry.

(*Tuc looks at the basket.*)

EMMA: What baby?

IZZY: Some say it's a foster child she's raising. Some say it's her own.

EMMA: What does she say?

IZZY: Nothin' about nothin'

EMMA: Now, don't that beat all!

JONAS: She sure is a beautiful child.

NELL: That she is, Mr. Tucker.

IZZY: (*Overlap with Nell.*) I rented her my guest house at the south end of town.

NELL: *(Overlap with Izzy.)* I rented the Ricks house at the south end of town.

EMMA: You rented her a house?

JONAS: You rented a house from Izzy?

IZZY: A house is a house, Emma.

NELL: A house is a house.

(Lights out on Izzy and Emma.)

JONAS: Midwife business must be booming.

NELL: There's always babies and those who need nursing.

(Tuc dips his finger in the honey and offers it to May -ry.)

JONAS: Tuc!

NELL: She's a little young for honey, Tuc, but I could use some for a honey cake.

JONAS: We're taking this for barter at the store, but we got plenty to share.

NELL: Much obliged, Mr. Tucker. Much obliged, Tuc.

(Tuc repeats the gesture of thanking the bees.)

JONAS: Don't thank us, thank the bees.

NELL: Much obliged, bees.

(Nell repeats the gesture and exits as Jonas and Tuc continue on the path to town.)

TUC: **From Father's shoulders**
I see as far as I can see.
Everyone in town
Looks small to me.

(As Jonas and Tuc make a wide circle around the playing area, townspeople stand on the upper platforms and wave as they go by.)

JONAS: Morning, Miz. Ward.

ALMA: That poor unfortunate boy.

JONAS: Hello, Mr. Eudy.

CLOVIS: Deaf as a fireplug.

JONAS: Howdy, Miz Ricks.

IZZY: Dumb as a post.

EMMA: It's not kind to stare at him, just because he's afflicted. *(Emma crosses down to join Jonas and Tuc.)*

JONAS: Tuc and I'll get the fertilizer at the Feed and Grain, while you do the shopping at the General Store.

EMMA: Let me take Tuc with me, Mr. Tucker.

JONAS: Why?

EMMA: Show your father, Tuc.

TUC: *(Struggles to speak in a very distorted voice.)* Ice cream cone.

JONAS: *(Very surprised.)* Ice cream cone?

EMMA: We've been practicing at home, haven't we, Tuc? Clovis P. Eudy has just put in a brand new soda fountain and I thought Tuc and I might…

TUC: Ice cream cone!

JONAS: I don't like Tuc going places without me.

EMMA: Then come with us.

TUC: Ice cream cone.

JONAS: I got a whole field of winter rye won't wait for ice cream.

EMMA: It's a soda fountain, Mr. Tucker. The whole town's talking bout it.

TUC: Ice cream cone! Ice cream cone!

JONAS: All right, all right! I see I'm out numbered. Go on, but take care of him, Emma.

EMMA: Well, of course!

(Jonas exits as Emma and Tuc cross downstage. Clovis sets up the soda fountain by placing a board between two chairs. Two patrons sit sipping sodas.)

EMMA: Clovis, I believe you know Jonas Tucker; this is his son, Tuc.

CLOVIS: *(In a loud voice.)* Why, Tuc, I haven't seen you in a long time! *(To Emma.)* He doesn't look deaf.

EMMA: Clovis, you give Tuc anything he wants from the fountain, while I finish the rest of my shopping.

(Emma turns away. Patron two rises and shouts at Tuc.)

PATRON TWO: YOU CAN HAVE MY SEAT. *(Patron two points and gestures.)* SEAT, MINE, YOU HAVE! DONE, FINISHED, ALL EATEN UP…I AM. OKAY? *(To Clovis.)* I'm not sure how much of this he's getting.

CLOVIS: *(To Patron.)* I'm not sure how much of that *I'm* getting. *(To Tuc.)* Have a seat. What will you have?

TUC: *(Very distorted speech.)* Ice cream cone.

CLOVIS: What did you say? Say it again.

TUC: Ice cream cone.

PATRON ONE: Why Clovis, I heard him plain as day; he said "Root beer float."

PATRON TWO: That's not it, he said "Hot fudge…Hot fudge sundae"…

PATRON ONE: *(Shouting.)* Have some root beer!

PATRON TWO: Try a bite of this. It's great!

TUC: Ice cream. Ice cream! Ice cream!

(Patrons offer Tuc tastes of their treats but the overall effect is terrifying. Emma enters with a parcel Tuc runs out of the scene.)

EMMA: Tuc, I'm sorry, I am so sorry!

(Tuc runs to the forest. There is the sound of water running, birds singing, wind rustling in the trees.)

TUC: **Here in forest, here in trees**
   Everything I know speaks to me.
   Wind rustle in leaves, I see.
   Water splash, birds fly.
   Sunset colors sing.
   In town, all they see is deaf.
   Here, I am only me.
   (Jonas enters and sits next to him. They point to the stars.)
TUC: **Stars come, one by one.**
   Father talk, has no need of words.
   (Lights change. There is the sound of honking. Dr. Graham enters, wearing a cap and goggles. She sits in a chair. Tuc creates the car around her in sign language, as Dr. Graham mimes the action.)
TUC: **Clouds of dust**
   Rattle down the road.
   Shining headlights,
   Gleaming fenders,
   Wheels, turning
   Faster, faster.
   Honk, honk,
   Rattle, bump, rattle, bump
   Psheeeeeewwwwwww!
   (Emma enters.)
EMMA: Mr. Tucker, another one of them Model T's has blown up near your driveway!
   (Emma exits. Jonas and Tuc cross to the car.)
GRAHAM: This blasted machine overheats every time I get her over fifteen miles per hour.
JONAS: Need some help?
GRAHAM: Just some water, thanks.
JONAS: Tuc will fix you up in a jiffy.
   (Jonas gestures to Tuc, who exits the playing area, and crosses upstage.)
GRAHAM: These Lizzies are pretty temperamental.
JONAS: The boy has seen an overheated car before. Come up to the porch and sit a spell.
   (They cross to a seating area on a porch.)
GRAHAM: I'm looking for the Tucker farm.
JONAS: You found it.
GRAHAM: I'm Doctor Alexis Graham. *(She hands him a card.)*

JONAS: Doctor?

GRAHAM: I'm an otologist but I'm also a teacher at the Central Institute for the Deaf and I understand that you have a very bright boy here.

JONAS: How did you hear about my son?

GRAHAM: From the county Medical authority. Scarlet fever cut quite a path through this county about seven years ago.

JONAS: Tuc and I had our fill of Doctors. He's had every test you can think of. Every Doctor's got some new cure, but they all come out just the same.

GRAHAM: I'm not here about tests or cures; I'm here to talk about a school.

JONAS: I tried sending him to school in town, the other kids whispered behind his back and the teacher shouted at him all the time.

GRAHAM: A school for the Deaf.

JONAS: I've seen the Deaf School in Jacksonville! Too big, too far away.

GRAHAM: Ours is a new school, much smaller than the State School in Jacksonville. It's a private, residential research facility, totally committed to oral communication. *(She hands him a brochure.)*

GRAHAM: How does your son presently make his needs known to you?

JONAS: He points and gestures, but mostly, I just know.

GRAHAM: What if he could talk to you?

JONAS: Talk?

GRAHAM: We can teach Tuc to speak and to read lips. Oral speech is the sole power to rekindle the light of intelligence.

JONAS: Tuc's intelligent. He knows the land. He can feel the ground and understand the soil. He can look at the sky and tell tomorrow's weather. He can touch a leaf and know the whole life of the plant. He's got the gift. He'll be twice the farmer I am.

GRAHAM: That's exactly why he needs training! Your son communicates by instinct and mimicry, but without training his intelligence is locked in a tiny room, without concepts, without ideas, without ways of sharing thoughts and feelings. Language is the key to unlocking that room.

JONAS: He could speak to me?

GRAHAM: Think of it, Mr. Tucker. Think of being able to say everything you ever wanted to tell him. Think of his being able to tell you his hopes, his fears, his dreams.

JONAS: *(In awe.)* You can do that?

GRAHAM: If you send us a quick curious lad, we will send you back a boy who can speak and understand those who speak to him.

(Tuc returns to the "car" and honks. Jonas and Graham rise and cross back to the car.)

JONAS: He'd have to go away wouldn't he?

GRAHAM: For a while.

JONAS: He's never been off the land. *(Beat.)* I don't know what I'd do without him.

(Tuc hands Graham a glass of water.)

GRAHAM: *(Enunciating very clearly.)* Oh, No, Tuc. The water was supposed to be for my automobile.

(Tuc gestures.)

JONAS: This is for you. He's finished with the car.

GRAHAM: Oh, well…I see.

JONAS: I told you he was intelligent.

GRAHAM: Thank you, Tuc. Thank you, very much!

JONAS: You say, he could talk to me?

(Tuc moves away, sits in the car, and pretends to drive.)

GRAHAM: Yes, and understand what you say to him. What would you think of that?

JONAS: I'd think it was a miracle.

GRAHAM: Think about it, Mr. Tucker. Good-bye, Tuc.

(Tuc cranks the engine. The sound of Model T starting up is heard. Both Tuc and Jonas wave. Lights out on Graham.)

TUC: **Car starts,**

Drives away.

Leaves behind

Dust and doubt.

(Emma enters with a small suitcase.)

TUC **I've had ten years of summer and winter,**

Ten years, planting and harvesting

Ten years, walking and sleeping.

My life, so small

It fits inside a suitcase.

EMMA: Now, you be a good boy and practice the words I taught you.

(She hugs him. Nell enters holding her baby. She gives a small parcel to Jonas.)

NELL: We came to say good-bye, and to bring you some fresh honey cake for your journey.

JONAS: That's very kind of you. Thank Miz. Hicks.

NELL: Don't thank us, thank the bees.

(Nell crosses to Emma. Jonas kneels beside his son. He scoops up a handful of soil.)

JONAS: This is your land, son. It's where you're from. It's where you'll come back to. *(Jonas pats Tuc's pockets.)* Fill your pockets with it. Fill 'em up, so you can carry it with you. *(He looks at him deeply.)* You can't understand one word I'm saying can you? But you will! They promised me, you will. *(He touches the boy's pockets.)* Home, always here.

(A train whistle blasts. The scene swirls around and changes to Central Institute for the Deaf. Dr. Grindly Mann enters. Roscoe stands nearby.)

MANN: Mr. Tucker, I am Dr. Grindly Mann, Superintendent of the Central Institute for the Deaf, and you must be Tuc. We've been expecting you.

JONAS: I'm sorry we're late but Tuc wanted to ride the streetcar to the end of the line and back. He's never seen a streetcar before.

MANN: *(To Tuc.)* Did you enjoy the streetcar?

(Tuc looks to Jonas who gestures pulling the bell of the streetcar. Tuc nods.)

MANN: After he's been here a while, your son will be able to read my lips and answer that question. *(Mann offers his hand.)* I'm very pleased to meet you, Tuc.

(Tuc turns back to Jonas and rubs his hand over his head and points to Mann's bald head. If the actor is not bald use any exaggerated physical characteristic such as glasses, weight, height, mustache, etc. Both men understand this gesture but pretend they don't.)

JONAS: He's pleased to meet you as well.

MANN: Tuc, this is Roscoe. Roscoe this is Tuc. *(To Jonas.)* We always try to match a younger boy with an older one; it helps the young ones settle in.

(Roscoe comes forward. Tuc shies away, hiding behind Jonas.)

JONAS: *(To Tuc.)* That's Roscoe, he's going to be your friend. *(To Mann.)* He's never had a friend before…other than me, that is.

MANN: Mr. Tucker, there are a few papers to sign before you go. Please sit down.

(Jonas nudges Tuc toward Roscoe.)

MANN: This paper authorizes the medical personnel of this institution to examine your son and to remove his tonsils and adenoids if necessary. Please sign here.

(While Jonas and Mann are talking, Roscoe points to his ears and makes a questioning expression asking Tuc if he can hear. Tuc shakes his head, "No." Roscoe points to his own ears and then shakes his head, "NO." Tuc points to his ears and to Roscoe again as if to ask, "Are you sure you can't hear?" Roscoe answers in gesture with great drama and animation.)

MANN: *(To Tuc.)* Roscoe will take your suitcase to the dormitory so we can get started on the auditory testing.

(Roscoe turns away to pick up the suitcase and Tuc claps his hands near Roscoe's ears…just testing. Roscoe exits.)

MANN: I'll give you some privacy to say your good-byes. Most parents find it best if it's done quickly.

(Mann steps aside. Jonas kneels down to Tuc.)

JONAS: I gotta go home now…I'm going to miss you, son. I don't know how to tell you that. *(Jonas pats the boy's pockets tenderly.)* Home, always…here. *(Tuc traces the pattern of a tear on his father's cheek. Jonas turns away suddenly and starts to exit. Tuc holds onto his arm.)*

JONAS: I gotta go, Son. I gotta go.

(Jonas struggles to free himself from Tuc. Mann crosses to help Jonas.)

MANN: No, Tuc you're staying here.

JONAS: I'm sorry.

MANN: This is the hardest part, Tuc, the hardest part. Soon it will be better. I promise you.

(Jonas pulls away and exits. Tuc reaches after him. Mann crosses downstage. Audiologists One and Two enter. Graham crosses down from the opposite side.)

MANN: Come along and we'll examine your ears and test your hearing.

(Audiologists mime conducting their tests. As they all speak at once, signer interprets gibberish.)

GRAHAM:	AUDIOLOGIST ONE:	AUDIOLOGIST TWO:
Outer Ear		
Tragus		
Ear Canal	Just a little squirt in	
Tympanic Membrane	each ear	
Eustachian Tubes	This will be a little	
Ossicles	warm.	Just a little jolt of
Incus	This will be a little	electricity
Stapes	cold.	behind the right ear
Cochlea		and behind the
Inner ear		left ear.

(All three ring tuning forks near Tuc's ears.)

GRAHAM: Raise your hand when you hear the tone.

AUDIOLOGIST ONE: Raise your hand when you hear the tone.

AUDIOLOGIST TWO: Raise your hand when you hear the tone.

MANN: Diagnosis: Profoundly deaf. No residual hearing whatsoever.

(Mann, Graham, and Audiologists exit leaving Tuc facing full front, totally bewildered. Maizie enters the playing area. She carries a mop, a pail, and a feather duster. She trips and drops everything. Tuc, unaware of her presence, does not move.)

MAIZIE: I'm sorry! I didn't know anyone was here.

(Maizie walks up behind Tuc and plucks a feather from her duster. Maizie releases a single feather, which drifts slowly down in front of Tuc. Tuc watches it fall and lifts one finger on his right hand to catch it. Maizie lets another single feather fall. Tuc watches this one as well and catches it with one finger of his left hand. Maizie lets a third feather fall. Tuc is momentarily hesitant, then sticks out his tongue and catches the third feather. Maizie crosses to face him.)

MAIZIE: You're new? Just arrived? Can you read my lips?

(She blubbers her lips. He smiles.)

MAIZIE: That's it, give Maizie a smile. You're gorgeous, you are. *(Maizie looks around to be sure no one is coming. She signs, Ensemble Member voices.)*

MAIZIE: **Do you sign? Do you know sign language?**

(He does not understand her signs. Tuc points to his ears and then to Maizie, questioning.)

MAIZIE: **Me, deaf? Yes and no. Mother-Father Deaf. I came here with my Momma who'll be cookin your dinner and my Daddy who mows the lawns. I hear and I speak, but deep inside I'm deaf.**

(Dr. Graham enters. Maizie stops signing immediately.)

GRAHAM: It's almost time for lunch; your mother needs you in the kitchen. Run along, Maizie.

MAIZIE: Yes, Ma'am.

(Maizie ruffles Tuc's hair and exits but not before giving Tuc a thumbs-up. A bell rings. Students in the deaf school enter. They set up the chairs in a neat row indicating a classroom.)

GRAHAM: Today, we welcome a new student: Jonas Tucker, Junior. I ask you all to welcome Tuc to our school.

(Led by Graham, the entire group repeats this greeting in a toneless, singsong rhythm.)

ALL: Welcome, Tuc, to our school.

GRAHAM: Tuc, that will be your seat, over there.

(Tuc walks down the row as all eyes follow him.)

GRAHAM: Now, all together…Ahhhhhhh!

(At the signal, students open their mouths and put their heads back. Graham crosses to each one and puts the stick in their mouth to touch their windpipes.)

STUDENTS: AHHHHHHHHH!

GRAHAM: Open wide to feel the vibration of the windpipe!

(When she gets to Tuc he spits the stick high into the air.)

GRAHAM: Ahem! And now, the vowels!

(Students face forward as if looking into a mirror.)

GRAHAM: AAAAAAA, EEEEEEEEEE, IIIIIIII, OOOOOOOOO, UUUUU!
> (In a somewhat exaggerated manner, Graham stresses facial expressions to indicate proper placement of lips, tongue, teeth, and jaw. Class repeats in a toneless drone.)

STUDENTS: AAAAAAA, EEEEEEEEEE, IIIIIIIIIII, OOOOOOOOO, UUUU
> (Graham moves down the aisle correcting and checking each student. Tuc is making faces and cracking up the other students.)

GRAHAM: (Directly to Tuc.) AAAAAAAAA, EEEEEEEEEEEE, IIIIIIIIII, OOOOOOOOOOOO, UUUUUU!
> (Graham gives him a harsh look. He smiles angelically.)

GRAHAM: And now the plosives! (Graham produces a large red feather and demonstrates making the feather move with the force of the plosive.) PAH, PAH, PAH, BAH, BAH, BAH, TAH, TAH, DAH, DAH, DAH!, (She goes back down the line until she gets to Tuc. Directly to Tuc.) PAH, PAH, PAH, BAH, BAH, BAH, TAH, TAH, DAH!
> (He folds his arms and glares at her.)

GRAHAM: Try to move the feather, Tuc…Move the feather. Come on Tuc, try, at least try!

CLASS AND GRAHAM:	TUC:
PAAAAAAA	**Over and Over**
BAAAAAAA	**Again and again**
TAAAAAAA	**Day after Day**
DAAAAAAA	**Again and Again**

> (A bell rings loudly; lights flash and change. The students briskly turn their chairs around so the backs look like headboards.)

GRAHAM: Light's out! Everyone to sleep!
> (Students pretend to sleep.)

TUC: **Light's out**
> **World disappears**
> **Smell of earth and sky, not here**
> **No grass, no leaves, no smell of rain…**
> **Lights ON!**
> (The room erupts in pandemonium of sign language.)

TUC: **Hands come alive.**
> **Fingers fly.**
> **Arms spin like windmills.**
> **Hands, hands everywhere.**
> **Weaving pictures in the air.**

(During this speech, Roscoe tells the following story entirely in sign language. This scene is not voiced.)

ROSCOE: *(Not voiced.)* Hearing father and son deaf go to the forest to cut down trees.

Hearing Father takes an ax. Chops, chops, chops.

Yells "Timber." Tree falls.

Deaf son takes ax. Chops, chops, chops. Tree does not fall. Hearing father says "Yell Timber."

Deaf son says, "I can't yell timber, I'm deaf!"

Deaf son says, "Maybe tree is deaf."

(Finger spells T. I. M. B. E. R.)

TREE FALLS.

(Students laugh. Tuc turns away.)

ROSCOE: *(To Tuc.)* What is wrong?

(Tuc has no idea what the signs mean and turns away.)

ROSCOE: *(Not voiced.)* What is wrong?

Are you sad? No.

Are you happy? No.

Are you scared? No.

Are you angry?

(Tuc turns away, irritated.)

ROSCOE: YES! *(Roscoe signs the sign for "ANGRY," stamps around, and shows Tuc the sign for anger.)* You are seething,

mad,

furious,

blow your top!

(Tuc begins to copy, connecting meaning to sign.)

ROSCOE: Are you sad?

TUC: *(Copying the sign.)* Sad. Yes, sad.

ROSCOE: Are you scared?

TUC: Scared.

ROSCOE: Are you angry?

TUC: Angry!

BOTH: Seething,

Mad,

Furious,

BLOW MY TOP!

(Students pick up the sign and "blow their tops.")

TUC: *(Voiced.)* **Feeling has name,**

Has shape. Has sign.

I am angry, sad, scared, happy!

Sign, sign, sign, sign!

I see, I sign, I know

Before no deaf I ever see

Whole world hears, I think,

But me.

(Roscoe teaches Tuc to finger spell his own name and gives him a name sign.)

ROSCOE: *(Voiced.)* Your name is Tuc. T.U.C.

Name sign…Tuc.

(Tuc solemnly repeats the name sign.)

TUC: **After this night**

Nothing ever same.

This night I learn

I have a name.

(Tuc and students exchange name signs. This part of the scene is not voiced. Maizie enters playing space wearing a black headband and clutching a movie magazine.)

MAIZIE: Oh, no! Oh, no! Oh, no! Oh, woe!

(Maizie wails and kisses the magazine. Dr. Graham enters.)

GRAHAM: Maizie? What's the matter?

MAIZIE: Oh, Dr. Graham. It's just too sad. Too sad for words.

GRAHAM: You'll be too sad for words if Dr. Mann catches you with a movie magazine again.

MAIZIE: Dr. Graham! I am in mourning!

GRAHAM: I'm sorry. Who died?

MAIZIE: Why, Rudolph Valentino, of course!

GRAHAM: You are in mourning for a movie star?

MAIZIE: The Orpheum is having a special matinee of *The Sheik,* today at 2:00 and I promised the kids I'd take them…out of respect for the dead.

GRAHAM: I'm sorry, Maizie, that won't be possible.

MAIZIE: Why not? The picture show is great for Deaf kids, I mean they don't need to hear or nothing, because the words is written up there on the screen; and it's educational…it's all about Arabia or someplace. I made my boyfriend sit through *The Sheik* fourteen times last month. The kids will love it.

GRAHAM: Dr. McRee called to say he could take your mother and father this afternoon at 2:00.

MAIZIE: Oh, no! Not the dentist!

GRAHAM: Come on, Maizie, he's the only dentist in St. Louis who will take deaf patients.

MAIZIE: Last time I got in so much trouble. My mother had to have a tooth pulled and I told him the wrong tooth…twice.

GRAHAM: They're depending on you.

MAIZIE: My mother thinks he's out to kill her, one tooth at a time!

GRAHAM: Be a good girl, Maizie. *(Graham exits.)*

MAIZIE: I'm always a good girl! I'm so good it hurts!

(Maizie signs. Ensemble Member voices.)

MAIZIE: **That's a real flat tire, ain't it?**
Sorry, kiddo, no go to the picture show.
(Students crowd around.)

MAIZIE: Hey, hey, hey. Sorry. No. We can't go. No.

(They pull at Maizie's dress and beg her. Roscoe taps her on the shoulder, but cannot get her attention. The kids continue to clamor. Finally, Roscoe stamps on the floor, and everyone looks at him. Ensemble Members voice as Maizie and Roscoe sign and act out the following scene.)

ROSCOE: **We do movie here.**

MAIZIE: **You seen it?**

ROSCOE: **Six times!**

MAIZIE: **BUT we need all of Arabia!**

ROSCOE: *(Indicating the other kids.)* **They can be Arabia!**

MAIZIE: **Great! Maybe we can do it here!**

(She pulls a dust rag out of her cleaning supplies and using one of her black garters snaps it on Roscoe's head as the Sheik's headdress. Old Time Movie Music.)

MAIZIE: **"IN THIS WORLD OF PEACE AND FLAME, LIES A PALM GARDEN. A BLESSED OASIS OF THE SANDS."** *(Maizie dances around a little and presents Roscoe.)* **"The Great Sheik Ahmed, like a page from the Arabian Nights!"** *(Dramatic voice.)* **"Lady Diana, orphan daughter of an English Poet,"** *(In her own voice.)* **So the next day, she rides into the desert…and he…**

(She gallops around as she and Roscoe act out the capture.)

MAIZIE: **Captures her and takes her to his oasis in the sand.** *(As Diana.)* **"Why have you brought me here?"**

ROSCOE: **"Are you not woman enough to know?"**

MAIZIE: *(As Diana.)* **"You cannot keep me here."** *(In her own voice.)* **So she runs away into a sandstorm. Whoosh, whoosh, whoosh! And he rescues her!**

(Maizie and Roscoe act out the rescue. As the rest of the kids get into the act as the sandstorm.)

ROSCOE: **"You are so pretty, if I choose I can make you love me!"**

MAIZIE: *(As Diana.)* **"I would rather you had killed me!"** *(In her own voice.)* **Anyway…she loves him, she hates him. She loves him. She hates him. So she tries to run away again.** *(Maizie acts out running away.)* **But this time, she is captured by OMIA THE BANDIT!**

(Maizie indicates Tuc who enters the fray.)

MAIZIE: *(As Diana.)* **"Help! Help! Help! Ahmed, where are you?"**

(Pandemonium breaks loose. Mann enters into the melee and stamps for order to no avail. Finally, he flashes the lights.)

MANN: Stop it! Stop it! Stop it at once!

(The melee ends as quickly as it began. All signing stops.)

MANN: MAIZIE, what is going on here?

MAIZIE: Cleaning?

(Roscoe and Tuc whip the rags off their heads and scrub the floor.)

MANN: You know the school policy regarding the use of manual expression. Any staff member caught conversing with students in sign language will be dismissed.

MAIZIE: Yes, sir. I know, sir.

(Students obediently line up in a single line and hold out their hands.)

MANN: There is to be no sign language in public, in private, in the classroom, in the dormitory!

(Mann marches briskly down the line and snaps a ruler down smartly on their hands. Tuc puts out his hands and awaits the blow.)

MANN: You must understand, Tuc. Sign language is the enemy of speech! We cannot permit you to sign or it will ruin your speech forever.

(Mann does not punish Tuc. The last one in line is Roscoe. Mann and Roscoe lock eyes in defiance.)

MANN: Roscoe, will you never learn?

(Mann lifts the ruler and brings it down, just as Roscoe moves his hands away. Roscoe signs rudely right in front of Mann.)

MANN: One hour detention.

(Roscoe's hands are tied tightly in front of his chest. Tuc signs encouragement. Mann turns just in time to catch him.)

TUC: **You tie our hands,**
Tie our minds, never!

MANN: Mr. Tucker, that's one hour for you as well. Sit on your hands! As for the rest of you, since you have such an abundance of energy, I suggest three laps around the playing field.

(*Students exit briskly. Mann starts to exit.*)

MAIZIE: Dr. Mann, I gotta take my parents to the dentist this afternoon and since I gotta leave early…I was wondering if I could have a little help with all this…cleaning? (*Maizie looks at the boys.*)

MANN: Very well, Maizie, but just this once.

(*Mann exits. Maizie unties Roscoe's hands. Maizie signs to the boys. Ensemble Member voices.*)

MAIZIE: **Scram, before I actually make you do some work!**

(*Roscoe exits. Tuc hangs back pretending to dust.*)

MAIZIE: **Thank you, Omir.**

(*They clean for a moment together.*)

MAIZIE: **I ain't always gonna be here running errands for my parents, and taking orders from old pickle face. My boyfriend and me, we're gonna get married and he's gonna take me to Chicago and I'm gonna work in a palace, a movie palace. You ever seen a movie palace?**

TUC: **No.**

MAIZIE: **My boyfriend took me for my birthday, to the Fox right here in St. Louis. Outside, it's got about a million lights, so you feel like a movie star just goin' in. It's got these big doors made of solid gold and a huge staircase, like the kind queens come down. Inside the theater there's this painting on the ceiling. I swear that's what heaven looks like. Your whole stupid little life disappears when you sit there, it just blows away like fuzz off a dandelion; and there you are, your shiny self, clean and new. When they turn out the lights, you look up and see a heaven full of stars twinkling like they was alive. They made me sad, them stars, I don't know why.**

TUC: **Stars make me sad, too.**

MAIZIE: **Why?**

TUC: **They're not the same stars I see at home with my father.**

MAIZIE: **But they are; they're the very same stars.**

TUC: **Don't look the same.**

MAIZIE: **That's because there's only one pair of eyeballs lookin' at them. When you see them stars, you gotta put your Daddy right there next to you.**

TUC: **How?**

MAIZIE: **When I was kid, I'd play this game where I'd sneak all over town** and peek in people's windows and then I'd imagine my whole self inside the family I liked best.

TUC: **Imagine?**

MAIZIE: **See it in your mind live and true. So now, when you see them stars, think about your Daddy real hard and he'll be there.**

TUC: **You promise?**

MAIZIE: **I promise.**

(They "pinkie-swear." Lights change. Maizie exits. Tuc comes forward.)

TUC: **At School I dream of home.**

Christmas come, too much snow.

Stay at school.

Easter come, too much rain.

Stay at School.

Summer come, too much nothing

GO HOME!

(Jonas and Emma enter.)

JONAS: There's that city boy!

EMMA: Land, how big you've grown!

JONAS: Emma, bring my boy a chair We're gonna have ourselves a talk!

(Emma brings a chair. Tuc and Jonas sit opposite each other and grin.)

JONAS: I missed you son I really did

(Tuc nods and smiles.)

JONAS: Do you understand me?

(Tuc shrugs. Jonas plunges on in his excitement.)

JONAS: I don't know what to tell you first…

(Tuc continues to smile at him and struggles to read his lips.)

JONAS: Well uhhh…The forty acres up on Dug Hill you know, Dug Hill…DUG HILL…that's some of the best land we got. I thought we might plant it this summer with…

(Tuc is totally confused by this and shakes his head. He waves his hands to get Jonas' attention.)

JONAS: Oh. too fast…sorry. I'll slow down *(Jonas speaks very slowly, over-compensating.)* I uhhh, missed you son I really did

(There is an awkward pause. Tuc eagerly signs to Jonas.)

TUC: *(Voiced.)* **I tell you a joke, Father.**

JONAS: *(Over-enunciating.)* Can you understand me, son?

TUC: **It's a good one. My friend, Roscoe, tell me. I tell you!**

(Emma notices Tuc signing.)

EMMA: Look what's he doing, Mr. Tucker.

TUC: **Hearing father**
     and son, deaf
     go to the forest to cut down trees.

JONAS: Read my lips, Tuc…Read my lips

TUC: *(Voiced.)* **Hearing Father takes ax**
     Chops, chops, chops
     Yells, "TIMBER"
     Tree falls.

EMMA: You're not supposed to let him do that.

TUC: **Deaf son takes ax.**

JONAS: Do what?

TUC: **Chops, chops, chops;**
     Tree doesn't fall.

EMMA: *(Overlapping with Tuc.)* That fingering around. Dr. Graham said if we let him do that it will ruin his speech.

JONAS: Look at me, son…

TUC: **Look at me, Father…**
     Hearing Father says
     "Yell timber."

JONAS: I think he's trying to tell me something.

TUC: **I can't yell "timber" I'm deaf…**

EMMA: Tell him to use his words *(To Tuc.)* USE YOUR WORDS, Tuc.

TUC: **Deaf son says,**
     Maybe tree is deaf…

JONAS: *(Overlapping.)* Use your words, son.

TUC: **Look at me, Father**
     This is sign…
     Sign is talking. You and me, together
     Sign is UNDERSTANDING.

JONAS: Read my lips, Tuc. Use your words.

TUC: **I teach you**
     I teach you sign!

EMMA: *(Overlapping with Tuc.)* It will ruin his speech. *(To Tuc.)* Use your words, Tuc, speak, speak, speak!

JONAS: For God's sake, Emma, it sounds like we are talking to a dog!

TUC: **Look at me, Father!**
     LOOK AT ME!!!

EMMA: Hold his hands, Mr. Tucker. Hold his hands!
     (Jonas grabs Tuc's hands to stop him signing. Tuc recoils as if he has been slapped.)

TUC: **DON'T SILENCE ME!**

    You want to talk to me?

    Learn SIGN!

    (Tuc pulls away. Jonas is stunned by Tuc's fury.)

JONAS: Tuc, come back here. Talk to me, son. Talk to me!

    (Lights change.)

TUC: **I go to fields;**

    Wind whispers, not.

    Stream laughter, none.

    Home is not home.

    Father talk is gone.

    (Lights change.)

TUC: **Years pass.**

    More and more I stay at school,

    Less and less I long for home.

    Half and half do not make whole.

    (Maizie crosses down into the playing area. She wears a coat and carries a small duffel bag. Tuc runs to her with a small box.)

TUC: **Maizie, look what Father sends for Christmas!**

    Honeycomb, sweet and good, taste like summer.

MAIZIE: **Ain't you goin' home for vacation?**

TUC: **I stay here with you and Roscoe and…**

MAIZIE: **Go home, Tuc, while you still can.**

TUC: **I stay with you and…**

MAIZIE: **I ain't gonna be around here no more. Tuc. I gotta go.**

TUC: **Where?**

MAIZIE: **Away.**

TUC: **Why?**

MAIZIE: **Cause I do.**

TUC: **Are you going to Chicago to work in that Palace?**

    (Maizie smiles and lies to him.)

MAIZIE: **Yeah, Tuc. That's just where I'm goin'.**

    (He hands her the box.)

MAIZIE: **See ya, in the movies.** *(Maizie exits.)*

TUC: **Time pass slow**

    After Maizie go.

    (Lights up on Emma on the upper platform.)

EMMA: Dear Dr. Mann, I am writing to you at the request of my employer, Mr. Jonas Tucker

(Lights up on Mann in the playing area.)

MANN: Tuc, I've had a letter from your home.

EMMA: There has been a serious outbreak of influenza here Three adults and seven children have died.

TUC: *(To Mann.)* **Something is wrong.**

I see by your eyes.

Tell me what is wrong!

EMMA: Things have been very bad here...

MANN: If you have questions, you must use your words.

EMMA: But everyone says the worst is over,

TUC: **Tell me what is wrong!**

MANN: I can't answer if I don't understand you.

EMMA: Unfortunately, Mr. Tucker was one of the last to be stricken. The Doctor says that Tuc should be sent for at once. I have enclosed money for his train fare. He will be met at the Jonesboro station, pray God it is in time.

TUC: **FATHER!**

(Tuc runs in a wide circle of the playing space as Mann exits. The sound of Nell's singing is heard, echoing. Izzy and Clovis appear in harsh light on the upper platform. Jonas sits in two chairs indicating a bed. A blanket covers his legs. Far downstage, Nell comes slowly down into the playing area, carrying the bundle that has signified May -ry.)

IZZY: She nursed Gussie Hatfield and she died.

CLOVIS: And the Bridges boy...

EMMA: And Alma Ward's, Sara Beth.

IZZY: Seems like when Nell Hicks starts singing, people die.

(Nell kneels and slowly unwraps the bundle. Nell holds the empty cloth open in her arms and wraps herself in the cloth. She rocks back and forth. Lights change. Emma crosses down near to Jonas' chair. He is very ill.)

EMMA: I'm sorry to disturb you. It's that Hicks woman at the door. I told her you were resting, but...

JONAS: Show her in, Emma.

EMMA: Nobody in town will let her in. Nobody in their right mind. Izzy Ricks just turned her out of her rent house.

JONAS: I sent for her.

(Nell enters, unseen by Emma.)

EMMA: And people are dying all over town. Some people say she is witching our children.

JONAS: For God's sakes, Emma, her own child just died.

EMMA: She wouldn't let the doctor touch it; tried to cure it herself with herbs and potions, spells and charms more likely.

JONAS: Emma!

EMMA: She sang to those babies and they died.

NELL: I sing when the fever burns away the will to live. I sing to bring the dying home, or let them go. They decide, the song just lets them go.

(Emma is surprised and embarrassed.)

EMMA: That's the kind of talk, makes some people think about witchcraft.

JONAS: That's nonsense and you know it!

EMMA: I said, some people…

JONAS: Some people are fools. *(Jonas starts coughing.)*

EMMA: Mr. Tucker.

(He waves her away angrily.)

JONAS: Bring Mrs. Hicks a chair.

(Emma fetches a chair.)

NELL: I brought bayberry and shepherds purse for the bleeding and a poultice of river mud for your chest.

JONAS: Thank you for coming, Nell.

NELL: Thank you for what you said.

JONAS: You shouldn't have to hear that nonsense.

(Emma brings her the chair and exits.)

NELL: It's all over town.

JONAS: Where will you go?

NELL: No one in town will rent to me, but I won't go far.

JONAS: I was sorry to hear about your little girl.

(This hits her hard, she turns her face away.)

JONAS: Is there anyone…near to help you. No one should grieve alone.

NELL: There's no other way to grieve.

(There is an awkward pause.)

JONAS: They've sent for Tuc and the whole town's been over with casseroles, so I guess I must be dying.

NELL: Jonas…

JONAS: Doc. Gunner says it's just a matter of time.

NELL: It's never just a matter of time. It's a matter of sickness and doing everything that God and nature give us to fight it with.

JONAS: It's tuberculosis.

NELL: I know. I heard it in your cough. But I brought a poultice and…

JONAS: Please, Nell, listen. I need a favor from you. I've sold the farm to pay Tuc's school fees until he's eighteen. I won't have him in the Orphan Home.

NELL: Jonas…

JONAS: See that he goes back to school.

(Nell nods.)

JONAS: I sold everything but the forty acres on Dug Hill. Some of our best pasture land is up there. When he's done with school, Tuc will come back and farm that land. There's a summer cabin up there. It just needs a little fixing up. You can stay there as long as you want. After I'm gone, I…

NELL: *(Interrupting.)* You're going to wear yourself out talking nonsense. You are going to get well, Jonas Tucker. I have nursed plenty of people with tuberculosis in my time and I can tell just by looking in a person's eyes that they are going to get well.

JONAS: You can?

NELL: I most certainly can.

JONAS: Then look in my eyes and tell me.

(She looks in his eyes and turns away.)

JONAS: That's what I thought. *(After a beat.)* There's a trout stream and good soil for a garden. You can stay up there for as long as you like.

NELL: Why are you doing this for me? You hardly know me.

JONAS: I want you to take care of Dug Hill for my boy.

NELL: *(After a beat.)* I will.

JONAS: One other thing. When the time comes, I want you to sing to me.

(Nell smiles and nods. He nods back. She rises, touches him on the shoulder and exits. Tuc crosses down to playing area. Lights change.)

TUC: **Doctor comes,**
Then men in white.
They go to hospital in Jonesboro.
Father promise to come back to me.
Father promise to come back.

(Ensemble enters with open umbrellas They surround Jonas' chair. Lights come up on Nell in another part of the playing space. She clears a spot on the ground, kneels and sings as Tuc signs.)

TUC: **Singing spell.**
Children ride her voice away.
Past the mourning,
Past the pain,

(The mourners slowly leave, taking Jonas with them. The chairs stand empty, except for Jonas' hat on the back railing.)

TUC: **How can there be world,**
And father not?

How can there be earth and sky?
How day?
How light?
How breath?
How life?
How can there be Tuc,
And father not?

ACT II

On the upper platform is a representation of a tree. Tuc sits in the tree. A rocking chair, a few stools and a campfire are in the playing area.

TUC: *(Not voiced.)* Wind.
   (The sound of wind is heard as gust of golden light illuminates the space.)
TUC: (Not voiced.) Water.
   (The sound of water is heard as a ribbon of blue light establishes the stream area.)
TUC: (Not voiced.) Bird.
   (The sound of birds is heard. Tuc watches their flight, reaching slightly toward a soaring bird. Lights up. Graham and Nell enter and stand in the playing space at the foot of the tree.)
GRAHAM: *(To Tuc.)* Come along, Tuc. Time to go.
   (Tuc turns his head away from her.)
GRAHAM: Tuc, I need you to come with me. *(She moves to keep eye contact.)* Tuc, I mean it…Please, Tuc, come with me now.
   (He places his hands over his eyes, so he cannot see her.)
GRAHAM: I know that trick. Well, I'll wait right here until you come down out of that tree.
   (Nell is amused and pulls over a chair for Graham.)
GRAHAM: You must be Nell Hicks.
NELL: I am.
GRAHAM: I've heard a lot about you.
NELL: I expect you have.
GRAHAM: You've got quite a view from here.
NELL: I do.
GRAHAM: There's nobody around for miles.
   (Tuc lowers his hands and watches.)
NELL: He's peeping.
   (Graham quickly waves to get his attention.)
GRAHAM: Tuc. Look at me…Don't cover your…
   (He covers his eyes again.)
GRAHAM: *(To Nell.)* The first time I tried to take him back to school, I got all the way to Carbondale before I realized that he jumped out of the rumble seat. The second time, I got as far as the Jonesboro road. This time, I stopped at the end of his driveway and he was gone. I've been looking all night. The Housekeeper told me to try looking up here.

(Nell sees Tuc lower his hands. She points to Graham who turns back to him. He starts to cover his eyes, but Graham signs and voices to him. Tuc is astonished.)

GRAHAM: Come down from that tree!

TUC: *(Not voiced.)* You sign?

GRAHAM: Just because I do not sign, does not mean I can't sign. Why are you sitting in a tree?

TUC: *(Not voiced.)* I'm waiting!

GRAHAM: Waiting, for what?

TUC: To turn into a bird.

GRAHAM: *(To Nell.)* He says he's waiting to turn into bird.

TUC: To fly away.

GRAHAM: To fly away.

NELL: You understand those…air pictures?

GRAHAM: At school sign language is forbidden. If we permit the children to communicate in sign it will ruin their speech.

NELL: Seems to me talking's talkin'.

GRAHAM: Tuc, come down this minute!

(He turns away.)

GRAHAM: I can't force him to return to school with me if he doesn't want to.

NELL: *(Looking at Tuc.)* My Grandmother used to tell me that the Cherokee believe that when someone you love dies, part of you dies…

GRAHAM: *(Not listening.)* There is no one in town who'll take him…

NELL: …and wanders in the land of the dead.

GRAHAM: …no friends, no relatives.

NELL: The living part has to stay in one place until the dead part returns.

GRAHAM: What did you say?

NELL: The living part has to stay in one place and wait for the dead part to return. The grieving is the waiting.

GRAHAM: For how long?

NELL: As long as it takes.

GRAHAM: *(The idea dawns.)* That is very kind of you.

NELL: Me?

GRAHAM: Here is my card. When Tuc is back among the living, contact me. I'll come for him.

NELL: You're going to leave him here?

GRAHAM: Isn't that what you just…

NELL: I promised Mr. Tucker I would see to it that Tuc went back to school.

GRAHAM: That was Mr. Tucker's intention in his will, but that boy has jumped out of a moving car three times, it seems like he's got a will of his own.

NELL: How will I care for him?

GRAHAM: I'll see to it that you are sent the money put aside for his room and board.

NELL: How will I talk to him?

GRAHAM: He reads lips…some.

NELL: *(Resisting.)* I'm sorry, I…

GRAHAM: If the authorities discover that he is not in school, he'll be sent to the State Orphan Home.

NELL: Oh, no. Not that. Never that.

GRAHAM: If there were any other alternative, believe me, I wouldn't ask.

NELL: You said you've heard stories about me in town.

GRAHAM: I have.

NELL: And you still want me to care for him?

GRAHAM: I don't believe everything I hear.

(Nell smiles ruefully.)

GRAHAM: In his will, Mr. Tucker indicated that you were to be contacted if Tuc were to have an illness or injury.

NELL: He did?

GRAHAM: Isn't grief a kind of injury?

NELL: Worse than any broken bone.

GRAHAM: So he can stay?

(Nell nods. Graham smiles.)

GRAHAM: As soon as he's ready to go back to school, I'll come for him.

(Graham looks at Tuc who is peeking through his fingers. He quickly covers his eyes.)

GRAHAM: Thank you.

(Nell nods again. Graham exits. Nell looks up at Tuc who looks back at her quizzically.)

NELL: I must be out of my mind!

(Lights change. Nell turns upstage and picks up a bowl. Tuc signs and Ensemble Member voices.)

TUC: **Day One.**

(Nell crosses to Tuc who is still in the tree.)

NELL: We got black beans and fatback. Come on down for supper.

(Tuc turns away. Nell turns upstage.)

TUC: **Day Two.**

(Nell crosses to the other side of the tree.)

NELL: We got pinto beans and cornbread tonight.

(*Tuc turns away to the other side. Nell sighs and turns back upstage.*)

TUC: **Day Three.**

(*Nell crosses back downstage with the bowl.*)

NELL: Butter beans and biscuits.

(*Tuc turns away a third time.*)

NELL: You can't eat grief, Tuc. I know, I've tried.

(*Nell places the bowl at the foot of the tree and exits. Tuc climbs down and eats a bit. Ensemble Member playing Jonas enters on the top platform. Throughout this scene when Tuc signs, Jonas voices. Tuc is remembering his father, but at no time do they look at each other or make any visual contact.*)

TUC: **Mouth eats, taste nothing.**

Eyes look, but do not see.

No word, no sign to touch this feeling.

Father promise to come back to me.

(*Tuc reaches in his pocket and pulls out a handful of soil. He lays his cheek in his hand and closes his eyes. Jonas kneels on one leg and scoops up a handful of soil.*)

TUC: **Week One. Earth begins to call to me.**

(*Nell enters the playing area with a hoe.*)

NELL: We gotta plant something other than beans or we're both going to blow up and fly away from the gas!

(*Nell looks around finds a likely spot and raises the hoe. Jonas shakes his head. Tuc pounds on the ground and stops her mid-swing. She looks at him. He shakes his head "NO."*

NELL: No?

(*Jonas squints at the sun. Tuc signs.*)

TUC: **Too much sun.**

(*Nell selects another spot and lifts her hoe. Jonas shakes his head again and Tuc waves his arms to stop her.*)

NELL: Why not?

(*Jonas points to the tree.*)

TUC: **Too much shade.**

(*Getting a bit frustrated, Nell finds a third spot.*)

NELL: Here?

(*Jonas kicks the ground where he is on the upper platform. Tuc shakes his head "NO" and signs.*)

TUC: **Too much rocks and sand.**

NELL: (*Exasperated.*) All right then, where?

(Jonas moves to a position center stage, still on the upper platform. He places both hands on the ground. Tuc signs.)

TUC: **Father used to ask the earth where to garden dig.**

(Tuc moves to a place center stage in the playing area and places his cheek on the ground.)

NELL: There?

TUC: **Worms are happy, yes!**

Earth says, plant here!

(Tuc dives down and buries his face in the soil. Nell laughs.)

NELL: Thank goodness we haven't spread the manure yet.

(Lights change. There is the sound of running water and intense blue light from the stream area.)

TUC: **Week two. Stream begins to sing to me.**

(Jonas crosses to the stream area on the upper platform, bathed in blue light. He squats and places his hands over the platform's edge. Tuc crosses to the stream area. He squats and puts his hands in the light. Nell watches him for a moment. She waves to get his attention and makes a puzzled expression.)

NELL: What are you doing?

TUC: **Father used to show me how to sit and think like river.**

(Tuc nods and motions her over to where he is. With a sigh Nell joins him. He shows her how to place her hands in the water.)

NELL: Like this? Oh! It's cold.

TUC: **Fish come, swim between hands**

Ask fish: Will you be our dinner, please?

No. Swim away.

(Tuc makes his hand into a fish that "swims" between Nell's hands.)

NELL: Tuc, this ain't gonna...

(Tuc motions for her to be still.)

TUC: **Soon another come.**

(Jonas and Tuc mirror the motions of the fish.)

TUC: **Soft, soft, belly rub.**

Will you be our dinner please?

Fish turn over...

Yes!

Take him home for...

(Tuc lifts the "Fish" in Nell's hands and Nell puts it in a pail.)

NELL: Supper!

TUC: **Week three. Stars come out to welcome me.**

(Nell hands him a blanket.)

NELL: You can sleep inside if you want.

>*(Tuc gestures that he will sleep there. Jonas lies down on the platform with his arms behind his head.)*

NELL: Stars are better company.

>*(Nell exits, as Tuc beds down.)*

TUC: **Stars cover me**

>**So close, so warm.**
>
>**I remember father's arms.**
>
>**Can father see same stars as me?**

>*(Sound of crickets and a distant hoot owl. Lights change. Jonas exits. Nell enters on the upper platform, bathed in moonlight. She carries a small basket. She kneels, clears a small patch of ground. She begins to sing a low keening song. She removes several articles of clothing from the basket and places them lovingly on the ground. They are baby clothes. Tuc rises and crosses to the area. He stands just outside the circle of light, watching, not daring to go further. When the clothes have been laid out in a human shape, Nell slowly lowers her whole body on top of them.)*

TUC: **Days pass,**

>**Slow and Fast.**
>
>**Waking to the taste of sunrise,**
>
>**Sleeping with the smells of night,**
>
>**Sadness covers us like rain.**
>
>**When will heartbeat start again?**

>*(Nell crosses back to Dug Hill and hides the basket under one of the upstage chairs. She turns and is startled to see Tuc awake and looking at her.)*

NELL: You're up early.

TUC: *(Not voiced.)* Are you sad?

>*(Nell understands but pretends she does not.)*

NELL: I was just out for a walk.

TUC: *(Not voiced.)* I'm sad, too.

NELL: Gathering mushrooms. Dawn's the best time for mushrooms. I'll get us some breakfast. *(She hustles past him and exits.)*

TUC: *(Voiced.)* **Don't be sad.**

>**I find something to make you happy.**
>
>**I find something…** *(Suddenly, Tuc has an idea. He finds the bucket and signs.)* **HONEY!**

>*(Lights change as Tuc circles the stage. During his honey hunt, set elements for Dug Hill are removed. The hive is created as before, either with light or by an Ensemble Member. Tuc salutes the bees and begins the slow process of*

reaching into the hive and bringing up the honey. He is flooded with golden light. Hunters one and two enter the playing area. Buzzing is louder.)

HUNTER ONE: What's a kid doing way out here?

HUNTER TWO: Look, there s bees on his hands and arms.

HUNTER ONE: *(Shouting.)* Careful of those bees, kid!

HUNTER TWO: Don't shout! It might scare him and they'll sting him.

(Tuc turns around to put the honey into the pail and finds himself face-to-face with the hunters. The buzzing is very loud.)

HUNTER ONE: Don't move, kid! Don't move!

HUNTER TWO: It's okay. We're gonna help you. Just hold still.

HUNTER ONE: Look at those BEES!

HUNTER TWO: All over him!

HUNTER ONE: Don't be scared!

(Hunter one takes off his jacket and holds it in front of him.)

HUNTER ONE: HOLD STILL. JUST HOLD STILL!

TUC: *(Voiced by Tuc.)* NOOOOOOOO!

(In a great rush of total stupidity, Hunter one knocks Tuc to the ground and starts rolling him over and over. The buzzing is terrifying!)

TUC: Aaaaaaaaaggrrrahhhhhhhhhhhh!

HUNTER ONE: It s okay, kid! I got ya! I got ya! I got ya!

HUNTER TWO: *(From a distance.)* You all right?

HUNTER ONE: Of course I'm not all right. I'm stung to Jesus! Come here and help me!

TUC: **Pain, all over body hot.**
Breathe not.

(Hunter two crosses to them batting at the bees. Tuc struggles as he signs.)

HUNTER TWO: He's stung to pieces.

TUC: **Chest tight.**
Breathe not.

HUNTER ONE: He must be in shock.

TUC: **Throat close.**
Breathe not!

HUNTER TWO: We gotta get him to a Doctor.

(Hunters grab Tuc under his arms and move him to the area designated as the Illinois State Home. Tuc shakes them off. As they move, the rest of the Ensemble sets up the Illinois State Home: a hospital stretcher in a screened off cubicle.)

TUC: **Strange place, room white,**
Too much light.

Go, I want to GO!

Hands force me down.

I want to go.

Tie my hands.

LET ME GO!

(Tuc moves onto the stretcher. Doctor and Nurse strap his hands down. They exit. There is a beat of silence. A voice is heard from behind the screen.)

VOICE: Psssssssst. Psssssssst.

(An elaborate shadow puppet show appears on the screen. Rabbits hop by and are squashed. A duck quacks and is eaten by another duck. Two guns shoot each other and explode.)

VOICE: That's some of my best stuff, kid. You gotta be made of stone if you don't think that's funny.

(A hugely pregnant Maizie walks out from behind the screen.)

MAIZIE: Tuc! What are you doing here? *(She signs as Ensemble Member voices.)* **Tuc! Tuc! Don't ya remember me? It's Maizie! From the deaf school!**

(He sees her and struggles against his restraints.)

MAIZIE: **Look at you, they got your arms in these restraints.**

(He calms down a bit. She takes off the restraints. Tuc signs and is voiced by Ensemble Member.)

TUC: **Are we in a movie?**

MAIZIE: **This ain't a movie, Tuc. Not one you'd like to see anyway. Four months ago, my Momma made me pack up all my things and she brought me up here to the State Home and dropped me off. All she said was, "Here's where girls like you belong" and she drove away. I was so sad and alone I thought I was going to die, but I didn't.**

(He points to her stomach.)

TUC: **Baby?**

MAIZIE: **Dreams. That's where I keep my dreams for safekeeping. I filled my whole self up with dreams and I kin feel them moving around. I feel them kicking me, telling me to keep moving, to get going, to keep running till I find...**

TUC: **What?**

MAIZIE: **I don't know.**

(Nurse enters with a small quilt and tray containing a shot needle.)

NURSE: Maizie! What are you doing? The Doctor has ordered these are not to be removed. *(Nurse refastens the straps.)*

MAIZIE: Uhhhhh...All the girls in my ward was talking about baby names. Too boring, so I come to play with the orphans.

NURSE: Well, leave this one alone. He's violent.

MAIZIE: No, he ain't!

NURSE: He tried to jump out of a second story window. The Doctor has ordered him transferred to the State Asylum for the Mentally Deficient in Peoria.

MAIZIE: I know this kid. He's not mental; he's just deaf.

NURSE: We have tested him and while there may be some hearing loss, his IQ measures at the level of imbecile.

MAIZIE: He's deaf as a doorknob! You gotta take these things off him so he can sign.

NURSE: Return to the girl's ward, Maizie. If the Doctor finds you...

MAIZIE: Call the Central Institute for the Deaf...Call Dr. Mann. I used to work there.

NURSE: I need to give him a sedative.

MAIZIE: Don't dope him! He can't sign, if he can't think!

NURSE: Go back to your ward! The State Asylum is where this boy belongs. We know what's best.

MAIZIE: You don't know... *(She signs "SHIT" and exits.)*

TUC: *(Voiced by Tuc.)* MAIZIE, MAIZIE! MAIZIE!

(Nurse gives Tuc an injection, covers him with the quilt, and exits. Lights change. It is night. A bell tolls midnight. Maizie creeps into the space holding a lantern and a small duffel. She crosses to Tuc. She signs Ensemble Member voices.)

MAIZIE: **Tuc, you gotta wake up. This is serious. They are going to send you some place much worse than here, somewhere you don't belong. I gotta get you outta here.**

(Tuc wakes as Maizie takes off the restraints.)

MAIZIE: **Are you all right?**

(He stands; his legs are a bit rubbery. Maizie supports him as he gets his balance.)

MAIZIE: **We can't go back to the Deaf school; we'd never make it that far, besides I'm a week overdue.**

TUC: **I know where to go. I know someone to help.**

MAIZIE: **Why the heck not? I don't want my baby born in here. Nobody ever laughs in here. Let's get going before they put us both in the loony bin.**

(He shivers.)

MAIZIE: **You're shivering! Here, let's take this quilt. It's the only pretty thing in this whole place. Come ON!**

(As they run, set pieces for the State Home are removed. Maizie lopes along, trailing the quilt behind her.)

TUC: **Ribbon of moonlight**
Runs down the road.
Maizie and me
Follow the road.
Follow the moon.
Find something familiar
Sometime soon!

(Maizie is exhausted. She stops and waves the quilt to get Tuc's attention.)

MAIZIE: **Tuc, slow down. Slow down. I gotta stop and catch whatever breath I got left.** *(Maizie lowers herself to sit on the quilt.)* **I gotta sit a minute. This is like running with a bowling ball in your britches.** *(Maizie feels a kick from her baby.)* **Ouch! No offense! Quiet down in there!**

(Maizie places Tuc's hand on her stomach.)

MAIZIE: **Feel that?**

(Tuc's eyes grow wide as he feels the kick.)

MAIZIE: **Like Red Grange kicking a field goal. Sure wish I had me a cold Coca-Cola right now. I got some chocolate-covered goobers, you want some?** *(Maizie pulls a box of chocolate-covered peanuts out of her pocket.)* **I thought I'd be working the candy stall of the Avalon Theater in Chicago by now. But here I am in the middle of nowhere, big as a barn, eating candy in a cow field.** *(She experiences a contraction. Spoken by Maizie, not signed.)* Whoa…

(He looks at her, concerned.)

MAIZIE: I'm okay, least I think I am.

(Tuc points to her belly and signs.)

TUC: **Baby deaf?**

MAIZIE: **In my dreams, my baby's always deaf.** *(Maizie eats a goober.)* **Hey, how come you're not in school?**

TUC: **I left.**

MAIZIE: **You going back?**

TUC: **I'm waiting. Father promise to come back to me.**

MAIZIE: **Where is that star-gazing Daddy of yours?**

TUC: **Hospital.**

MAIZIE: **He been gone a long time?**

TUC: **Father go, box come home.**

MAIZIE: **Tuc, did he die?**

TUC: **I think so.**

MAIZIE: **Don't you know?**

TUC: *(Points to his head.)* **In here, I know.** *(Points to his heart.)* **In here, I wait.**

MAIZIE: **For what?**

TUC: **To tell him what is in my heart. I am so bad. Not read his lips. Not Speak. Father hurt. Father sad.**

MAIZIE: **Father sign?**

TUC: **No.**

MAIZIE: **Tuc, you can hold him live inside your mind and tell him everything you want to say. In real life parents understand nothing. In your mind, everything!**

TUC: **Promise?**

MAIZIE: **Promise.**

(They "pinkie-swear" and Maizie has a contraction.)

MAIZIE: **Speaking of which…we better get a move on or I'm gonna have this baby smack in the middle of Route 146!**

(Tuc and Maizie start their journey again and make a wide loop around the playing area. Set pieces for Dug Hill return.)

(Tuc runs to the garden. Maizie experiences a contraction.)

MAIZIE: **I hate to interrupt this touching reunion with your vegetables, but we gotta find some help here…fast!**

(Nell enters the playing space. She sees Tuc and runs to him.)

NELL: Tuc! There you are!

(Tuc runs to her and hugs her.)

NELL: I was worried. I was so worried! You've been gone almost a week! *(She takes him by the shoulders and speaks directly to him.)* I've been everywhere, to your house, to the town, I couldn't tell anyone you were gone, because you're not even supposed to be here. I just kept looking and looking. Are you all right?

(Tuc is confused by the torrent of words.)

NELL: Are you sure you're all right?

(Tuc motions to Maizie to interpret for him.)

MAIZIE: *(Speaking and signing.)* **She wants to know if you're all right.**

(Tuc signs and Maizie voices as indicated.)

TUC: *(Signs.)* I'm okay now, but I wasn't.

MAIZIE: He says, I'm okay now but I wasn't. *(Maizie experiences a contraction. As herself.)* Uhhhhh, Tuc…

(Tuc continues to sign. Maizie tries to keep up voicing despite quickening labor pains.)

TUC: *(Signing only.)* Then I got stung all over and…

MAIZIE: *(Interpreting for Tuc.)* Then I got stung all over and… *(Maizie has a contraction. As herself.)* Uhhhhh Tuc…

TUC: But Maizie, she rescued me and…

MAIZIE: *(Interpreting for Tuc.)* But Maizie, she rescued me and *(Maizie interrupts herself and signs to Tuc. Speaking and signing.)* **Hold It!** **I gotta say something myself here!** *(To Nell.)* **My name's Maizie, I knew Tuc from the Deaf School and well it's a long, long, story…** *(She experiences a contraction and stops signing.)* But I don't think I've got the time to tell it right now…

NELL: *(Appraising the situation.)* I can see that! Come inside, right away. *(Speaking to Tuc and gesturing.)* Stoke up the fire! Fill the pot with fresh water!

(Nell escorts Maizie upstage and into the cabin. Tuc paces back and forth.)

TUC: **All day, I wait and wait.**
All night, I wait and wait.
I wait and wait.
Finally…sun rise.

(There is the sound of a baby cry. Tuc continues to pace.)

TUC: **Still I wait, and wait, and wait.**

(Finally, Nell enters and gestures "Baby." Tuc leaps in the air, and runs in a circle.)

TUC: **So excited, body cannot hold it all!**

(Lights change. Nell and Maizie enter the playing space. Nell holds the wrapped bundle signifying the baby. Maizie sits in the rocking chair with her arms stiffly outstretched. Nell brings the baby to Maizie. Maizie holds the baby at arms length.)

NELL: You're holding her like she was a stick of dynamite.

MAIZIE: That's exactly how she feels to me. I'm afraid I'm gonna drop her.

NELL: You're sitting down. How are you going to drop her?

MAIZIE: I'll find a way.

(Tuc gestures a request to hold the baby.)

MAIZIE: *(Handing him the baby.)* Here, Tuc. You've been dying to do this for days.

NELL: Now, hold her head. Good.

MAIZIE: Of course, he can't hear if she explodes!

NELL: You can't go on being spooked by your own child.

TUC: *(Voiced.)* **Baby deaf?**

MAIZIE: *(Signs and speaks.)* **No, Tuc, she's hearing.**

TUC: *(Voiced.)* **She looks deaf.**

MAIZIE: *(Signs and speaks.)* **She may look deaf, but she's hearing…Nothin'** ever turns out like you think it will. Like romance, for instance. I dreamed it would be all beautiful, like Valentino. My boyfriend said we'd get married, he'd take me to Chicago, no big deal, just like a movie. But it ain't a movie and it's about the biggest deal there is.

(Nell crosses to Tuc with a large basket for a cradle.)

NELL: *(To Tuc.)* Put her in here when your arms get tired.

(Tuc holds the baby closer. Nell sits and begins to sew.)

NELL: Suit yourself.

(Tuc rocks the baby.)

MAIZIE: Strange thing about having babies, first nobody tells you anything about it. Then, after you've gone and done something you shouldn't do, all anybody does, is tell you what you shouldn't have done.

NELL: Do you want to hold her now?

MAIZIE: Later, I'll hold her later. Tuc's doin fine, ain't you, Tuc?

(She motions to him and he grins back at her and gives a thumbs-up.)

MAIZIE: So, ain't you gonna tell me what to do next? Like keep her or take her back to the State Home?

NELL: You got your own choices to make.

MAIZIE: I never make choices, see; I just do things one at a time and pretty soon that's my life.

(Nell chuckles and shakes her head.)

MAIZIE: If she was deaf, I'd know what to do. I'd know to care for her, just like I done for my Momma and my Daddy. I'd be her ears. I'd be her voice. But this baby can hear, Nell, and she scares me to death.

NELL: But you can hear.

MAIZIE: Only on the outside. My family was deaf and I was brought up deaf, so inside I'm...Never mind, you wouldn't understand.

NELL: Once I knew a baby porcupine that got itself raised up by a family of rabbits. That porcupine thought it was a rabbit and spent its whole life trying to hop. Is that what you're trying to say?

(Tuc sniffs the baby and waves to Nell and Maizie. He holds the baby at arms length.)

MAIZIE: You're pretty smart for a hearing person.

NELL: Smart enough to know when a baby needs changing.

(Nell exits into the cabin with the baby. Maizie signs Ensemble Member voices.)

MAIZIE: **Nell cut up that quilt we brought with us. Sure makes a fine baby blanket. I sure wish I grabbed a handful of those baby clothes they had at the State Home. They got gobs of charity clothes up there.**

(Tuc finds the basket of baby clothes, where Nell has hidden them.)

MAIZIE: **This baby can't stay naked forever.**

(Tuc presents her with the basket.)

MAIZIE: **Look, this dress and this bonnet and these tiny little shoes. These are great.**

(They play back and forth with the clothes. Tuc lifts out a rattle and shakes it.)

MAIZIE: **Look at this cute little rattle made out of buttons.**

(Nell enters from the house with the baby.)

NELL: *(Sharply.)* What are you doing?

MAIZIE: We found these here baby clothes in this basket like some kind of picnic.

NELL: Put them back! *(Nell crosses downstage and snatches up the clothes, dropping the bonnet and scattering the shoes. Very angry.)* Don't you touch them. Give them to me!

MAIZIE: I didn't hurt them. I just…

NELL: You mind your own things, and leave mine alone!

(Nell gives the baby to Tuc, gathers up the dropped clothing and holds them close.)

MAIZIE: *(Signs and speaks.)* I'm sorry, I…

NELL: Too late for sorry now.

(Tuc picks up the bonnet and gives it to Nell.)

MAIZIE: *(Signs and speaks.)* You lost a baby, didn't you? I can tell by the way you hold mine, by the way your hand just fits the back of her head. When you look at her, I see another baby in your eyes. How old was she?

NELL: Three years, twenty-seven days, fourteen hours.

MAIZIE: It must be hard on you to have us here, me and the baby.

NELL: We're a pair, aren't we? You can't pick your baby up and I can't put mine down.

MAIZIE: I'm scared, Nell. Scared that if I ever pick her up, I won't be able to put her down.

NELL: Once you hold her, really hold her, you'll never let her go. She can go away, live a whole different life from yours or no life at all; but she's always part of you. Every day you wake with her in some part of your mind; every day you look for the piece of you that's missing.

MAIZIE: I want to do what's right for her.

(Nell picks up the baby.)

NELL: When my baby was so sick, I knew the only way to heal her was to let her go. So I sang to her and let it be her choice. Whatever choice you make will be right, because you're going to spend the rest of your life making it right. *(She hands the baby to Maizie.)* Go ahead, hold her. You can't remember what you never know. No matter what you choose, you owe it to yourself to know.

(Nell smiles as Maizie sits and rocks the baby. Lights change. Tuc stands above Maizie and the baby. Nell exits.)

TUC: **In my pocket still I keep**
Soil from home,
From Father's hand,
All I have of my own land.
All I have of family.

(Tuc crosses downstage to his sleeping area.)

Baby sleeps and wakes
And cries and eats.
At night I'm the only one who sleeps.

(Tuc lies down and sleeps. Lights up on Maizie with her baby. As she speaks, she lovingly wraps the baby in a piece of the quilt. Maizie signs and voices.)

MAIZIE: **I ain't givin' you a name, because you don't want something stupid like Maizie to weigh you down. I ain't givin' you my past or my future, cause you got your own. I ain't givin' you money, or brains, or very good looks, cause I can't give what I don't have. But I am givin' you somethin' I never had: One world to grow up in your whole life long. I let you go, little one, to find your very own self. But if you ever go to the movies in Chicago, buy the goobers from the lady who smiles at you. Cause I'll smile at every kid who might be you, just in case.**

(Maizie rises. She starts to wake Tuc, then thinks better of it. Maizie exits. Tuc sits up and signs.)

TUC: **That night I dream**
The baby turns into a bird and flies
High into the sky
Where Father waits for me.

(Nell enters the playing area with a lantern. She looks about, and finally crosses to Tuc.)

NELL: Tuc, Tuc. Good! You're awake. I'm sorry to bother you, but I can't find Maizie.

(Tuc pulls the lantern so he can see her lips.)

NELL: I can't find Maizie or the baby. Have you seen them Tuc?

(Tuc shakes his head "no.")

NELL: I'll look down by the river. You check near the garden.

(Nell exits as Tuc runs to the area designated as the garden. Maizie enters. Maizie and Tuc sign. Ensemble Members voice.)

MAIZIE: **I couldn't leave without saying good-bye...and thank you.**

TUC: **Where is baby? Where is...**

MAIZIE: **Well, that's what I come to tell you...You know, I been pondering and pondering what do to about her and then it come to me clear as Christmas. I seen it in a movie...about this baby that gets left on a doorstep and these rich people take it in and raise it up to be happy and...**

TUC: **Doorstep?**

MAIZIE: **I found the perfect family in town. Just like in the movie. There's a Momma with a kind face and a Daddy who laughs all the time...**

TUC: **You left your baby on doorstep?**

MAIZIE: **Isn't it a great idea?**

TUC: **No! What if they don't want baby?**

MAIZIE: **They did in the movie!**

TUC: **Don't leave her there alone. Alone is sad and scared and...**

MAIZIE: **I found her a good home!**

TUC: **This is good home. Stay here!**

MAIZIE: **Here?**

TUC: **Here is flowers and trees, here is people who care.**

MAIZIE: **It ain't that simple. Besides, I can't sit up here on this mountain and watch my whole life go by.**

TUC: **Why not?**

MAIZIE: **I am sixteen years old. I want to dance the Charleston and play a trombone, and go up in one of those airplanes way up in the air.**

TUC: **Then go, but leave baby here.**

MAIZIE: **I can't do that either.**

TUC: **Why not?**

MAIZIE: **Because you are deaf and Nell is hearing.**

(He turns away from her. She forces him to face her.)

MAIZIE: **Look at me, Tuc. This is hard to explain...Part of me is deaf and part of me is hearing, and all my life I never felt like I belonged in either world. Now, that family in town is hearing and my baby is hearing and she has a chance to belong to one world her whole life long.**

TUC: **Baby can have two worlds.**

MAIZIE: **Two worlds is too hard!**

(Nell enters.)

NELL: There you are. I was beginning to get worried.

(Tuc crosses to Nell and signs frantically. The following is signed with great animation but not voiced. Leaving Nell confused.)

TUC: Tell her to bring the baby back...Tell her baby can stay here. Tell her...

NELL: Hold it, Tuc. What's going on, here?

TUC: *(To Maizie, not voiced.)* Go back, get her, bring her back here!

MAIZIE: *(Signing and voicing.)* I can't do that! They already took her in! I saw them take her in!

(The following is voiced but not signed, leaving Tuc frustrated, as he cannot understand what is being said. He pulls at Maizie to interpret.)

NELL: Would someone please tell me what is going on here?

MAIZIE: I found the baby a good home in town.

NELL: You what?

TUC: *(To Maizie, voiced.)* **What she say? What you say? Sign for me!**

MAIZIE: *(To Nell, not voiced.)* I been watching them all week. They got a big house and lots of kids and a dog and plenty of room...

NELL: People in that town are fools. People in that town are hypocrites!

TUC: *(To Maizie, voiced.)* **Sign for me! Sign for me!**

MAIZIE: *(Signs and voices.)* **Just a minute, Tuc...**

(Maizie turns away from Tuc to face Nell.)

NELL: *(To Maizie, very angry.)* You can't just drop a baby off like so much laundry! Not in that town. Not to those people!

TUC: *(Signing to Nell.)* We keep baby here! Tell her, Tell her!

NELL: *(Frustrated.)* I don't understand you, Tuc. Maizie, tell me what he's saying!

TUC: *(Pulling at Maizie.)* SIGN FOR ME! SIGN!

MAIZIE: *(Signing and speaking.)* **STOP IT! I can't do this anymore.** *(To Tuc.)* **You want sign.** *(To Nell.)* **You want voice.** *(To both, signing and voicing.)* **If I leave my baby here with you two, she'll be right where I am, caught between deaf and hearing.** *(To Nell.)* **Nell, I can't be the Momma that baby needs. I'm too young. I can't be a Mother to her until I can be a whole person to myself.**

NELL: But...

MAIZIE: **And I can't leave her here with you, 'cause you got your own baby to grieve. You told me to make a choice. Well this is it...Choice is choice.**

TUC: But I want...

MAIZIE: **Tuc, you can't make up for that Daddy you lost by turning yourself into one.**

TUC: **I want a family.**

MAIZIE: **We can't turn ourselves into a fairy tale family, just cause that's what you want.**

TUC: **I want you to stay here with Nell and with me.**

MAIZIE: *(To Tuc, signing and voicing.)* **Someday, when my baby is old enough to understand, I want her to know you. I want her to have you for a friend. If you stay, will you keep an eye on her for me? Promise?**

(Tuc shrugs.)

MAIZIE: **Promise?**

(Tuc turns away without promising. Nell turns him to look at her.)

NELL: Stay here? But Tuc, you're going back to school.

(Maizie interprets for him.)

TUC: *(Voiced by Maizie.)* **I can't go back until I find what I lost.**

NELL: What?

TUC: *(Voiced by Maizie.)* **A home where I belong.**

MAIZIE: **First you gotta belong here…** *(She slaps her own chest.)* **to yourself. If you don't belong to yourself, you don't belong anywhere.**

NELL: *(To Tuc.)* You want to stay here, with me?

(Maizie signs this to him.)

TUC: *(Voiced by Maizie.)* **Maybe, for a while…Do you want me to stay here with you?**

NELL: *(Smiles.)* Maybe…for a while.

(Maizie interprets. Tuc smiles.)

NELL: Maizie, before you go. Will you ask Tuc one last thing for me? It's important and I want to get it right.

MAIZIE: Sure.

NELL: Tuc, I want Maizie to ask to you for me…

MAIZIE: Just talk to him, like I ain't here.

(Maizie signs as Nell speaks directly to Tuc.)

NELL: Teach me your talk, boy. Teach me your air pictures.

TUC: *(Voiced by Maizie.)* **Teach you?**

NELL: *(Signed by Maizie.)* I can't know you; you can't know me unless we build ourselves a talking way.

(Jonas enters. He stands behind Nell.)

NELL: Teach me.

TUC: *(Voiced by Ensemble Member.)* **Father?**

JONAS: Teach me.

TUC: *(Voiced by Maizie.)* **What do you want to know?**

JONAS AND NELL: Everything.

(There is the sound of wind. Tuc looks up and signs "wind" Nell looks confused. Tuc blows on her cheek and signs again.)

NELL AND JONAS: Wind?

(Maizie steps back into the shadows. Ensemble Member, voicing for Tuc, exits.)

TUC: *(Not voiced.)* That's right!

(Nell makes the sign for wind. Tuc is delighted. He takes her hand and pulls her to the stream area. He signs "water.")

NELL AND JONAS: **Water! Water!**

(Maizie sees her chance to slip away. There is the sound of birds. Tuc points to a bird and signs a soaring bird. Nell, Jonas and Tuc sign "bird.")

NELL AND JONAS: **BIRD!**

(Tuc follows the bird and catches sight of Maizie who stops and waves. He returns her wave.)

MAIZIE: **Promise?**

TUC: *(Signs broadly.)* PROMISE!!!

(Maizie exits. As dawn paints the cyclorama, Nell and Jonas sign and voice.)

NELL: **Teach Me.**

TUC: *(Voiced by Jonas.)* **Home.**

(They sign "Home" together.)

JONAS AND NELL: **Teach me.**

TUC: *(Voiced by Jonas.)* **Forgive.**

(They sign "Forgive" together.)

JONAS AND NELL: **Teach me.**

TUC: *(Voiced by Jonas.)* **Sunrise.**

(They all sign "Sunrise" together.)

TUC: *(Voiced by Jonas.)* **Teach me. How does Sunrise sound?**

NELL: **Some things are so beautiful they don't need sound.**

(With the glory of the sunrise fully behind them, lights dim on Nell, Jonas and Tuc.)

THE END

PRODUCTION NOTES

1. The script you have in your hands is only half the play. It is my intention that every moment on-stage be fully bilingual in both spoken English and American Sign Language. To produce this play you will need to create or find a translation in American Sign Language. I encourage you to get in touch with Billy Seago, through the Seattle Children's Theatre, who may be able to assist you.

2. After two successful large-scale productions of this play, complete with multiple actors playing Tuc at a variety of ages and cinematic approaches to the various locations, I decided to simplify the play so that it might be able to be produced by eight actors on two elevated platforms with eight chairs. The staging suggestions in this script are a result of that experiment. Although this degree of simplicity was a bit draconian—the director felt that nine actors would facilitate the necessity of Ensemble Members playing several roles *and* serving as interpreters for signing for hearing characters—I do encourage producers to keep things as simple as possible and to realize the play in the metaphoric language of the theater as opposed to the cinematic realism of film.

3. In this draft all Ensemble Members will play a variety of roles and will sign for hearing characters and/or voice for Deaf characters. I have deliberately not done a breakdown on who could play which roles. I have indicated specific actors to voice particular scenes where there is a dramaturgical reason for doing so.

4. Potential producers are encouraged to remember that both sight lines and lighting levels must be taken into consideration so that Deaf audience members might actually see the language of the play at all time. It does little good to have beautiful, evocative lighting if it makes it impossible for the actors/interpreters to be understood.

5. It is possible to do this play with a minimum of two Deaf actors, one for Tuc and one for Roscoe, but I encourage you to use more Deaf actors to sign the speeches of hearing characters. Under *no* circumstances may this play be produced without a Deaf actor for Tuc, no exceptions, end of discussion!